# MOTHERLESS CHILDREN

# MOTHERLESS CHILDREN

*a screenplay*

# Hal Hartley

ELBORO

MOTHERLESS CHILDREN
Copyright © 2020 by Hal Hartley

All rights reserved. No part of this book may be used or reproduced in any manner whatsoever without written permission except in the case of brief quotations embodied in critical articles and reviews.

ISBN: 978-1-7321817-4-8

Published in New York City by Elboro Press

Elboro Press books may be purchased in bulk for educational, business or sales promotional use. Please address enquiries to:

office@elboropress.com

First Edition, 2021 – Second Printing

# CONTENTS

*Index of Principal Characters*
*vi*

Episode One
*3*

Episode Two
*61*

Episode Three
*121*

Episode Four
*177*

Episode Five
*241*

Episode Six
*299*

Episode Seven
*369*

Episode Eight
*421*

# INDEX OF PRINCIPAL CHARACTERS

### Jim & Audrey Fulton's Family
*Jim Fulton*, union architectural ironworker
*Audrey*, his wife, deceased but remembered
*Richard*, their first son, unskilled
*Billy*, second son, college-bound
*Joseph*, third son, a celebrated liar
*Natalie*, their daughter, youngest

### Mike & Ruthy Fulton's Family
*Mike Fulton*, Jim's older brother, ironworker
*Ruthy*, his wife, Audrey's childhood friend
*John*, their first son, also an ironworker
*Edward*, second son, an apprentice ironworker
*Bobby*, their third son, an aspiring chef
*Other children*

### John Fulton's Family in Newfoundland
*John Fulton*, captain of fishing fleet, Jim and Mike's father
*Louisa*, his wife
*Leonard*, their eldest son and ship's captain
*Nell* and *May*, their daughters
*Mike* and *Jim (as children)*, their younger sons

### Tom & Marie Dolan's Family
*Tom Dolan*, ironworker
*Marie*, his wife, Audrey Fulton's half-sister
*Maggie*, their sixteen-year-old daughter
*Anna*, their thirteen-year-old daughter
*Other children*

### Paddy Dwyer's Family
*Paddy Dwyer*, Audrey and Marie's widowed father
*Cecile*, his second wife, deceased but remembered
*Ned*, his eldest son, deceased but remembered
*Eleanor*, Audrey's older sister, deceased but remembered

**Paul & Trish Fiore's Family**
*Paul Fiore*, floor manager at a printing works
*Trish*, his wife, works at a department store
*Catherine*, Richard Fulton's girlfriend, pregnant with his child
*Karen*, older daughter
*Diane*, younger daughter
*Lizzy and Maria*, little sisters

**Eliot & Agnes Wilson's Family**
*Eliot Wilson*, black lawyer and civil rights activist
*Agnes*, his wife, white art gallerist and publisher
*Julia*, their daughter, Billy Fulton's girlfriend

**Ironworkers**
*Clarence*, black Vietnam vet
*Bear*, Oneida Indian
*Jackie-Neal*, Canadian Cree Indian
*Kevin*, union shop steward
*Dizzy, Wally and Chet* – journeymen

**Rehab Detention Center**
*Amy*, nurse administrator, later Jim's girlfriend
*Hallahan*, an angry patient
*Robert*, a nervous patient
*Morris*, philosopher, patient, sex offender

**Others**
*Uncle Leo*, close relative, esteemed singer
*Constantine Giordano*, Jim's parole officer
*Desmond Saint-Just*, black radical activist lawyer
*Sister Ann-Margaret*, Catherine Fiore's teacher
*Sister Justine-Marie*, parish school principal
*Father Russell*, pastor
*Rashid & Yosef*, proprietors of a deli in New York
*Pete Barrows*, Little League baseball coach
*Corrigan & Hopkins*, retired cops
*Schmidt*, bartender
*Lonnie and Edgar*, impoundment lot employees
*Rachel Lambert*, manager of a volunteer community school

Motherless children have a harder time.
When the mother is dead, Lord!
Motherless children have a harder time.
When the mother is dead, Lord!

Father will do the best he can.
But there's so many things that he don't understand!

Motherless children have a harder time.
When the mother is dead, Lord!

*"Motherless Children"*
*gospel blues song*
*traditional*

# Motherless Children

# Episode One

01. EXTERIOR, FIELD AND POND—DAY

It's raining. An eight-year-old boy, Joseph Fulton, is dressed for a funeral in a white shirt and clip-on tie, a jacket and dress shoes. He's trudging dreamily through the mud of a vacant field beside a highway, mumbling to himself.

A title card announces: Long Island 1969

Joseph stops and looks off at two boys his own age—Mitch and Ed—working carefully to tie a sturdy length of twine to the leg of a duck they have captured and hold securely in their arms. The terrified duck struggles to get free, but it's no match for the two dangerous and concentrated boys. The pond is really only a big ditch, a runoff for the rain water from the nearby parking lot. Car parts and old shopping carts break the surface of the brown water. Joseph approaches and looks in through the chain-link fence that surrounds it. He studies what the other boys are doing. While Mitch holds the panicked duck, Ed measures the depth of the pond with a stick. Drawing it out of the water, he sees the pond is about five feet deep. Then he trails out the twine to match the depth of the pond against the water mark on the stick. Joseph pushes in through a break in the fence and comes closer. Meanwhile, cutting the twine at the right length, Ed ties its free end securely around a piece of a busted cinder block. Mitch looks over and sees Joseph on the opposite side of the pond.

> MITCH
> *(surprised)*
> Ain't you supposed to be at your mom's funeral?

Joseph shrugs. He watches Ed lift the cinder block and approach the water's edge, Mitch following close behind with the duck as they are now tied together. Concentrating and practiced, the boys toss both the brick and the duck towards the center of the pond. Joseph looks on, troubled, at the fluttering of wings, the squawking and the splash. Mitch and Ed step back, anxious, eagerly assessing the outcome of their handiwork. The water settles and the duck is only able to keep its head above water. The boys watch, riveted.

                    ED
Just a matter of time.

                    MITCH
Fuckin' A!!!

                    ED
They say it's gonna rain till tomorrow morning.

                    MITCH
              *(explains to Joseph)*
And all the water off the parking lot flows down
into here.

The duck throws its head from side to side.

                    ED
                *(excited)*
Inch by inch. Slow death. How long you think?

                    MITCH
Fuck if I know.

                    ED
Joseph, how long you think?

Joseph looks at the sky, the parking lot, the duck.

                    JOSEPH
Couple of hours maybe.

                    MITCH
Shit.
         *(pulls cash from his pocket)*
Ed, go get that pervert who hangs around
the deli to get us a bottle of Thunderbird.

Ed walks away with the money. Mitch lights a cigarette, glancing at Joseph's dress clothes. Church bells ring out in the distance. Hearing them, Ed stops and looks back. Mitch looks from the unseen bells to Joseph who looks down at his feet.

                              MITCH
                You're gonna catch hell for skipping out on
                your mom's funeral.

                              JOSEPH
                Shut up.

And he walks into the pond towards the duck. Mitch is outraged. The cigarette falls from his mouth.

                              MITCH
                Hey!

Ed comes running back—

                              ED
                Don't be a fucking asshole, Joseph!

Joseph makes his way shoulder deep in dirty water towards the duck.

                              MITCH
                We spent all morning capturing that
                fucking animal!

The duck is thrashing around. Joseph holds his breath and goes under.

02. INTERIOR, JIM FULTON'S HOME—DAY

Forty-five-year-old Jim Fulton comes in the back door of his home holding his four-year-old daughter, Natalie. He's followed by a crowd of family and friends all dressed in mourning.

                              NATALIE
                        *(innocently preoccupied)*
                So why don't people have wings like birds?

                              JIM
                          *(exhausted)*
                I don't know, Natalie.

NATALIE
Where does dust come from?

JIM
From, you know, things. Here, quiet a minute. Let's sit.

It's a working-class home. Jim is drawn and, despite some effort, unshaven. The other adults are making coffee, opening liquor and laying out sandwiches. Jim's father-in-law, Paddy Dwyer (70), enters, pats Jim on the shoulder consolingly and sits on the couch, stunned.

NATALIE
Why is everyone sad, Daddy?

JIM
Because Mommy's gone.

NATALIE
But she's gone to heaven, right?

JIM
Yeah. That's right. Mommy's gone to heaven.

NATALIE
But that's a good thing, right? It's nice in heaven. They have built-in swimming pools in heaven, right?

Jim looks to someone for help. A teenage girl comes by.

JIM
Catherine's got some cookies she made.

NATALIE
Okay!!!!

CATHERINE
*(takes the child)*
You come with me.

JIM
Go on.

As Catherine carries Natalie away Jim turns to the table and holds his head. Someone puts a glass of whiskey down beside him. He looks at it, pauses, then picks it up and throws it back. Once the glass is back on the table, it is refilled. His sister-in-law, Marie Dolan (37), sits across from him.

JIM
I'm not ready for this, Marie.

MARIE
None of us are.

JIM
I don't know how to deal with these kids.

MARIE
The older ones will help out.

Another sister-in-law, Ruthy Fulton (35), puts a sandwich in front of him.

RUTHY
Eat something.

JIM
*(looks around)*
And where the hell is Joseph?

RUTHY
He'll be okay. He'll turn up.
*(calls to her own son)*
Brian, go look for your cousin.

BRIAN
I just got a sandwich.

RUTHY
Knock it off! Find Joseph or I'll smack ya!

Jim drinks his second whiskey. His older sons, Richard (18) and Billy (16) crack open cans of beer where they sit on the staircase and continue a conversation from earlier.

                    BILLY
Have you told Dad yet?

                    RICHARD
               *(glances at Jim)*
No.

Billy looks across the room at Catherine who sits with Natalie on her lap. Then he turns back to his brother.

                    BILLY
How pregnant is Catherine, anyway?

                    RICHARD
Two months and some.

                    BILLY
Fuck. What are you gonna do?

                    RICHARD
Marry her, I guess.

                    BILLY
And live where?

                    RICHARD
I don't know. Here?

                    BILLY
               *(skeptical)*
That would be brave.

                    RICHARD
Maybe her house.

Billy starts to drink his beer but is distracted by a particularly lovely teenage girl, Sheila, passing by the staircase on her way to the bathroom. She smiles at him and he follows her with his eyes. Meanwhile—

                      RICHARD
        Dad's in bad shape, I think.

Billy looks off at Jim at the kitchen table where friends of his are talking and trying to keep him upbeat.

                      BILLY
               *(looking for solutions)*
        You could go to work with him.

                      RICHARD
               *(shakes his head)*
        I can't go to work with Dad.

                      BILLY
        As an apprentice you'd be earning like twenty-five dollars an hour. And then there's the annuity.

                      RICHARD
        I don't want to work with Dad.

                      BILLY
        Yeah, I get it.

                      RICHARD
        It's not my kind of thing.

                      BILLY
        But, Richard, you gotta do something. I mean, it means nothing to me, but in the job market you're what's called unskilled.

Richard looks over at Catherine. She smiles back. At the kitchen table, Jim is with Marie's husband, Tom (40).

                      JIM
        Jesus, what am I gonna do with these kids?

TOM
Easy, Jim. They're kids. They take care of themselves.

Billy comes over and leans down to Catherine, kissing her cheek.

BILLY
Congratulations, beautiful.

CATHERINE
Oh! Billy! Thank you. Thank you.

BILLY
And everything's gonna be alright.

CATHERINE
Yeah? You think so?

BILLY
Have you told your folks?

CATHERINE
My mom.

BILLY
And your dad?

CATHERINE
*(worried)*
She'll talk to him.

Sheila walks by again and she and Billy share a smile.

BILLY
Who is that?

CATHERINE
Shelia?

BILLY
She related to me?

CATHERINE
She's your aunt Theresa's niece.

BILLY
So, we're not, like, related?

CATHERINE
*(rolls her eyes)*
Billy!

BILLY
What?

CATHERINE
This is a funeral.

BILLY
I know that, Catherine.

CATHERINE
It's your mother's funeral.

Meanwhile, Jim is shaking his head and scratching his chin, still amazed, stunned. Someone pours him another whiskey. Ruthy is rubbing his shoulder.

RUTHY
You just go ahead and cry if you want to, Jim.

Jim just looks at her. He has no intention of crying. He looks at his older brother, Ruthy's husband, Mike Fulton (48).

MIKE
We're just family here and God knows there ain't none of us is perfect.

This is equally unhelpful. Besides, Jim is preoccupied.

JIM
Where the *hell* is Joseph you think?

                    RUTHY
        Poor boy.

                    JIM
        How can he just bolt on a day like this?

                    RUTHY
        He's confused.

                    JIM
                *(drinks)*
        That kid's unusual.

                    MARIE
        Jim, this is a bad day for him too. He's just
        finding his own way. Leave him be.

03. EXTERIOR, JIM FULTON'S HOME—DAY

It's still raining. Joseph shuffles up alongside the house carrying the wounded duck. He hugs the wall and overhears the gathering inside. There's a pile of building supplies against the garage and he locates a ladder. He climbs up onto the roof with the duck but pauses to sneeze.

04. INTERIOR, JIM FULTON'S HOME—DAY

Billy and Sheila are making out on Joseph's bed upstairs. Sheila pulls away.

                    SHEILA
        What was that!

                    BILLY
        What?

                    SHEILA
        I heard something.

Billy doesn't care but she scrambles up and drags him out of the room anyway.

Downstairs, Jim and another relative, Leo (45), are hunched over the edge of the kitchen table.

> LEO
> You gave her a good life, Jim. It's a tragedy, of course. But while she lived, she had the things she wanted. Well-brought-up kids, a good house.

> JIM
> I could never make her happy, Leo. She was never satisfied. Not with me anyway.

Leo pours the man another shot.

> LEO
> Now you're talking like a madman, son.

Richard is carrying Natalie, who is asleep, up the stairs. He turns off to the left and enters one of the two upstairs rooms and places her on the bed. He covers her with a blanket. Coming back out, he hears something in the opposite room. He crosses the landing and, opening the door, finds Joseph just stepping in the window with the duck.

> RICHARD
> What are you doing?

> JOSEPH
> They were gonna kill it.

> RICHARD
> Get the fuck in here.

Moments later, Richard comes to the bottom of the stairs and looks across at Catherine. He gestures for help and she moves towards him. She follows Richard upstairs and into the room, sees Joseph and sighs.

> CATHERINE
> Joseph! My God, what happened to you!
> *(aside)*

Richard, go get some towels.
>    *(to Joseph)*
Your father is furious. Everyone is worried. What have you been doing? What is this?

#### JOSEPH

A duck.

#### CATHERINE

I know it's a duck, Joseph.

#### JOSEPH

Its leg is broken.

Down in the kitchen, everyone is singing the chorus to an old ballad, Leo leading. Richard comes past and into the first-floor hallway. He throws open a closet and starts collecting towels. Catherine's mother, Trish Fiore (50), sees him and pulls him aside.

#### TRISH

What's with the towels? My daughter okay?

#### RICHARD

What? Oh. Yeah. It's Joseph. He fell in a creek or something.

#### TRISH

You tell your father yet?

#### RICHARD

About Joseph?

#### TRISH

No! About Catherine.

#### RICHARD

Sorry. No. No. I didn't.

#### TRISH

Probably just as well. It's okay. Scat.

He runs off. Trish drifts up the hall towards the kitchen where Jim is surrounded by people singing.

Fade to black.

05. INTERIOR, JIM FULTON'S HOME—NIGHT

A month later: Joseph and Natalie are watching TV in the living room. The place is a mess. Jim is standing at the kitchen sink, staring out into the backyard. A bottle of whiskey stands on the counter. He knocks back a shot and cocks his head when he hears, far off in the distance, the screeching of car tires. Joseph and Natalie hear it too and look away from the TV.

> JIM
> *(checks the time)*
> That'll be your aunt Marie.

06. EXTERIOR, STREETS—NIGHT

Behind the wheel of her 1967 Chevy Impala, Marie comes speeding around the corner, smoking—a lot on her mind.

07. INTERIOR, JIM FULTON'S HOME—NIGHT

> JIM
> Come on, clear this mess up off the floor.

> JOSEPH
> That's my homework.

> JIM
> Go wash your face and hands.

The kids scramble away while Jim attempts to straighten up.

08. EXTERIOR, JIM FULTON'S HOME—NIGHT

Marie skids to a stop before the house and gets out. She throws open the backseat door and lifts out a big pot of something still hot.

09. INTERIOR, JIM FULTON'S HOME—NIGHT

Marie comes in the front door with the steaming pot.

                  MARIE
Hello! Richard? Billy?

                  JIM
Good evening, Marie.

                  MARIE
                 *(surprised)*
Oh, you're here. Didn't you go to work today?

                  JIM
No.

She puts the pot on the stove and expertly removes the whiskey bottle from the counter and replaces it in the cabinet beneath the sink. Jim doesn't notice this as he throws back another shot.

                  MARIE
Where are the boys?

                  JIM
I think Richard's up the street at his girlfriend's house. Not sure about Billy.

Joseph and Natalie come into the kitchen and, as Marie turns away to greet them, Jim reaches for the bottle, finds it's not there, then bends down to remove it from beneath the sink again.

                  MARIE
Joseph, your shoe's untied. Natalie, what have you done to your hair?

                  NATALIE
Joseph did it.

                  JOSEPH
She said it was in her eyes.

Marie carefully removes an old rusted clamp from Natalie's tangled hair.

>                    MARIE
> What is this rusted old clamp?

>                    JOSEPH
> I found it.

>                    JIM
> Hey, that's from my tool box. I need that.

Marie hands it to Jim.

>                    MARIE
>                 *(to Joseph)*
> Run and go get me a hair brush.

>                    JIM
> Joseph, I told you to stay out of my tool box!

Marie lifts Natalie and sits her on the counter, nudging Jim out of the way. He sits at the table as Marie once again places the whiskey beneath the sink and, when Joseph returns with a brush, begins neatening the little girl's hair. Everything is comparatively quiet and peaceful. Jim watches Joseph who is entertaining himself by trying to sit upside down in a chair.

>                    MARIE
>                 *(to Natalie)*
> Poor girl, you'll have to try and civilize
> these men.

>                    NATALIE
> Okay.

Marie glances over at Joseph.

>                    MARIE
>            *(bangs brush on counter)*
> Hey! Cut that out and sit up straight!

>           *(then)*
> Jim, that stew's hot. Get some for him before
> he sets the house on fire.

Jim moves mechanically to the stove and grabs a ladle. He opens the pot.

>                     JIM
> Where's your brood? Don't they have to eat?

>                     MARIE
> The girls are on some sort of starvation diet. I
> gotta get back. The boys have a football game.

>                     JIM
>             *(of stew)*
> This will last us till the weekend.

>                     MARIE
> You going down to the hall tomorrow?

>                     JIM
> Joseph, bring me over your dish.
>             *(then answers)*
> Yeah. I think so.

>                   JOSEPH
> What is it?

>                     JIM
> Shut up. Lift the dish higher. Thank your
> Aunt Marie.

>                   JOSEPH
> Thank you, Aunt Marie.

Jim ladles out a portion of stew.

10. INTERIOR, JIM FULTON'S HOME—DAWN

The alarm clock is beeping. Five in the morning. Jim reaches out and stops it before falling back to sleep. But Richard leans in the doorway.

> RICHARD
> Dad. Dad.

> JIM
> Huh?

> RICHARD
> Dad. Get up.

Jim sits up again and looks around him. Natalie is in the hallway, whimpering.

> JIM
> Oh Jesus, we've woken her up now.

> RICHARD
> Come on, Natalie, back to bed.

> NATALIE
> I want cereal.

> RICHARD
> It's too early for cereal.

She starts crying as Jim staggers across the hall and into the bathroom.

> JIM
> Shut her up for crying out loud.

Then Joseph appears carrying a hockey stick as a weapon.

> JOSEPH
> *(excited)*
> Is something wrong? What's happening? Are there thieves?

Richard hands him the child.

RICHARD
Shut up. Here, give her some cereal and put her back to bed.

JOSEPH
It's the middle of the night!

RICHARD
*(takes hockey stick)*
Knock it off. In two hours you have to be up for school anyway.

Jim comes back out of the bathroom and looks at the kitchen sink.

JIM
What have I told you about leaving the dishes in the sink! When I come home from work tonight...

RICHARD
*(rattles car keys)*
Dad, come on, you're gonna be late. Your train leaves in ten minutes.

JIM
What are you doing with my keys?

RICHARD
I need the car today. I'll pick you up at the station. We talked about this.

JIM
We did?

RICHARD
Yeah. Billy has to take his scholarship test in Hempstead today.
*(aside to Joseph)*
Take that knife away from her.

Natalie is toying with a carving knife the size of her arm. Just as

Jim and Richard head out the back door, Billy wanders in after a night of partying.

> BILLY
> Ah... hey.

> JIM
> Where the hell have you been all night?

> BILLY
> Uhmm. We ah. You know.

> RICHARD
> *(annoyed)*
> Get some sleep.
> *(to Jim)*
> Come on.

> JIM
> *(glares at Billy)*
> I'll deal with you when I get home.

Richard and Jim leave. Billy looks around at the kitchen and the two little kids.

> BILLY
> Wow, this place is a mess!

The kids crack up. Billy grabs a can of beer out of the fridge and sits with them at the table.

> BILLY
> Ain't it a little early for you to be up and about there, princess?

> NATALIE
> In two hours Joseph's got to go to school.

> BILLY
> Yeah, I guess there's no point risking being late, huh.

JOSEPH
You going to college today?

BILLY
I just gotta take the test.

JOSEPH
Just to get into college? I thought you had to take a test to get out of college.

BILLY
To get this scholarship. Money. If I get a high enough grade they give me money to pay for college.

JOSEPH
Is it a hard test?

BILLY
No sweat. Ask me something. Anything.

JOSEPH
*(thinks, then)*
When was America discovered?

BILLY
Ah! Good question. But which discovery?

JOSEPH
What?

BILLY
Of course, there was the famous Italian working for the Spaniards, but then, way before that, there was Leif Erikson, from Iceland.

JOSEPH
Iceland?

BILLY
A Viking.

                    JOSEPH
        You mean with the helmet and the horns?

                    BILLY
    Exactly.

                    NATALIE
    Exactly!

Meanwhile—

11. INTERIOR, MIKE FULTON'S HOME—DAWN

Ruthy screws on the top of Mike's thermos, puts it in his lunch box, clips it shut and hands it to him just as he zips up his coat.

                    MIKE
                *(kisses her)*
        Thank you, dear.
                *(then, to his sons)*
        Come on, you two!

And he goes out. Two of their sons, John (19) and Edward (17) are half asleep over their tea and toast. Ruthy takes their cups and plates away.

                    RUTHY
        Let's go. Go on! Your father'll leave without
        ya, don't you worry about that. Take your
        lunches.

She kisses them both and they stumble out the door. Tossing her lunch supplies back into the fridge, she notices the lights on next door and hears Billy and the younger ones laughing. She goes over to her kitchen window and can see directly over into Jim's kitchen. She frowns.

12. INTERIOR, JIM FULTON'S HOME—DAWN

Billy listens, fascinated, as Joseph elaborates on his own invented history of the world—

JOSEPH

Because Erikson was the strongest and meanest of all the Vikings and he broke the law, he... he...
*(invents something)*
He stole someone's lunch money and... and... he was exiled. He had to go out into the wilderness and no one was allowed to talk to him or give him a place to stay... but...

BILLY

He was outlawed!

JOSEPH

Yeah! He was outlawed. But... but even though he was mean and super tough he was afraid of the dark!

BILLY

Get outta here!

JOSEPH

It's true! And you know in Iceland—way up there, you know, at the top of the world...

BILLY

The Arctic.

JOSEPH

Yeah, in the Arctic, in the winter it's like night time all day long!

BILLY

Bad news for a Viking who's afraid of the dark.

JOSEPH

Yeah, and so he built a boat and rowed all the way to Florida!

RUTHY
*(entering)*
What's going on in here!

BILLY
*(stands, caught)*
Oh! Aunt Ruthy! Sorry. We...

She lifts the beer can out of his hand and puts it in the sink.

RUTHY
It's too early for her to be eating breakfast.

NATALIE
Joseph has to go to school in two hours.

RUTHY
That's right and he should still be asleep. Come here you.
*(picks up Natalie then, to the boy...)*
Joseph your face is filthy. You went to bed like that?

JOSEPH
There were burglars. I was setting a trap. But Richard took my hockey stick.

Bewildered, Ruthy knows enough not to reason with this kid. She shakes her head clear and addresses Billy.

RUTHY
And what? Did you just get in?

BILLY
*(pretends to be in charge)*
Joseph, come on, we'll get your face clean.

RUTHY
*(not fooled)*
Don't bother with that now. What time is your test?

BILLY
Eleven.

RUTHY
Go to bed. Now. I'll wake you at nine thirty.
Where's Richard?

BILLY
He drove Dad to the station.

RUTHY
Scram.

Billy takes off towards his bed. Ruthy looks at Joseph.

RUTHY
And what are we gonna do with you?

The kid just shrugs.

RUTHY
Can you stay awake until it's time for school?

JOSEPH
Yeah. I suppose.

As long as she's there anyway, she steps over, opens the fridge and checks inside. She sighs in dismay at what she sees. Then, returning to Joseph—

RUTHY
If you go back to sleep now there'll be no
waking you at all.

JOSEPH
*(full of ideas)*
I could clean the dishes.

RUTHY
*(considers this)*
Without hurting yourself?

JOSEPH
Yeah.

                        RUTHY
            Without breaking anything?

                        JOSEPH
                    *(thinks about it)*
            Probably.

                        RUTHY
            Okay. Call out the window here to me when
            you're done.

She leaves. Joseph leans down and opens the cabinet beneath the sink. He looks at Jim's bottle of whiskey. The kid makes sure the coast is clear, then reaches in and grabs the bottle. He goes to the fridge and takes out various liquids: syrup, vinegar, steak sauce. He carries them to the sink and begins mixing a potion that begins to resemble the whiskey.

13. EXTERIOR, TRAIN STATION—DAWN

The sun is just coming up. Jim gets out of the car and approaches the suburban train station along with dozens of other local workingmen. He gets in line to buy a coffee from a little truck at the foot of the stairs leading up to the elevated tracks. Tom Dolan is in line already.

                        TOM
            Morning Jim.

                        JIM
            Tom.

They pay for their coffees and start up the stairs reaching the platform, just as the train pulls in. Mike is already there, scanning the headline of his newspaper.

                        TOM
            Mike.

                        MIKE
            Tom.

                             TOM
                    *(to Mike's sleepy sons)*
                    Rise and shine, boys!

                             MIKE
                          *(to Jim)*
                    You going down the hall?

                             JIM
Yeah.

They all board the train.

14. EXTERIOR, JIM FULTON'S HOME—DAWN

Ruthy carries Natalie back across the lawn towards her house as Richard pulls up in the driveway. She stops and waits for him to get out of the car.

                           RICHARD
                    What happened now?

                            RUTHY
                    Get Joseph ready for school and come see
                    me later.

And she storms off with the child. Richard heads on inside.

15. INTERIOR, JIM FULTON'S HOME—DAWN

Joseph finishes pouring Jim's whiskey down the sink. He finds a funnel and pours his concoction into the bottle. But then he hears Richard coming in the front door. He tries to hide the bottle and accidentally knocks a bowl to the floor. It smashes to bits. Richard stops in the doorway and looks at the broken crockery strewn across the kitchen. The duck waddles by with an ice-cream stick splint taped to its broken leg.

                           JOSEPH
                    That's the old salad bowl that nobody likes
                    anyway.

                    RICHARD
I won't tell you again: this duck cannot be
in the house.

He turns away, goes into the living room, and falls on the couch, asleep immediately.

16. INTERIOR, UNION HALL—DAY

The Union Hall is exactly that: a long tall hallway in an old building in lower Manhattan. Workingmen are sitting around waiting. There's an office with a burly man at a desk on a phone: Flood.

                    FLOOD
Yeah. Right. Okay.
          *(hangs up and reads from a
          list of names)*
Carter! Johnson!

Two men at different ends of the hall stand and approach.

                    FLOOD
Cam-Ron job, corner of Sixth Avenue and
Forty-Third. See Tommy Maher.

Carter and Johnson crowd into the office and sign their names in a log book. Flood looks past them and is surprised to see Jim in the hallway.

                    FLOOD
Jesus fucking Christ, Jim!

                    JIM
Flood.
          *(then, to Carter)*
Hey, Dennis.

                    CARTER
Hey. How's everything, Jim? Family alright?

Jim nods and lightens things up with a joke at Johnson's expense.

JIM
Yeah. Yeah. Thanks. Don't worry about us.
We're fine. You just look after yourself
boltin' up with this failure here.

Johnson laughs and punches Jim affectionately in the arm as he passes back out through the doorway.

JOHNSON
Welcome back, Jim.

The two men move off and Flood offers Jim a seat.

FLOOD
What are you doing back here so soon?

JIM
*(sits, shrugs)*
I gotta work.

FLOOD
You can take your time. There's always
gonna be work for you. And if there's any
kind of financial hassle in the meantime
you know the union's not gonna let you sink.

Jim hears this out and nods, but—

JIM
I'm going crazy at home.

Flood notices Jim's state: unshaven, jittery. He stands and closes the door.

FLOOD
*(sits back down)*
Tough time with the kids?

JIM
No. Not really. I just—I don't know how to
do it, to deal with them. Audrey raised them.

>           I played with them when they were little and
>           everything but now—they're a mystery to me.

Flood taps a cigarette out of his pack and offers one to Jim.

>                          FLOOD
>           Who's the oldest one, Richard?

>                           JIM
>           Yeah, Richard. He's out of high school
>           now and has no idea what he wants
>           to do with himself. Just hangs around with
>           his girlfriend from up the street. Hoping for
>           something to come along. He'll probably
>           get drafted. Then the second one, Billy, he
>           wants to go to college, for Christ's sake.

>                          FLOOD
>           He's the smart one, right?

>                           JIM
>           As a whip. But reckless. And how would I
>           know. It's just what the teachers told Audrey:
>           the kid's bright, gotta encourage him and
>           whatnot.

>                          FLOOD
>           Yeah, I told my kid, I says, if you're so smart
>           why you gotta go to college for anyway?
>           Answer me that!

They both laugh. They smoke. Finally, Jim shakes his head—

>                           JIM
>           No, he should go to school if he can—Billy
>           should. I don't want him doing this.

>                          FLOOD
>                    *(pretends to be insulted)*
>           What's wrong with this? It's been good enough
>           for the likes of us!

                    JIM
Yeah, it's good when it's good. When there's
work. And we got the union. But when the
work's thin on the ground it makes a guy worry.
          *(sits forward)*
I mean, Flood, I have a four-year-old girl. Len,
my brother, he's got two girls—older—girls are
expensive. Boys you can just throw out of the
house when they're working age. Can't do that
with girls.

Flood rifles through some papers on his desk, looking for the list of jobs. Jim smokes and continues—

                    JIM
And then there's Joseph. He's seven—or eight...
He might be ten. Anyway, this one's gonna be
a lot of trouble.

                    FLOOD
          *(looks up)*
Sickly?

                    JIM
          *(mystified)*
No. He's a liar.

                    FLOOD
          *(laughs out loud)*
Whoa! Them is fightin' words, Jim!

                    JIM
He just makes things up! All the time. Lies
without flinching. Even when he ain't done
nothing wrong. Flood, I'm telling ya, this
kid will not give you a straight answer if his
life depended on it. Oh, and Audrey, she
loved it. Creative, she called him. Artistic.
Spoiled him rotten. And he's a bad influence
on his little sister. She believes everything
he says.

Flood leans over the desk with the log book.

> FLOOD
> Okay, look. The Skanska job on Seventh Avenue at Fifty-Third. Jimmy Mullet's the shop steward. Just go boltin' up for a few weeks. We don't want you pushing a derrick till everything, you know, gets back to normal.

Jim signs the book.

> JIM
> *(glad)*
> Thanks, Flood.

17. INTERIOR, HIGH SCHOOL GYM—DAY

Billy is taking the test along with hundreds of other students. He moves confidently through a list of multiple-choice questions then yawns and contemplates the next page.

18. EXTERIOR, HIGH SCHOOL PARKING LOT—DAY

Billy comes out and finds Richard waiting for him. Richard looks irritated, concerned about the outcome. Billy leans against the car and avoids Richard's stare.

> RICHARD
> So?

> BILLY
> What?

> RICHARD
> How'd you do?

> BILLY
> I passed.

> RICHARD
> But passing ain't enough, is it?

                            BILLY
        Hey, back off!

Richard shoves him. Billy shoves him back. They start swinging.

19. EXTERIOR, JOB SITE—DAY

In the yard formed by tall wooden planks around the base of this building in progress, Jim straps on his tool belt and dons his hard hat while being greeted by the shop steward, Mullet. It's too noisy to hear anything. The din of the job site competes with the roar of midtown Manhattan. Jim steps over to a large steel toolbox and gets himself what he needs: two offset spud wrenches, an adjustable wrench, a bull pin, a four-pound sledgehammer, another piece of tapered iron called a "sleever bar" and a folding rule. Then he walks over to the iron cage elevator where an elderly worker lets him in and closes the gate.

                            TOMMY
        Where to, boss!?

                            JIM
        Forty-two, Tommy! Thanks!

The elevator kicks into action and rises, rattling up along the outside edge of the building. The yard falls away out of sight, revealing the facades of the office buildings around them. Then these, too, fall away as the elevator rises higher. Jim looks out and down at the rooftops of the city and sees even the Hudson River and New Jersey to the west. And, of course, this spectacular view hardly interests him. He studies the sky.

                            TOMMY
                        *(notices)*
        Bad weather over Westchester.

                            JIM
        It'll miss us, I think.

                            TOMMY
        Here we are.

And the cage jolts to a halt. Tommy drags open the gate and Jim steps out onto the forty-second floor, two floors below the top where steel columns and beams are being set still higher. Jim immediately meets a young black man, Clarence (30), who looks surprised to see him.

CLARENCE

Hey Jim!

JIM
*(shakes his hand)*
Clarence! What are you doing here? I thought you were in my brother Mike's gang over on the Grand Central job.

CLARENCE
Yeah, but they're finishing up over there. Sending guys back to the hall. I been here a week. You boltin' up?

JIM
Yeah. Can you set me up?

CLARENCE
Sure thing. All those points along there need to be done still.

JIM
I'll just make the points first and come back with the impact wrench later.

CLARENCE

Right.

Jim climbs a ladder up to the nearest "point" where four horizontal beams meet a vertical column. Clarence fills a metal basket with bolts and their corresponding nuts and washers. Jim straddles a beam right up close to a column and waits for the bolts. He looks around at a few other men doing the same work, though one of them is tightening the bolts with a compressed air impact wrench. Clarence tosses Jim up one end of a line of rope and knots the other end around the handle of the steel mesh basket. Jim is intrigued.

                    JIM
What kinda' knot is that!

                    CLARENCE
                    *(sagely)*
That would be your standard issue clove hitch, Mister Fulton! I'm doing the apprentice school two evenings a week now. All sorts of new knots to learn!

                    JIM
They made you an apprentice! But you're a journeyman for years now.

                    CLARENCE
                    *(shrugs, then)*
It's ah... I don't know. Some new rule. Hey, listen, Jim—my condolences. About your loss.

                    JIM
Thank you, Clarence. Look, I'll work this point and make my way towards the perimeter.

                    CLARENCE
Got it.

Clarence moves off to deliver bolts to the other men and Jim sets to work. But first he takes of sip of whiskey from his hip flask.

20. INTERIOR, JIM FULTON'S HOME—NIGHT

It's tense at the supper table. Jim is drunk and dangerous. Richard and Billy have cuts and scrapes on their faces. Joseph and Natalie look on and keep quiet.

                    JIM
You failed?

BILLY
I didn't fail. I just didn't score high enough.

JIM
But you failed to get the scholarship.

Billy just pushes his plate away and looks at Richard.

RICHARD
Let's talk about it later.

JIM
If you weren't out drinking all night with your asshole friends!

BILLY
Me! You're giving me shit about drinking?

RICHARD
Okay! Look! That's enough! Billy, get out of here!

JIM
You selfish little punk! You expect me to...

BILLY
I don't expect *anything* from you!

Billy stands up and walks out the back door. Jim looks to Richard. Richard looks to Joseph who sits wide-eyed and still before his plate.

RICHARD
Go watch TV. Take Natalie with you.

Joseph grabs Natalie by the hand to go.

JIM
They ain't done eating yet.

Joseph stops, worried, and looks back at Richard. Richard nods to go and Joseph flees with his little sister. Jim and Richard sit there in silence. Then—

                    RICHARD
          Aunt Ruthy and Aunt Marie want to take
          Joseph and Natalie.
                *(pauses as Jim bristles)*
          For a while, at least, until...

                    JIM
          No.

Richard, looks away, gathers his strength, and continues.

                    RICHARD
          I'm gonna marry Catherine.

Jim looks up from his plate and glares at him. Richard looks at his glass of water, reaches out to lift it, then changes his mind and drops his hands into his lap. Jim stands and crosses to the sink. He opens the cabinet beneath it and takes out (what he believes to be) his bottle of whiskey. Richard looks away and sighs. Jim pours himself a shot. He lifts it and is about to drink, but places it back down on the counter.

                    JIM
          She pregnant?

                    RICHARD
          Yeah.

Jim shakes his head and sighs. He almost drinks, but then stops and looks at his son.

                    JIM
          What more can we do to make the situation
          worse, Richard?

                    RICHARD
                *(pushes back)*
          You could keep drinking.

Jim drops the shot on the counter and lunges for his son. They crash down through the kitchen table. Joseph jumps to his feet in front of the TV, runs to the doorway and sees Jim and Richard beating the hell out of each other.

21. EXTERIOR, STREET—NIGHT

Joseph runs up the street dragging Natalie behind him

22. INTERIOR, DOLAN HOME—NIGHT

Joseph bursts in the back door and startles Marie.

> JOSEPH
> They're gonna kill each other!

23. EXTERIOR, DOLAN HOME—NIGHT

Marie strides to her car while Tom calls from the front door.

> TOM
> Marie, calm down! What do you think you're gonna to do?

But she just gets in her car and speeds recklessly around the corner to Jim's place.

24. INTERIOR, JIM FULTON'S HOME—NIGHT

Marie throws open the front door and comes through the house till she reaches the kitchen. Richard is alone, sitting on the floor, leaning against the counter with his head in his hands. Marie begins sobbing immediately and comes down over him, lifting his face. He is bleeding in a few places. She daubs at a cut on his forehead.

> MARIE
> Did he do this to you?

> RICHARD
> No. Billy did that. Dad hurt my jaw, though.

                    MARIE
Where's he gone?

                    RICHARD
I don't know. He took off in the car.

                    MARIE
You okay?

                    RICHARD
I think my ankle's busted.

25. EXTERIOR, JIM FULTON'S HOME—NIGHT

As Marie comes out of the house, Ruthy and Mike pull up into their own driveway.

                    RUTHY
What's wrong!

                    MARIE
He beat up Richard and took off!

Ruthy looks at Mike as if to say *I told you so.*

                    MIKE
We passed him on Hoffman Avenue pulling into the Station Cafe.

                    RUTHY
Where are the kids?

                    MARIE
            *(getting in her car)*
At my house.

                    MIKE
Now, where are you going?

                    MARIE
I'm gonna talk sense into that brother of yours

if I have to do it with a big stick!
*(turns back and adds)*
Richard needs to go to the hospital.

             MIKE
      *(hangs his head)*
Oh, sweet Jesus!

Marie puts her car into gear and peels out. Ruthy walks up the street to Marie's house.

             RUTHY
I'll go get the kids.

26. INTERIOR, STATION CAFE—NIGHT

Jim enters and the bartender, Schmidt, is alarmed.

             SCHMIDT
Jim, you okay?

             JIM
It's nothing. Whiskey.

             SCHMIDT
You're bleeding.

             JIM
You should see the other guy.

             STAN
      *(another regular)*
Who's the other guy?

             JIM
Richard, my oldest.

             STAN
Fuck no!

Jim sits and works out a kink in his neck.

JIM
Yeah. He can fight. Damn. He might've broke my rib.

Then Marie throws open the door and stands there in the entrance.

JIM
Fuck! Will you leave me alone!

MARIE
You oughta be ashamed of yourself.

SCHMIDT
*(to Marie)*
I can't serve him.

JIM
What! Schmidt... what the hell?
*(then to Marie)*
Look, Marie, you have no idea of the kinda shit I'm going through!

She comes in and stands a few feet away.

MARIE
Oh, spare me! You think you're the first man on earth to lose his wife and be saddled with a bunch of kids?

JIM
Did you know Richard's got Catherine knocked up?

Marie is blindsided by this. She glances at Schmidt who, understanding, turns away and motions to Stan.

SCHMIDT
*(moves off)*
Stan, down here.

Marie sets her bag on the bar and comes closer.

MARIE
No. I didn't. Is that why you beat him up?

JIM
I didn't beat him up. We fought.

MARIE
You dislocated his jaw. His ankle's busted.

JIM
You can't come in here and tell me how to run my home—how to raise my kids!

MARIE
Yes, I can.

JIM
Oh yeah? Who died and made you boss?

MARIE
My sister, asshole! Your wife.

Jim pushes away from the bar and heads for the door.

MARIE
Where are you going?

JIM
Fuck off!

MARIE
Jim, be sensible! You're in no condition to... drive!

But he's gone. Exhausted, Marie collapses onto a bar stool and hangs her head. Schmidt puts a glass down in front of her.

MARIE
Scotch and water. Thanks.

He's splashes the whiskey into the glass and shoots some water over it. Marie lifts the drink, sips it, and sighs in exhaustion.

27. EXTERIOR, STATION CAFE—NIGHT

Jim peels out from the parking lot and swerves dangerously into fast-moving traffic.

28. EXTERIOR, HIGHWAY—NIGHT

He drives along, talking to himself, pissed off. He sees the flashing lights of a police car in the rearview.

> JIM
> Oh, you gotta be kiddin' me!

A squad car comes up alongside and an alert and scowling young policeman, Armstrong (30), motions for him to pull over. Jim complies. The officer pulls up behind him. But Jim starts getting out of his car and Armstrong stands up out of his—

> ARMSTRONG
> Sir! Stay in the car! Sir!

> JIM
> Listen, you son of a bitch...

> ARMSTRONG
> Sir, get back in your vehicle!

But by then, they're both already standing on the roadside.

> ARMSTRONG
> Sir, this is a violation of...

And Jim throws a punch, connecting hard with Armstrong's jaw. The younger man staggers aside but then bounces back, shoves Jim against the car and cuffs him in a flash.

29. INTERIOR, MIKE FULTON'S HOME—NIGHT

Ruthy tucks Natalie in before getting Joseph settled in another bed across the room.

> RUTHY
> Now, go to sleep.

> JOSEPH
> Natalie's gonna cry when she wakes up in the night.

> RUTHY
> Never you mind about that. I'm right across the hall.

Ruthy dims the lights and steps out onto the staircase.

30. EXTERIOR, HIGHWAY—NIGHT

A little later: Jim is up against his car, his hands cuffed. Another squad car arrives and an older officer, Polansky, gets out and approaches.

> ARMSTRONG
> Speeding. Driving while intoxicated. Resisting arrest.

> POLANSKY
> Assaulting an officer of the law.

> JIM
> My taxes pay your goddamned salaries, you bastards!

> POLANSKY
> Yeah, it's a funny world, ain't it.

They throw him in the squad car.

31. INTERIOR, HOSPITAL—NIGHT

Richard comes out to the waiting room, accompanied by his uncle Mike. He's wearing a neck brace. Catherine stands up, horrified.

Her mother calms her.

> TRISH
> Easy, Catherine.

> CATHERINE
> *(runs to Richard)*
> Are you okay?

> RICHARD
> I don't even think I need this thing.

Mike steps away and leaves the young people their privacy.

> MIKE
> Hello Trish.

> TRISH
> Hi, Mike. Ruthy called us. She's got the little ones with her at your house.

> MIKE
> Where's Marie?

> TRISH
> Don't know.

> MIKE
> *(of Richard)*
> Can you drive him back?

> TRISH
> Yeah. Go ahead. I'll see you later.

> RICHARD
> *(to Catherine)*
> I told him we were getting married.

> CATHERINE
> *(appalled)*
> And he *hit* you?

**RICHARD**
No. He hit me when I told him you were pregnant.

**TRISH**
*(heads for the exit)*
Let's go, you two.

But they all stop when they see Paddy Dwyer entering from the sidewalk. He comes in and stops.

**MIKE**
Paddy.

**PADDY**
Mike. Missus Fiore.
*(turns to the boy)*
Richard, what's this I hear about you roughin' up your old man?

**RICHARD**
Grandpa, this is Catherine.

**PADDY**
Hello, Catherine.
*(then, to Richard)*
What is this contraption around your neck?

**RICHARD**
I don't think I even need it.

**PADDY**
Well, come on with me now. We've got to go bargain with the law for your father's freedom.

**MIKE**
Oh no! What? What happened?

**PADDY**
They got him driving drunk and he took a

swing at a cop is what I hear. Come on, Richard.

## 32. INTERIOR, MIKE FULTON'S HOME—NIGHT

Ruthy comes into the kitchen where Marie is at the table gazing out the window over to Jim's kitchen window forty feet away. Ruthy sits, pours more tea, and looks over as well.

MARIE
I miss her so much.

RUTHY
I can't get used to not seeing her there in the kitchen window.

MARIE
Jim's ruining himself.

RUTHY
He'll be okay once the smoke clears.

MARIE
Ruthy, he's out of control.

RUTHY
Marie, if you and me had a nickle for every man in both our families who ran off on a bender now and again and was locked out of the house by his own wife we'd be rich ladies with fur coats.

MARIE
*(smiles, then)*
We can't leave the kids in the house with him in that condition.

RUTHY
I can take Joseph. The boys won't even notice another one in amongst them all. Can you take Natalie?

                    MARIE
        She'd be better off with my girls.

Mike comes in the back door and stands at the kitchen counter.

                    MIKE
        The cops got him.

                    RUTHY
    Who?

                    MIKE
        Jim.
            *(then to Marie)*
        Your father's gone up to try and get him out.

33. INTERIOR, POLICE PRECINCT—NIGHT

In a holding cell, Jim sits on the edge of the hard, narrow bunk, elbows on knees, staring at the floor. Finally, he sighs and shakes his head.

                    JIM
            *(whispers weakly)*
        Jesus Mary and Joseph.

Out in the lobby, Paddy is dealing with the desk sergeant, Officer Whalen, while Richard tries to keep his dad in sight without letting him know it.

                    WHALEN
            *(explains)*
        Well, Mister Dwyer, the driving while
        intoxicated that can happen to anyone but,
        you know, he assaulted an officer of the law.

                    PADDY
        Oh, yes, that's bad, that is, assaulting an
        officer of the law.
            *(to Richard)*
        Remember that, lad.

**WHALEN**
It complicates things.

**PADDY**
It does, indeed, it does.

Paddy turns away from the desk and takes Richard aside. He looks down the hall to the cells, thinks a moment, then—

**PADDY**
What do you say we leave him in there for the night?

**RICHARD**
*(terrified)*
What?

**PADDY**
It'll do him a world of good.

**RICHARD**
*(worried)*
He'll be mighty pissed off.

Paddy steps over and takes a look at Jim as well.

**PADDY**
He's already mighty pissed off. But he can't do himself any harm in there. He needs some time to cool off.
*(to Whalen)*
That possible officer?

**WHALEN**
*(reading his newspaper)*
We have the room.

Paddy nods. That's settled. He leads Richard toward the exit.

**PADDY**
Come on. You're eighteen now, right?

                    RICHARD
Since yesterday.

                    PADDY
Let me buy you your first legal drink.

## 34. EXTERIOR, STATION CAFE—NIGHT

As it turns out, the Station Cafe is across the street from the Police Precinct, practically beneath the train station, and adjacent to the Roman Catholic church on the corner. Paddy and Richard approach.

                    RICHARD
                *(slows up)*
I don't know, Grandpa: The Station Cafe?

                    PADDY
Yeah, I know it's a place for retired cops.
                *(stops and turns)*
But you and I, we need some reliable
advice right now.

Richard hesitates, but then follows.

## 35. INTERIOR, THE STATION CAFE—NIGHT

Paddy and Richard enter and stop near the door.

                    PADDY
Excuse me, is there a policeman present!

The four old men present, all retired cops, turn away from the bar.

                    CORRIGAN
Goddamn it, Dwyer, you're under arrest!
And who's this delinquent you've got in tow?

                    PADDY
                *(approaches bar)*
This is Richard, my grandson.

SCHMIDT
Jim Fulton's boy?

PADDY
The oldest. He's legal. Give him a beer.

SCHMIDT
Sorry to hear about the loss of your mother, son. Your old man was in here just two hours ago.

CORRIGAN
How's he holding up? Must be a hell of a time these past months.

RICHARD
*(confused, embarrassed)*
Well, he's, ah...

Paddy knocks back a shot and smacks the glass back down.

PADDY
He's in the lockup across the street.

CORRIGAN
No!

PADDY
He got pulled over after having a few drinks and assaulting one of your confederates by the name of Armstrong.

HOPKINS
*(another retired cop)*
Oh, shit! Armstrong's an ass!

CORRIGAN
Armstrong wants to be mayor. It's this new breed of policemen. I don't know what they're teaching those punks at the academy these days.

Paddy nods, grateful for the intelligence. He gestures to Schmidt that he'd like to buy everyone a drink. Schmidt sets everyone up, then—

                    PADDY
Gentleman, what can we expect?

                    HOPKINS
Assaulting a cop is tough, Paddy. I know he's your son-in-law and everything and he's going through a rough patch, but the force goes ballistic when its guys are fucked with.

Richard is increasingly unsettled. Paddy sees this and gestures the boy should remain calm. Then, returning to the cops—

                    PADDY
Might we be able to plead emotional duress—perhaps temporary insanity?

                    HOPKINS
That could work.

                    RICHARD
Oh man, no, he'd never forgive us!

                    PADDY
Now, look, sooner or later everyone does a little time, Richard. It's not a judgment of your dad's character at all.

                    CORRIGAN
I myself arrested your granddad here twice in 1935 alone.

                    PADDY
Exactly! And what were the charges, Corrigan? Enlighten the young man.

                    CORRIGAN
Incitement to riot, I believe.

PADDY
Yes, that's right, we went on strike.

HOPKINS
Yeah, but remember unions were illegal back then, Mister Dwyer.

PADDY
Except for the cops.

HOPKINS
We were a Patrolman's Benevolent Association.

PADDY
With guns, yes, of course, but...
*(to Richard, concerned)*
You okay?

Finally, Richard states plainly—

RICHARD
I got drafted.

Now Paddy goes pale. Richard shows him his draft card. Paddy takes it and looks it over, speechless. He hands it to Corrigan.

CORRIGAN
*(reads)*
1-A. Front of the line. Wow.

PADDY
Well, at least you're fit and healthy enough to kill people.

HOPKINS
Now hold on! Wait a minute. They can't mobilize him because he'll be head of the household when his old man goes to jail.

RICHARD
What!

SCHMIDT
Yeah! Legal guardian and such of the little
ones.

HOPKINS
And if he ain't got no previous convictions
it'll most likely be time in a detox psychiatric
facility or something.

RICHARD
They're really gonna send him away for a
drunk and disorderly?

CORRIGAN
*(delighted, laughs)*
They might have to, son, just to keep you from
getting your ass shot to hell in Vietnam in a
few months! Ha!

But no one else finds this funny and Corrigan shuts up. Paddy pulls Richard away, further along the bar, for privacy.

PADDY
Look, this is not a bad plan. Let's try to keep
you out of the armed forces and your dad off
the streets somewhere to dry out for a while.

Richard looks aside, overwhelmed.

RICHARD
Why's he like this?

PADDY
Who, your dad?

RICHARD
Yeah.

PADDY
*(drinks, then)*
He feels cheated. He's been wronged. Life's

unfair. All that kind of thing. You gotta help him through it.

> RICHARD
> I'm trying! But he just keeps fighting me.

> PADDY
> *(hands back draft card)*
> Fight him back. Look, you're killing material. The US government says so.

> RICHARD
> I don't like fighting, Grandpa.

Paddy lays a hand on the young man's shoulder.

> PADDY
> Yeah, I know. You're a good guy, Richard. And that matters.
> *(drinks, then)*
> But so's your old man. He's just scared out of his wits. You and Billy and the whole lot of us, we gotta help him get through it.

Richard nods, agreeing, then drinks his beer and adds—

> RICHARD
> And my girlfriend is pregnant.

This almost knocks Paddy over. He buys time sipping his drink then finds a chair and sits down.

> PADDY
> You don't say.

> RICHARD
> *(bashful)*
> Yeah.

Paddy is unsure how to advise. He takes out his handkerchief and blows his nose. Returning it to his back pocket again, he studies his grandson.

### PADDY
And you, being the decent young fella you are—you're going to do the right thing?

### RICHARD
Well, yeah.
*(then, less certain)*
Right?

He comes and sits at the small table with his grandfather.

### PADDY
*(decides to be positive)*
Of course! Of course, lad.
*(turns away, as if for air)*
Schmidt, we'll have another round here.

As Schmidt pours, Paddy pats Richard on the back and shakes his head in amazement.

### PADDY
Damn. When it rains it does surely pour.

# Episode Two

01. INTERIOR, BORDER CROSSING, 1949—DAY

A long line of hopeful Canadians are in line to present their papers, make their case, and cross over the border into the United States.

A title card announces: US-Canadian Border 1949

Twenty-three-year-old Jim Fulton is among them. His turn comes and he approaches the border official's desk.

LAWRENCE
Declaration of Intention, please.

Jim hands over some forms he has filled out. Lawrence rifles through them, checking for errors.

LAWRENCE
*(reads)*
"Place of Origin: Placentia Bay."
*(looks up)*
Where is that?

JIM
*(thought it was obvious)*
Oh, ah, sorry. Newfoundland.

LAWRENCE
*(writes this in)*
New Found Land... Nationality: British. Okay. So, what do you intend to do in the United States?

JIM
Marry my girlfriend.

LAWRENCE
I see. And what's her name?

JIM
Audrey Dwyer.

Lawrence makes a note of this. Then—

> LAWRENCE
> And what will be your address in the United States?

> JIM
> I'll be staying with my sister, Nell, and her husband, Mister Mike Powers, in Brooklyn.

> LAWRENCE
> *(patiently)*
> Right, but, ah—where in Brooklyn? You got an address?

> JIM
> Oh, yeah. Second Street. 472 Second Street, Brooklyn.

> LAWRENCE
> Excellent.
> *(writes it in, then)*
> So apart from marrying your girl, what else you plan on doing?

> JIM
> Oh, I'm sure something will come up. I've worked on fishing boats and in a timber mill. I've had a little schooling.

Lawrence nods thoughtfully before deciding to continue.

> LAWRENCE
> Now, ah...
> *(reads and reminds himself)*
> James. You know it could be a few years before you become a naturalized citizen of the United States.

> JIM
> Yes. I understand. I read the pamphlet.

LAWRENCE
Right. Good. But—it's a new policy—you can become a citizen right away if you join the US Army.

JIM
*(intrigued)*
Is that so?

LAWRENCE
You ever think about the military?

JIM
Well, ah, yeah sometimes. My older brothers Richard and Leonard, they served in the Royal Navy.

LAWRENCE
God bless 'em. They helped save the world from the menace of fascism.

JIM
*(not sure what that means)*
Well, yes, I suppose they did.

LAWRENCE
Listen, Jim, I'm sure the US Army can use a man with your experience and skills. They might even teach you a new trade. There's a world of opportunity for a man in the Army during peacetime.

JIM
*(thinks it over)*
And I'll be a US citizen right now?

LAWRENCE
In no time flat! Here, just sign this form.

He slides a form across the desk and points to the signature line, offering Jim a pen. Jim looks the page over, thinks a moment then shrugs and signs happily.

> JIM
> Okay. Well, that sounds...

But as his signature is finished, Lawrence pulls the form back.

> LAWRENCE
> And I'll countersign it down here.
> *(does so and hands it back to Jim)*
> And now you just take this copy with you, fill in the rest and bring it over to the nearest recruiting station and the deal is done.

Lawrence stands and shakes Jim's hand.

> JIM
> Thank you very much, sir. Thank you.

> LAWRENCE
> *(looks past him)*
> Next!

And Jim is waved on into the United States of America.

02. EXTERIOR, PADDY DWYER'S HOME—DAY

It's late 1969. Joseph sits, riveted by this story told by his granddad as the old man fixes the kid's bike.

> JOSEPH
> And that's how Dad became an American?

> PADDY
> Well, there was more to it than that, lad. There was a little bit of a dustup afterwards.

> JOSEPH
> A dustup?

Paddy looks back over his shoulder in disbelief.

### PADDY
You don't know what a dustup is? What the hell are the nuns teaching you over there in the third grade if not the English language!

Joseph comes over with a dramatic huff, aggrieved, more than eager to expand.

### JOSEPH
Crazy stuff about how God is, like, three people: there's God the Father, then there's the Son, who I think is supposed to be Jesus, and then somebody called the Holy Ghost.

### PADDY
I want it known here and now between us I tried to talk your mother out of sending you to the parish school.

### JOSEPH
She says you're a communist and you don't believe in God or anything!
*(catches his mistake)*
I mean: she *said*.

This touches the old man. He lowers his wrench.

### PADDY
I am not a communist. Too many meetings. And though the Catholic church is a craven superstitious mob, if there is a heaven, I'm sure your mother's up there sorting it all out on my behalf.
*(hands him the wrench)*
Here, throw this in the box, get me the Phillips head screwdriver and we'll be done.

Joseph goes to the tool box and looks.

### JOSEPH
There's two. Which one?

> PADDY
> The long one with the red handle. Just the thing we need here.

Joseph brings it over and Paddy uses it to tighten a screw in a hard to reach place. Satisfied, he leans back and displays the screwdriver.

> PADDY
> This, Joseph, is a good machine.

> JOSEPH
> I think it's a tool, Grandpa.

> PADDY
> Who told you that, the Holy Ghost?

> JOSEPH
> Sister Marie Cecile. A machine has different parts. Like a bike. But a tool...

They're interrupted when a car pulls up in the driveway.

> PADDY
> Now that'd be your uncle Mike.

Mike climbs out of his car, clearly straight from work, waves to them and enters Paddy's house.

> JOSEPH
> What are they talking about in there, Grandpa?

> PADDY
> Oh, that's none of your business. Let's see if this vehicle is fit for the road.

03. INTERIOR, PADDY DWYER'S HOME—DAY

Richard is seated at the kitchen table with Ruthy on one side and Marie on the other. Mike and Tom pace back and forth through the small rooms.

MARIE
We can't let them put him in jail.

MIKE
How long are they saying it'll be?

MARIE
At least six months.

RUTHY
But he can go to the hospital instead, isn't that right?

MIKE
The detox unit at the whatever you call it out there on the highway in Bay Shore.

TOM
The State Mental Institution? Jim would rather go to jail.

RUTHY
Well, he can't do that!

MIKE
He can't be outta work for six months. He's got a mortgage.

MARIE
It's not *up* to Jim. The judge said one of us can admit him.

TOM
To an insane asylum? Are you kiddin' me?

MARIE
It's not an insane asylum, Tom. It's a psychiatric hospital.

TOM
You're his brother, Mike.

MIKE
*(carefully, to Marie)*
How long would he have to be in there?

MARIE
What did they say, Richard?

RICHARD
Three months.

MIKE
He'll never forgive me for signing him into a mental institution.

RUTHY
Would you rather see him in jail?

MIKE
*(frustrated)*
Of course not! I live next door to him, for cryin' out loud. His kids are in my house, our kids are in his house, all day long. I don't want to hassle with him the rest of my life.

MARIE
*(exasperated)*
I'll do it.

TOM
No! You and Jim are at one another's throats enough as it is!

MARIE
*(losing patience)*
We can't let him have this on his record, Tom! Even if he is stupid and pigheaded enough to let it happen. If he's admitted to the hospital he won't have a criminal record!

Tom gets a beer from the fridge, offers it to Mike, who declines, then opens it for himself. He looks out the screen door to Paddy.

## 04. EXTERIOR, PADDY DWYER'S HOME—DAY

The bike fixed, Paddy hands Joseph some cash.

> **PADDY**
> Now repeat that back to me.

> **JOSEPH**
> A pack of Marlboro and a six-pack of
> Ballantine beer, cold, in bottles.

> **PADDY**
> Good. You can manage that in this basket
> here, right?

> **JOSEPH**
> Sure.

Joseph rides off on his mission while Paddy turns and approaches the back door.

## 05. INTERIOR, PADDY DWYER'S HOME—DAY

He comes up the steps, opens the screen door and stands there.

> **TOM**
> If you do it, Paddy, Jim won't complain.

Paddy was expecting this. He nods, then comes in and places his hand on Richard's shoulder.

> **PADDY**
> Richard, you have to do it.

Richard looks up from the table, nodding. He knows this is true.

> **RUTHY**
> Is he old enough?

> **TOM**
> You eighteen yet?

                    RICHARD
    Yeah.

Tom sits across from him at the table, concerned.

                    TOM
    You okay with that?

                    RICHARD
              *(lies bravely)*
    Yeah.

Mike flips through his little address book.

                    MIKE
    Who's his mortgage with?

                    RUTHY
    The bank. On Wellwood Avenue. Amalgamated.
    The same ours is.

                    MIKE
    Mister Dwyer, it all right I use your phone?
    I should call my other brothers and work
    something out about paying Jim's mortgage
    and whatnot.

                    PADDY
    Go right ahead, Mike.

06. INTERIOR, MIKE FULTON'S HOME—NIGHT

Later that night, Joseph and Brian are sitting up in their adjacent beds. Brian is enthralled by Joseph's whispered but feverish narrative.

                    JOSEPH
    So then my dad finally makes it past these,
    like, murderous US Border Patrol guards.
    They're aiming their guns at him, watching
    his every move. But he pretends he doesn't

see them. And he's got this super important piece of paper in his hand—this paper that will make him a citizen of the United States of America!

07. INTERIOR, BORDER CROSSING, 1949—DAY

Contrary to Joseph's heated reinvention, Jim walks down a long hall to the exit. But he needs to check in with one more military desk clerk who examines his papers and, in particular, the Army form. He is a young black man about Jim's age.

> CLARKSON
> *(amused)*
> I suppose the guy up there told you to run directly to a recruitment office?
>
> JIM
> Yeah, well... I think he did so, yes.
>
> CLARKSON
> *(stamps the form)*
> You have a year to get yourself to a recruitment office. You're signed up, but you got a year before you report.
> *(hands back form)*
> These bastards at the border get points for how many new recruits they send in. Have a good day.

Jim wanders hesitantly into the United States, not quite sure what just happened.

08. INTERIOR, COURT ROOM—DAY

Jim sits with an attorney across the table from the judge. Adjacent to him is Richard. Marie sits a few feet behind her nephew. Jim just stares at his hands. Richard glances at his father a few times but is ignored.

> JUDGE
> So, Mister Fulton, it's decided. Your son here,

Richard, being of sound health and mind and on the advice of this court has agreed to sign the papers admitting you to Pilgrim State Mental Health Facility in Bay Shore, Suffolk County, the State of New York. During your stay at the facility, which is mandated to be no less than three months, he will assume all responsibility as head of household.

09. INTERIOR, REHAB DETENTION—DAY

Richard signs some forms a policeman holds out to him on a clipboard as Mike and Tom stand aside with Jim. Jim is silent and scowling. Richard finishes with the paperwork.

### RICHARD
Okay, Dad.

He extends his hand but Jim ignores it disdainfully. Tom punches Jim in the arm, hard.

### TOM
Knock it off.

Jim holds his arm and comes to his senses. He shakes Richard's hand just as the gates clang open and a nurse, Amy (37), motions for Jim to follow her in.

### AMY
Mister Fulton?

### JIM
*(to Richard)*
Come visit on Sundays. Bring the kids.

It's an order. Richard nods. Jim turns and is escorted inside.

10. INTERIOR, DWYER HOME, BROOKLYN, 1949—DAY

Marie—just sixteen at this point—comes slamming through the front door, excited, panicked and itching for drama all at once.

The first person she sees is her older half-sister, Audrey, who's twenty-three and breathlessly strapping on the latest fashion platform shoe.

> AUDREY
> *(looks up)*
> Is it true?

> MARIE
> He just got off the train! He's on his way!

Audrey stands and composes herself. She looks down the hall to her father, Paddy Dwyer, just forty-five. He's drying dishes at the kitchen sink.

> PADDY
> Audrey, relax. Marie, don't slam the door like that.

Meanwhile, their mother, Cecile, hurries down the stairs with a glistening faux diamond clip she starts to set in Audrey's hair.

> CECILE
> Now Marie you just make yourself scarce for a while! Where's he at?

> MARIE
> *(petulant)*
> I don't know! Bob Hicky said he saw him at the station!

She stomps off into another room. Paddy tucks in his shirt and rolls down his shirt sleeves. He checks his appearance in a mirror. He takes a bottle of whiskey from a high cabinet and finds two clean glasses. Cecile grabs Audrey by both arms and talks straight but lovingly.

> CECILE
> Now I know I'm only your stepmother but I love you like my own. And if this Jim Fulton is a good man your father will know it.

Audrey nods. They wait a second, then hug.

## 11. EXTERIOR, BROOKLYN STREETS, 1949—DAY

Jim is walking along with his older sisters, May and Nell, who are talking to one another across Jim. They are working class and very proper ladies, grooming Jim as they move along, knocking dandruff off his shoulders, straightening his jacket, making him stop to rub the dust off his shoe tops.

> NELL
> *(optimistic)*
> Missus Dwyer is a nice churchgoing woman.

> MAY
> *(the careful one)*
> But they say Mister Dwyer is a socialist.

> JIM
> A what?

> NELL
> He was arrested once or twice in his youth
> for union activism or something. But he's
> very polite.

> MAY
> Though he's never in church.

May stops Jim in his tracks and comes around in front of him, kind but firm.

> MAY
> Now Jim—here, fix your tie—Audrey
> Dwyer is a pretty girl and a lot of the local
> beaus—some of them from back home
> too—have tried to win her affections.
> Apparently, she's not so easy to please.

Jim is flattered but embarrassed and a little irritated. He moves on and they follow.

JIM
           We like each other.

May considers this and looks at Nell.

                    NELL
           Well, liking each other is a good start.

                    MAY
                  *(nods)*
           A lot of marriages start out with much less.

                    JIM
           Here it is: Seventh Avenue. That's their house
           over there.

Now Nell comes forward and holds her little brother (a foot taller than herself) at arm's length.

                    NELL
           You're such a man now! You were such a
           little weed when I left home.

                    MAY
           Keep your wits about you, Jim. Everything
           moves faster in the United States of America.

                    JIM
                  *(hugs them both)*
           Thank you, Nell. I'll be back before midnight.
           Don't wait up. Thank you, May. And tell Mister
           Shea I'll stop in to say hello before the weekend.

                    MAY
           Good luck, Jim.

They watch as he sets off for the Dwyer house.

12. INTERIOR, DWYER HOME, BROOKLYN, 1949—DAY

Marie is at an upper bedroom window, watching. She bolts into action, running downstairs.

> MARIE
> He's coming! He's here! He's got a new suit
> but it's badly made. He's really skinny!

Audrey and Cecile are watching as well, peeking out through the living room curtains.

> CECILE
> He is well mannered, Audrey.

> AUDREY
> Isn't he, though!

> CECILE
> You can see it.

Cecile walks into the foyer to receive Jim but stops and points at Marie on the stairs.

> CECILE
> *(stern)*
> And you behave yourself!

Paddy bides his time at the kitchen table. Cecile opens the front door just as Jim has his knuckles raised to knock.

> CECILE
> Hello, Jim!

> JIM
> How do you, Missus Dwyer.

> CECILE
> I'm well, thank you. And call me Cecile.
> Nice to see you again. Come on in. Here's
> Audrey.

Jim and Audrey haven't seen one another in some time. They're both tongue-tied and self-conscious. Marie, up on the stairs, is relishing it all like it's a movie.

> MARIE
> *(can't help herself)*
> What took you so long? God, I thought Audrey was gonna blow a gasket!

> CECILE
> *(warns)*
> Marie.

> JIM
> I had to... Hello Marie... I had to...
> *(to Audrey)*
> I dropped my suitcase off with my sister, Nell.

> AUDREY
> Of course.

Cecile cocks her thumb at her younger daughter and Marie skulks away. She leads the lovers into the living room.

> CECILE
> Now you two have some catching up to do, so just make yourselves comfortable in here and I'll go see what Mister Dwyer wants to do about supper.

They sit side by side on the couch and fumble helplessly with their hands before finally kissing chastely—then a little less chastely. They look around to make sure no one is watching. Cecile lingers in the kitchen doorway, listening to make sure the lovers are getting along. Then she looks in at Paddy who is casually perusing the newspaper.

> CECILE
> We'll leave them alone for a bit.

> PADDY
> That'd be the civilized thing to do, I'm sure.

Meanwhile, back in the parlor—

> AUDREY
> *(being kind)*
> That's a nice suit.

> JIM
> It's a little big on me. It belongs to my brother, Bill, up in Boston.

> AUDREY
> We expected you last week. What happened?

> JIM
> It took longer than I thought to get all the paperwork done. Did you get my postcard? Anyway, I wanted to come over the border legally this time. Seeing as how, well, as how we want to get married and all.

She smiles. He's relieved. They fall into one another's arms and make out properly. Marie is watching from the top of the stairs, hugely entertained. Behind her, across the room, is another older sister—Eleanor.

> ELEANOR
> *(scolds)*
> Marie, come away from there and leave them alone.

Back in the parlor, post kiss—

> AUDREY
> And how did it go? Everything work out okay?

> JIM
> Yes, it did. I'm a US citizen.

> AUDREY
> *(confused)*
> You are? How?

                    JIM
          I joined the US Army and they let me in
          for free.

Audrey goes white and stands. At the top of the stairs, Marie, too, looks astonished.

                    AUDREY
               *(screams)*
          You what!

In the kitchen, Cecile drops a plate. Audrey comes stomping up the hall in her platforms.

                    AUDREY
               *(furious)*
          He went and joined the Army!

And she slams out the backdoor.

13. EXTERIOR, DWYER HOME, BROOKLYN, 1949—DAY

On the back porch, Audrey kicks a garbage can over, stomps her foot, and marches down into the paved yard. She sits on an overturned milk crate and sobs.

14. INTERIOR, DWYER HOME, BROOKLYN, 1949—DAY

Jim appears in the kitchen doorway, his hand raised in mute apology. Cecile studies him a moment, then throws away her dishtowel and goes out to Audrey. Marie and Eleanor appear from behind him and glare at the young man.

                    MARIE
          Idiot!

The sisters run out the back door as well. Jim looks to Paddy.

                    PADDY
          Jim! Nice to see you again. Come on in and
          sit down.

Shell-shocked, Jim wanders to the table and sits. Paddy pours two shots of whiskey.

>                    PADDY
> So, what's all this about the Army, son?

>                     JIM
> I thought it would be a good thing. Become a
> citizen right away. Easier to find work and
> all that.

>                    PADDY
>                *(lifts his shot)*
> Not unreasonable. Not unreasonable at all. But
> women, Jim, wives in particular—I've had
> two in my time—they like to be... Oh, what's
> the word: consulted.

## 15. EXTERIOR, DWYER HOME, BROOKLYN, 1949—DAY

Flanked by her sisters who are crying tragically and her stepmother who is just frowning, Audrey is inconsolable.

>                   AUDREY
> How could he do this! Soon I'll be too old
> to marry and no one will ask anymore! I
> mean, at least, not anyone I like and, and...
> I want to have babies and get a place of our
> own like you and Dad, Cecile. And Jim...
> now he'll go off to a war somewhere and
> get himself blown to pieces!

The sisters sob in concert and Cecile has had enough.

>                   CECILE
> Now just settle down, Audrey. Settle down.
> And you two knock it off! Eleanor, give
> me your handkerchief.
>              *(attending to Audrey)*
> You'll be a rare sight with your makeup all
> running down your face like this.

## 16. EXTERIOR, REHAB DETENTION—DAY

Back in 1969: Richard shakes hands with his uncles and they all return to their cars. Billy is waiting in the passenger seat as Richard approaches, sits in behind the wheel, and catches his breath. He tries to sound encouraging.

> BILLY
> Well, it's done.

> RICHARD
> Yeah. I guess.

Richard starts the car and drives out of the parking lot.

> BILLY
> When's the baby due?

> RICHARD
> April or thereabouts.

> BILLY
> So, you got to get married in the meantime?

> RICHARD
> Yeah.

> BILLY
> What now?

> RICHARD
> I gotta find a job.

> BILLY
> Any ideas?

They stop at a traffic light.

> RICHARD
> I guess I'll just start going in to each of these factories along the highway here.

Billy looks out at the endless bleak rows of small manufacturing plants lining either side of the highway.

>BILLY
>Okay. I'll leave you to it. Let me off here, then. I'll see you back at the house.

>RICHARD
>Where you going?

>BILLY
>Nowhere. Just feel like walking. See you later.

Richard pulls over and Billy gets out. He watches as his brother crosses the highway and disappears. Then he cuts the engine and stands out of the car as well. He checks his appearance in the windshield, pauses, then approaches the nearest factory.

17. INTERIOR, DWYER HOME, BROOKLYN, 1949—DAY

Things have settled down. Jim and Audrey are back on the couch again: she, contrite and embarrassed, he being as sensitive and careful as he can.

>AUDREY
>A year?

>JIM
>I don't have to report for duty till a year from yesterday.

>AUDREY
>So we have to start making plans for the wedding.

>JIM
>Yes. Absolutely. But I have to find work too.

>AUDREY
>Oh, no more of the fishing out of New Bedford,

please! That's as bad as the Army!
Away for a month at a time! All the men
missing fingers and toes if they manage to
get back home alive at all...

JIM

No. No. I'll find something here in New
York.

Just then, a tall, lanky young man a little older than Jim appears in the doorway—Ned Dwyer.

NED

Jim!

Jim looks over and stands. Audrey smiles and looks on.

JIM

How are you, Ned!

NED

Good as gold. So, it's true, you're to marry
my kid sister?

JIM

If she'll have me.

AUDREY
*(sardonic)*
He joined the Army.

NED
*(skeptical, to Jim)*
Did you now?

JIM

I suppose.

NED

And what Army would that be? You're still
a Britisher, technically.

                    JIM

Here. The US.

                    NED
            *(knowingly)*
And they made you a citizen straight off,
didn't they?

                    JIM

Right.

                    NED
            *(leads Jim away)*
Audrey, excuse us.
            *(then turns back)*
You know there's not a few lads down the
corner bar who'll be throwing themselves off
bridges when this gets out.

                  AUDREY

Oh, stop it.

## 18. INTERIOR, ARMY RECRUITING STATION—DAY

Billy is sitting with a recruiting officer, Powell, and listening carefully.

                   POWELL
              *(dubious)*
Well, of course, the Army will make it possible
for you to go to college after your service time
is up. But there are plenty of things you can
study while doing your service. What are you
interested in?

                    BILLY
              *(shrugs)*
I'm good at math.

                   POWELL

Oh yeah?

BILLY
I got my best grades last year in a special course on abstract geometry. Statistics, I'm good with that too.

POWELL
You sound like an engineer to me.

BILLY
Will I go to Vietnam?

POWELL
Whoa! Hold on. First of all, you'll need your parents consent as you're not yet eighteen.

19. INTERIOR, DWYER HOME, BROOKLYN, 1949—DAY

Paddy and Ned have commandeered the kitchen to advise Jim. Whiskey is poured.

PADDY
Now, Jim, the thing is Audrey don't want to be a widow at her age. If she were eighteen, okay. She'd get another chance. But she's not the youngest gal in Brooklyn anymore. And she wants to start a family.

JIM
I don't have to report for a year.

PADDY
Good.
*(to Ned)*
In the meantime, why don't we introduce him to the union and get him set up as a journeyman, straightaway. Can you see your self being an ironworker, Jim?

JIM
Whatever's needed. Audrey's not eager to see me back on the fishing boats.

PADDY
She's a sensible girl. This way you'll learn
a trade closer to home and get union benefits.

JIM
*(curious)*
Union?

PADDY
Yeah.

JIM
Is that legal?

PADDY
More or less—not uncommon since the war.
*(to Ned)*
Now, Ned, tell him what you know.

Ned sits, drinks, and explains.

NED
Well, about the Army: don't report until the
last minute. Things are getting bad in this
Korean conflict we keep reading about in the
papers.

JIM
Where's that exactly, Korea?

NED
Part of China. Near Japan. We're losing men
by the thousands, week after week.

JIM
Coming over the border, he told me it was
peacetime.

PADDY
*(smirks)*
Peacetime? Jesus. That'll be the day!

## 20. INTERIOR, REHAB DETENTION—DAY

Jim kicks a chair across the recreation room and Billy dives for cover.

**JIM**
No! Fucking! Way!

**BILLY**
*(careful)*
Well, what do you want me to do?

**JIM**
I don't know! You're the goddamn genius! But don't go joining the fucking armed forces! Damn!

One of the other inmates, a grizzled older man named Hallahan, steps forward to intercede.

**HALLAHAN**
Fulton, don't mess with the kid's patriotic impulses.

**JIM**
Hallahan, not now. Go away.

**HALLAHAN**
The Army needs smart guys like him. When I was in the Navy...

**JIM**
I don't want to hear it! Back off.
*(then, to Billy)*
You got a cigarette?

**BILLY**
No.

**JIM**
Candy? You got any chocolate?

              BILLY
No.

              JIM
Let's go get some coffee.

21. INTERIOR, REHAB DETENTION—DAY

They sip coffee in the cafeteria.

              JIM
They're all nuts. That's the worst part of it. There's no one to talk to who's not insane.

              BILLY
How about the doctors?

              JIM
              *(needs to know)*
I'm not crazy. You know that, right?

              BILLY
Yeah.

              JIM
I fucked up. That's all. And I'm paying the price.

              BILLY
Are you... I mean, do you feel like... are you getting better?

              JIM
Better? Better than what? There's nothing wrong with me.

              BILLY
Well, I mean, the drinking.

              JIM
You think I have a drinking problem?

Billy is speechless. He looks aside, clears his head, then returns to the issue at hand.

### BILLY
Can I join the Army?

Jim just stares at him a moment, then leans back and concedes.

### JIM
Okay. Maybe I have a drinking problem.

### BILLY
I don't know how else I can pay for college.

Jim nods. He's been thinking about this too.

### JIM
*(sits forward)*
Come to work with me. I can have the union get you on as an apprentice. I mean, when I get outta here.

### BILLY
*(astonished, but)*
I'd rather go into the Army, Dad.

### JIM
Well, you're not going into the Army. Do what you want when you're eighteen, but I'm not giving you permission.

### BILLY
You were in the Army.

### JIM
Yeah, and now I'm in a fucking nut house and my brothers are paying the goddamn mortgage on my house! If I cut my left hand off with an axe, would you do that too?

Billy just looks away. Jim calms down.

                    JIM
        Finish up school and graduate. Plan on iron-
        working through the summer and we'll figure
        something out about the college tuition.

22. EXTERIOR, JEWELRY STORE—DAY

Richard and Billy are looking in the window at wedding rings.

                    BILLY
        So what's the job?

                    RICHARD
        Loading dock stuff. It's a factory. They make
        electrical fixtures.

                    BILLY
        Full time?

                    RICHARD
        Yeah.
            *(points)*
        How about that one?

Billy comes over and looks closer.

                    BILLY
        That's a wedding ring. You've got to let
        Catherine pick that one out herself.
        Engagement rings are over here.

They move to a different part of the window.

                    RICHARD
        Two rings? Why is that?

                    BILLY
        The first one's just to make sure you're
        serious. A guy spends...
            *(points)*
        ...four hundred bucks on a...

                         RICHARD
No way!

                          BILLY
Okay.
           *(finds another)*
A guy spends a hundred and eighty bucks on
a ring and the family thinks, okay, he's
invested. He's not gonna run away at the last
minute.

                         RICHARD
Where the hell would I run away to?

                          BILLY
           *(scheming)*
What's the pay?

                         RICHARD
Minimum to start with. Three-sixty an hour
minus taxes.

                          BILLY
One-forty-four minus taxes per week. Not
even enough to buy the cheap-skate
engagement ring.

                         RICHARD
Hey!

                          BILLY
I've got an idea.

## 23. EXTERIOR, BASEBALL FIELD—DAY

Richard is pitching a hardball to Joseph who generally pops up to Billy out by second base.

                         RICHARD
           *(throws, then)*
Who is this guy Steve?

#### BILLY
He's a friend of Bobby's. He buys like ten pounds of pot from this guy in the city each week and sells it in one pound and half pound sections.

#### RICHARD
How much is a pound?
*(then)*
Joseph, hit higher on the ball. Keep it on the ground.

#### BILLY
*(answers)*
Two hundred and forty bucks. But we can buy a half pound for a hundred and twenty. Besides, the idea is to get rid of it quickly.

#### JOSEPH
*(pops one up again)*
You're pitching too high.

#### RICHARD
No, I'm not. That's the top of the box. Focus.

Richard takes a hit off a joint as Billy catches the fly ball.

#### RICHARD
How much you pay for this?

#### BILLY
Twenty.

#### RICHARD
For an ounce?

#### BILLY
*(approaches and tokes)*
Yeah. So, do the math: we buy a half pound—eight ounces—for 120 and we sell those eight ounces for 20 we make...

JOSEPH
A hundred and sixty!

BILLY
Right. One-sixty. A profit of forty bucks.

RICHARD
And we might get arrested.

BILLY
We won't get arrested.

RICHARD
Risking it for forty bucks isn't worth it.

Richard pitches again. Joseph connects and hits a line drive towards right field. Billy has to run and dive for it, but misses.

RICHARD
There you go!

JOSEPH
*(with certainty)*
That was low and outside.

RICHARD
That was right down the middle!

JOSEPH
That was low and outside of this, whatever, imaginary box you keep talking about!

24. INTERIOR, JIM FULTON'S HOME—DAY

Billy and Richard are at the kitchen table while Joseph does his homework and Natalie scrawls in a coloring book. Billy continues his discussion with Richard while he oversees Joseph's geography studies.

BILLY
We can maximize profits by selling nickels

and dimes. People pay more for quick
disposable highs. Classic market capitalism.
I read about it in school. You can break an
ounce up into three dimes. That's ten dollars
times three per ounce.

### JOSEPH
Thirty dollars per ounce.

### BILLY
Thanks.
*(of Joseph's homework)*
That's Austria, not Australia.

### JOSEPH
*(realizes)*
Oh.

### BILLY
So, we'll be paying 15 an ounce but, because
we're selling in smaller, more conveniently
disposable amounts, we'll be earning 30 an
ounce. Doubling our investment.

He goes to the fridge for another beer, checking first to make sure his aunt Ruthy is not watching from her own kitchen window. Richard finishes eating and pushes his plate away.

### RICHARD
*(concerned)*
Is that fair?

### BILLY
*(drinks, then)*
Hey. This isn't the produce department of the
local supermarket, Richard. We're hardened
criminals trying to make an honest buck.
Right, Natalie?

### NATALIE
Right!

25. INTERIOR, FACTORY—DAY

Richard works dragging around pallets stacked with boxes of electrical fixtures. He loads the boxes onto a truck at the loading dock then drags the pallet away and stacks it with others. A bell rings, signaling quitting time. Elsewhere, a little later: he is handed his paycheck. Coming down the hall towards the exit, he stops at a pay phone.

26. INTERIOR, DOLAN HOME—DAY

*(Intercut with previous scene)* Marie is shouting at her sobbing teenage daughter, Maggie.

> MARIE
> Sit down!

> MAGGIE
> It wasn't my fault!

> MARIE
> You're not going anywhere for a month!

The phone rings and she moves to answer it, passing her thirteen-year-old daughter, Anna.

> MARIE
> You take that skirt off and put something decent on, you hear me!

> ANNA
> Ma! Come on!

> MARIE
> Go!

> MARIE
> *(grabs phone)*
> Yeah?

Richard is alert to his aunt's bad mood.

                    RICHARD
               *(carefully)*
Hi. It's me. I'm gonna be a little late getting
Natalie.

                    MARIE
               *(unyielding)*
No.

                    RICHARD
What?

                    MARIE
Get over here by six like we planned.

                    RICHARD
I gotta cash my paycheck.

                    MARIE
Cash it fast and get over here. Maggie got
the car towed away and I need you to drive
me over to motor vehicles or wherever and
get it back before your uncle Tom gets home.

Richard holds his head and tries to think. He looks at the wall clock and calculates.

                    RICHARD
               *(decides, then)*
Okay.

                    MARIE
Get moving.

27. EXTERIOR, FACTORY—DAY

Richard jumps in the car and pulls out.

28. INTERIOR, HIGH SCHOOL—DAY

Billy and Ruthy both sit obediently across the desk from the boy's guidance counselor, Mister Roberts.

       ROBERTS
You've got the grades. But your test scores
were terrible. What happened?

       RUTHY
He was sick.

       ROBERTS
    *(respectful but unmoved)*
That's unfortunate.
    *(to Billy)*
You can't be sick anymore. You won't
graduate if you miss anymore classes. And
if you don't graduate you won't be able to
take another crack at these scholarship
exams in June.

29. INTERIOR, BANK—DAY

Richard waits impatiently on line for a teller. He is summoned forth and signs the back of his paycheck at the counter.

30. EXTERIOR, BASEBALL FIELD—DAY

Joseph and his Little League teammates file in off the field. The other kids meet up with their parents or wander away on their own. Joseph sits in the bleachers. The manager, a middle-aged man named Pete Barrows, notices Joseph as he passes by on his way to his car.

       BARROWS
Joseph, you got a ride?

       JOSEPH
Yes, Mister Barrows, my brothers are coming.

31. EXTERIOR, BANK—DAY

Richard hurries back out to his car and meets Steve, a guy about his age. They get in the car and Steve shows Richard a large bag of marijuana.

                STEVE

Half pound.

                RICHARD
              *(counts out cash)*
One hundred and twenty.

                STEVE

Wanna taste?

                RICHARD

No. Go ahead, though. I gotta get my kid sister at my aunt's.

                STEVE

Oh, hey, can you drop me at the station?

Too polite to refuse, Richard pulls out as Steve rolls a joint.

                RICHARD

Sure.

32. EXTERIOR, HIGH SCHOOL—DAY

Ruthy smacks Billy in the head.

                RUTHY

Now, look at me! Look at me!
              *(he does, then)*
Now we all know you're smart! Okay, there's no denying that!

                BILLY

Is that why you're hitting me?

                RUTHY

Shut up, wise guy! Your brains was given to you. And all you do is go showing disrespect!

                          BILLY
                      *(entertained)*
            Given to me?

                          RUTHY
                    *(nods vehemently)*
            That's right.

                          BILLY
            By who, God?

                          RUTHY
            Don't be making fun of me!
                        *(then)*
            By your mother, obviously. Now get on the
            bus. Sister Justine-Marie will be waiting for
            us by now.

A bus arrives and they climb up into it.

## 33. EXTERIOR, DOLAN HOME—DAY

Richard pulls up and steps from the car. But Marie is already striding from the front door with Natalie in her arms and her bag over her shoulder. Maggie and Anna are both sobbing in the doorway. Richard throws his jacket over the marijuana. He looks worried and Marie, seeing this, assumes—

                          MARIE
            Don't mind them. They cry about everything.
            Come on, hurry up. What's that smell?

Richard shoves the pot and the jacket covering it into the back seat where Natalie grabs it. He looks back at her and winks. She smiles and clutches it tight.

## 34. EXTERIOR, BASEBALL FIELD—DAY

Joseph is content to be sitting alone on the bleachers, alternately daydreaming and flipping through the pages of *The Odyssey*, by Homer. Two older kids, Ron and Gus, come by with Joseph's old nemesis, Mitch.

**RON**
Hey, give us your mitt.

**JOSEPH**
What?

**MITCH**
Give us your mitt, scumbag.

**JOSEPH**
Why?

**GUS**
Because Mitch needs it. He's joining the Little League.

**JOSEPH**
It's my older brother's.

**RON**
So what.

**JOSEPH**
It was given to him by Jackie Robinson.

**RON**
Get outta here!

**MITCH**
Liar.

**GUS**
Who's his older brother?

**MITCH**
I don't know.

**RON**
How many brothers you got?

JOSEPH
Twelve.

GUS
Bullshit!

RON
Fucking Catholics.

JOSEPH
They oughta be here anytime now.

MITCH
He's lying! He's a famous liar! He skipped out on his own mom's funeral!

GUS
That don't make him a liar.

MITCH
He's just got a little sister.

RON
So, you're an orphan, huh?

JOSEPH
*(unsure)*
I don't think so. Maybe.

MITCH
His dad's in prison.

JOSEPH
Is not.

MITCH
Is so. That's what people say.

JOSEPH
*(adamant)*
He's in a state mental institution.

This impresses the boys. They come closer and Ron sits on a lower bleacher, eager to know more.

> RON
> *(genuinely curious)*
> What did he do?

Joseph looks around, scanning the horizon for Richard, but sees nothing. He looks back at the thugs and prepares to elaborate.

> JOSEPH
> Well, he killed some people.

> RON
> *(awed)*
> No.

> JOSEPH
> *(milks it)*
> Yeah.

Meanwhile—

35. INTERIOR, PARISH SCHOOL—DAY

Sister Justine-Marie (60, black), the principal, explains to Ruthy and Billy—

> JUSTINE-MARIE
> To put it simply: Joseph tells lies.

> RUTHY
> *(entertained)*
> Oh yes, he's got quite an imagination, that one! But he don't mean no harm by it.

The sister is not amused. She consults some notes.

> JUSTINE-MARIE
> He says his uncle Mike, for instance, your husband, is building an ark made of steel in

the backyard so the family can survive with
all its pets when the world gets flooded again
due to the use of automobiles and hair spray.

She looks back up at Ruthy. Ruthy is lost. She looks at Billy.

> RUTHY
>
> A what?

> BILLY
>
> An ark. You know, like a big boat.

> RUTHY
>
> Like in the bible story?

> BILLY
>
> Yeah.

> JUSTINE-MARIE
>
> Precisely.

Ruthy is relieved. She reassures the sister:

> RUTHY
>
> Oh, it's not really an ark, Sister! It's just a
> big ship. But it is all steel. So he's not lying
> about that. And I'm sure my husband won't
> allow any pets on board once she's done.

Sister Justine-Marie massages her temples. Ruthy is more trouble than Joseph.

36. EXTERIOR, IMPOUNDMENT LOT—DAY

Marie is at the caged-in cashier's office.

> MARIE
>
> A red Chevy Impala with a white roof.

> CLERK
>
> License plate: MBC-208?

> MARIE
> Yeah, that's it. How much?

> CLERK
> Seventy-five dollars.

> MARIE
> *(to Richard)*
> I've only got sixty.

Richard looks through his wallet and puts up all he's got left after buying the pot.

37. EXTERIOR, MARIE'S CAR—DAY

She speeds to the train station, lighting a cigarette and swearing under her breath.

38. EXTERIOR, PARISH SCHOOL—DAY

Billy and Ruthy come out of the building just as Richard pulls up with Natalie.

> RUTHY
> *(gets in car)*
> Now, Richard, the sisters are concerned about Joseph.

Richard and Billy both realize at the same time—

> RICHARD
> Joseph!

> BILLY
> Baseball practice.

> RICHARD
> *(checks the time)*
> Across town. Oh, man!

They pull out and drive off in a hurry.

### RUTHY
Drop me at the house. I have to get supper started. Drive slower! What's that funny smell?

## 39. EXTERIOR, BASEBALL FIELD—DAY

Mitch and his thug friends are captivated by Joseph's storytelling.

### JOSEPH
So, my middle, most beautiful, sister was being held captive by these Colombian drug dealers and my dad, who was a Green Beret in Vietnam and knows how to live underwater for days at a time... he...

But he looks over and sees Richard and Billy pull up.

### JOSEPH
Oh, those are my brothers. Two of them anyway.

The thugs all stand up and back away, wary.

### JOSEPH
It's okay. They're not the really dangerous ones. See ya!

And he runs off to the car with his mitt and copy of Homer.

### RICHARD
Hey, champ. Sorry we're late.

### BILLY
*(grabs book)*
Hey, I was supposed to return this to the school at the end of last semester.

### JOSEPH
*(indignant)*
You gave it to me!

                        BILLY
            Not forever. Get in.

Joseph climbs in and they drive off.

40. INTERIOR, JIM FULTON'S HOME—NIGHT

Down in the basement, Billy is busy with a scale, weighing out nickels and dimes of pot. Upstairs, Richard finishes drying dishes and looks out the window over the kitchen sink and into Ruthy's house. Uncle Mike can be seen smoking his pipe and playing solitaire at the table as Ruthy finishes her own after supper cleaning. She turns off the light as Mike and her leave the room. Richard waits a moment, then Joseph appears in the window and gives him the thumbs up.

                        JOSEPH
                      *(whispers)*
            They're gone to bed!

Now Richard hustles upstairs and looks out a bedroom window with Joseph's toy telescope across the few backyards that lay between him and Marie's house. He can see in through the back door and into the kitchen where Marie is buttoning Natalie into her pajamas. He waits. The pajamas fastened, Marie lets the child run off, turns off the lights and disappears. Richard comes down into the basement to join Billy just as there is a knock on the window. He goes over, reaches up and slides open the pane. It's Maggie.

                        MAGGIE
                   *(counts her money)*
            Hey. Can I get a dime? Here.

She hands him ten dollars and Richard reaches for a plastic bag of prepared contraband.

                        BILLY
            No, that's the nickels. Here.

Richard grabs the right bag and hands it up to Maggie.

**MAGGIE**

Okay. See you.
*(moves away but comes back)*
Oh! Vito Massalotti is playing with his band at the Pig & Whistle later.

**RICHARD**

Okay. Maybe.

**BILLY**

*(calls)*
I'll see you over there!

**RICHARD**

No, he won't.

**MAGGIE**

*(laughs)*
Ha! Look at you being all fatherly and shit!

**RICHARD**

*(all business)*
He's got school tomorrow. Get lost. See you later.

She runs off and before Richard can close the window someone else arrives. It's Edward from Ruthy's house.

**EDWARD**

Richard, gimme two dimes and a nickel.
*(counting out bills)*
This is for me and that's for these guys I know at the gas station.

Richard does the business and hands off the marijuana. He closes the window and returns to Billy.

**RICHARD**

*(worried)*
If it goes on like this, we won't be selling to anyone but relatives.

                    BILLY
              *(weighing)*
    That's what we call our targeted demographic,
    Richard.

                    RICHARD
    Shut up. Hand me a beer. We got enough of
    these plastic bags?

41. INTERIOR, REHAB DETENTION—DAY

Jim is trying to read a paperback while Hallahan argues about the weather with a nervous young man named Robert.

                    ROBERT
    Looks like rain.

                    HALLAHAN
    I doubt it.

                    ROBERT
    Yeah. It's gonna rain today.

                    HALLAHAN
    The TV says it'll clear up by noon.

                    ROBERT
    I doubt that. I doubt that very much.

                    HALLAHAN
    What?

                    ROBERT
    You can tell.

                    HALLAHAN
    Tell what?

                    ROBERT
    By the smell of the air. You can tell. There's
    rain coming.

                    HALLAHAN
            Robert, you're so full of shit.

                    ROBERT
            It's true. It'll rain and... and...

                    HALLAHAN
            You think you know more than Ted Danvers
            who does the weather on Channel Eleven!?
            Huh? Do ya?

Finally, Jim drops his book.

                    JIM
            Will you two shut the fuck up!

Nurse Amy comes to the door.

                    AMY
            Jim. You've got visitors.

                    JIM
            Thank God!

## 42. EXTERIOR, REHAB DETENTION—DAY

The kids are hanging around, nervously killing time on the steps outside. Jim comes out, pauses, then lifts Natalie in his arms and gives Joseph a pat on the head. He nods a stiff embarrassed greeting to the older boys. Nothing is said. He leads the way down into the garden. He sits on a bench with the kids. Richard and Billy look away, waiting for something to happen. Meanwhile, Joseph is curious.

                    JOSEPH
            Are all these people crazy, Dad?

Billy smacks him upside the head.

                    JOSEPH
            Oww!

But Jim just grins. He holds Natalie at arm's length.

> JIM
> I'm not crazy. You know that, don't you?

> NATALIE
> Yeah.

He sets the girl down, stands and takes Richard aside.

> JIM
> How's Catherine doing?

> RICHARD
> Okay.

> JIM
> She still in school?

> RICHARD
> Yeah.

> JIM
> You got work?

> RICHARD
> A factory. Loading dock stuff.

Jim is not optimistic but doesn't want to sound discouraging. So he looks at Joseph standing nearby.

> JIM
> You going to baseball practice?

> JOSEPH
> Yeah. They made me a pitcher.

Surprised, Jim looks at Richard.

> RICHARD
> Who knew! The kid's got a great arm.

                    BILLY
          Just gotta keep his mind in the game. Stop
          daydreaming.

                    JOSEPH
          Ain't no time to daydream now. Out in left
          field it was great. Nobody can hit out that far.
          Now it's like I have to be thinking constantly.

                    JIM
                  *(excited)*
          Right. Strategy.

                    JOSEPH
               *(glad someone understands)*
          Yeah. It's horrible.

                    BILLY
          But he's good at it, Dad. Really.

Jim is amazed and watches Joseph, grinning. Then—

                    JIM
          When's the season start?

                    JOSEPH
          I don't know. In April or May, I think.

                    JIM
                  *(to Richard)*
          You gotta get me outta here so I can see this.

Richard sighs, hard pressed, and looks away with a shrug. Jim looks at Billy instead.

                    JIM
          I mean it.

43. INTERIOR, REHAB DETENTION—DAY

Richard and Billy are with the head doctor, Harding.

RICHARD
But he is improving, right?

HARDING
He's a lot less violent. I mean, emotionally.

RICHARD
But that's good, right?

BILLY
He's gotta be safe to be out in society for a few hours at least. I mean he hasn't had a drink in six weeks.

HARDING
The risk is that he'll relapse as soon as he's in familiar environments. Sees people. Enablers, you know. You read the literature I gave you?

BILLY
Yeah. Enablers.

Harding moves on up the hall.

RICHARD
*(whispers)*
What's that mean?

BILLY
Us. I think.
*(follows doctor)*
Listen, Doctor, isn't it possible that this could be a sort of a therapeutic kind of thing?

HARDING
*(stops and turns)*
Elaborate.

Billy clears his throat and tries his level best to talk convincing nonsense.

                    BILLY
          Dad's really... identified with Joseph's athletic
          abilities. He derives... an enormous amount...
          of confidence and satisfaction and... self
          worth from the exercise of the kid's... skill.
          In baseball, I mean.

Harding is amused but not impressed. He removes his glasses, folds them, and puts them in his shirt pocket.

                    HARDING
          Your father is not yet well. And he's here in
          lieu of criminal charges. So, no, you can not
          take him on a field trip to see a Little League
          baseball game.

The doctor walks away.

44. INTERIOR, PARISH SCHOOL—DAY

Catherine, obviously pregnant, is in class with thirty other teenage students as a middle-aged nun, Sister Ann-Margaret, works out complicated math on the blackboard.

                    ANN-MARGARET
          If *this* times *this* squared by *that* equals 45
          what would the hypotenuse of this triangle
          be?

She turns and looks at the class and hopes for a response. Everyone is lost, except Catherine, who cautiously raises her hand.

                    CATHERINE
     Eleven?

                    ANN-MARGARET
          Exactly! Catherine, can you demonstrate that
          for us?

The sister holds out the stick of chalk to the girl and urges her to come to the front of the class. Catherine does come, nervous about

*115*

math only. But her classmates giggle because she's pregnant and Sister Ann-Margaret shoots them a look that shuts them up. Catherine takes the chalk and is about to demonstrate when another nun appears at the door:

> VERONICA
> Pardon me, Sister, Mother Superior needs a word with you and Catherine.

45. INTERIOR, PARISH SCHOOL—DAY

Catherine and Sister Ann-Margaret make their way to the principal's office.

46. INTERIOR, PARISH SCHOOL—DAY

Catherine sits across the desk from Sister Justine-Marie. Off to the side, Sister Ann-Margaret hangs her head in distress.

> JUSTINE-MARIE
> *(reluctantly)*
> We can't have an obviously pregnant girl in the school. It's just not done. It's making things difficult with the parent-teacher association.

> ANN-MARGARET
> But, Mother Superior, she's only got three months left to complete the tenth grade!

> JUSTINE-MARIE
> Sister! Enough.
> *(then, to Catherine)*
> My child, I'm sorry, but you must be able to understand our position.

Catherine is too overwhelmed to answer.

47. INTERIOR, JEWELRY STORE—DAY

Billy accompanies Richard as he buys the engagement ring. The clerk rings up the purchase and Richard counts out his money.

>                    BILLY
>     So you think we should retire now, huh?

>                    RICHARD
>     From being drug lords? Yes.

>                    BILLY
>     I mean, we've had a good thing going here
>     for a number of weeks.

Richard takes his purchase from the clerk along with his receipt.

>                    RICHARD
>              *(to clerk)*
>     Thank you.
>              *(then, to Billy)*
>     Enough is enough. I got the engagement ring
>     and I have more than half what I'll need if
>     Catherine goes for the expensive wedding band.
>     I can put aside a little of what I make at the
>     factory to pay for the hospital bills.

## 48. EXTERIOR, JEWELRY STORE—DAY

Exiting the store, they approach the car.

>                    BILLY
>     We gotta get Dad out to see Joseph pitch his
>     first game.

>                    RICHARD
>     I hate to disappoint him, but what can we do?

>                    BILLY
>     I have an idea.

>                    RICHARD
>              *(laughs, skeptical)*
>     No!

                    BILLY
                (offended)
What?

                    RICHARD
                (reaches car)
For one thing, I'm about to be a married man
with a family! I can't be breaking the law anymore!

                    BILLY
No, really, I've researched this. I've got it all
worked out! It'll be easy.

                    RICHARD
Come on, I gotta be back at work in ten minutes.

Billy is disappointed but lets it go. Still, he continues scheming.

                    BILLY
You can sell that special baseball mitt Dad got
you and be a rich man!

                    RICHARD
No way! Get in.

He does and they drive off.

49. EXTERIOR, BROOKLYN STREETS, 1949—DAY

Ned drives as Jim looks around, amazed at the life on the streets of downtown Brooklyn.

                    NED
                (rambling)
The idea is you stick with the union and the
union will stick by you. It's called collective
bargaining.

                    JIM
                (tries it out)
Collective bargaining.

NED
These corporations, they got loads of work,
all these building projects. But they'll go
with the lowest bidder—contractors hiring
cheap labor. These poor Mexicans and blacks
outta work now the German's are beat. They
don't need 'em in the factories no more. And
farming, I guess, is done for good. They come
flooding into the cities looking for work. And
they'll take anything, of course. It's like they're
slaves all over again for these rich white men.
Indians, too, from back up in Canada. But over
the years we forced a situation where there's
rarely a man, now, will go to work unless
it's union. It's all bluff and big talk, of course.
But you know what? It works! Ha!

Ned finds a place to park. They get out, lock the doors and follow a large crowd heading in one direction. There's excitement in the air.

NED
So, first thing here in the USA, Jim, is you
gotta have a team. A baseball team. And our
team's the Dodgers. The Brooklyn Dodgers.

They cross the street with the crowd and approach the baseball stadium, Ebbets Field, its name prominently displayed in lights up above them.

# Episode Three

01. EXTERIOR, REHAB DETENTION—DAY

In their dad's car, Richard and Billy drift to a stop at the edge of a road running behind the distant edge of the hospital grounds.

>                    BILLY
> This is it.

>                    RICHARD
> You sure?

>                    BILLY
> Yeah. Just by these trees.

They stop and wait. Then Billy stands out of the passenger side door. He's got an industrial strength bolt cutter a foot and a half long held alongside his leg. He looks up and down the deserted road to make sure the coast is clear as Richard waits behind the wheel. A few yards from the road, a ten-foot-tall chain-link fence rises up into the hanging branches of a few ancient spruce trees. Billy nearly disappears into the shadows beneath their boughs. He looks around once more, then through the fence and around at the grounds. All seems clear. He starts cutting a discreet slit in the chain-link fence.

02. INTERIOR, REHAB DETENTION—DAY

Jim stands from a cafeteria table and places his tray on a shelf near the kitchen.

>                    COOK
>                 *(surprised)*
> Hey, Jim! You're early today.

>                    JIM
> Yeah, I didn't have any lunch. See you later.

>                    COOK
> Later.

He steps outside and meets the supervising nurse, Amy.

                    AMY
          Good evening, Jim. You've eaten already?

                    JIM
          Yeah. I have that blood test in the morning
          and the doctor said...

                    AMY
          Right! You need to fast for twelve hours.

                    JIM
          Yeah. So, I thought I'd just hit the sack early.

She pats his arm and heads on into the cafeteria.

                    AMY
          I wish all the patients here were as on the
          ball as you, Jim! Thanks.

He waits for her to grab a tray and then slips out.

03. EXTERIOR, REHAB DETENTION—DAY

Jim crosses through the yard between a few buildings. Then, a moment later, he's double-stepping it out in a field behind those buildings. Finally, he's sprinting through the small woods at the back of the hospital grounds.

04. EXTERIOR, REHAB DETENTION—DAY

Back in the car, Billy sits low and keeps his eye on the fence.

                    RICHARD
               *(checks his wristwatch)*
          Game's already started.

                    BILLY
          Where is he?

                    RICHARD
          You sure these are the trees he meant?

#### BILLY
They're the only ones overhanging the fence.
That's what he said: the fir trees overhanging
the fence.

#### RICHARD
Those aren't fir trees.

#### BILLY
What?

#### RICHARD
They're spruce trees.

#### BILLY
Are you kidding me?

#### RICHARD
Wait! What's that?

Billy steps back out of the car and waits, listening, watching. Richard, too, steps out and looks over the car's roof. Billy takes a step toward the fence.

#### BILLY
Dad?

And suddenly Jim appears, thrashing his way through the underbrush. He stops at the fence.

#### JIM
Don't you know the difference between a
spruce tree and a fir tree!

#### BILLY
Sorry. Look, over here.

And he guides Jim over to the cut in the fence.

#### JIM
I've been waiting over there ten minutes.

                    BILLY
Sorry.

                    RICHARD
Dad, we gotta go.

                    JIM
I gotta be back by eight-thirty before Nurse
Amy does the rounds.

He's about to step into the passenger seat but stops and watches Billy comparing stands of trees. He grins and glances at Richard.

                    RICHARD
              *(calls to Billy)*
Hey, Professor! We gotta go. We'll do a nature
walk later in the week.

Billy returns to the car, cursing himself.

                    JIM
Game's already started?

                    RICHARD
Probably third or fourth inning.

                    JIM
Let's go.

05. EXTERIOR, HIGHWAY, JIM'S CAR—DAY

They race along, dodging in and out of traffic.

06. EXTERIOR, BASEBALL FIELD—DAY

Jim and the boys pull up and park at the curb. The boys get out of the car slowly, looking around like criminals. Jim just strides to the edge of the playing field, unconcerned. The bleachers are fairly empty and no one is paying much attention to the game. The coach, Pete Barrows, is hanging from the chain link fence of the dugout, smoking.

BARROWS
Jim! How's everything?

JIM
Good, thanks.
*(of game)*
What's the damage?

BARROWS
Stands a chance of pitching a perfect game.

JIM
Who?

BARROWS
Joseph.

Jim glances over at Joseph where he sits on the dugout bench. The kid just shrugs his shoulders, bewildered, and looks down at a page in his copy of *The Odyssey*. Richard and Billy arrive.

JIM
*(explains to them)*
They're up by one in the top of the ninth. And Joseph hasn't let no one get on base yet.

BILLY
Wow.
*(to Joseph)*
You stressed out yet, champ? You feeling the pressure?

Joseph glances at his terrified teammates. They all back away.

JIM
Come over here. You know what's going on, right?

JOSEPH
*(vaguely)*
Sort of.

                    JIM
You got three more outs to get and you've got
a perfect game!

                    JOSEPH
Yeah, I know. And they're all afraid of me.

                    JIM
Who is?

                    JOSEPH
These guys.

Jim looks past him to the other kids. They back away still further.
Barrows joins Jim and adds—

                    BARROWS
They've been all nervous and jittery since the
bottom of the sixth, afraid of making an error
and killing his no-hitter.

                    JIM
Who's pitching for the other team?

                    JOSEPH
              *(oppressed)*
Mitch Jaralski.

Jim looks at Barrows who smokes and shrugs.

                    BARROWS
Hard to tell with nine-year-olds. But Mitch
knows how to pitch and he's their best hitter,
far as I can see.

From out on the field, the thud of the ball in the catcher's mitt—

                    UMPIRE
Strike three!

Barrows wedges his cigarette in his teeth, claps his hands and calls to his team—

>                        BARROWS
> Okay, guys! Let's wrap this up! Get out
> there and shine!

Joseph grabs his glove but hangs back.

>                         JOSEPH
>                *(to Jim)*
> You back now?

>                          JIM
> I got some time to go. I just came to see
> the game.

Richard comes down beside his father and advises Joseph.

>                        RICHARD
> Just throws strikes.

>                         JOSEPH
> But change 'em up.

>                        RICHARD
> Right.

Joseph takes the field. Richard looks around, worried.

>                        RICHARD
> Dad, maybe you should put a hat on.

>                          JIM
> What do you think, I'm a wanted criminal?

>                        RICHARD
> Kind of. Yeah.

>                          JIM
> The only person I don't want to run into is
> your aunt Marie.

A huge kid from the opposing team named Polonksy steps up to bat.

> JIM
> Yikes. That kid looks sixteen if he's a day.

> RICHARD
> Polonsky's strong but he's not fast.

Out on the mound, Joseph is talking to himself—

> JOSEPH
> Polonsky. Man! Low and inside first, probably.
> Perfect game. This is a real pain in the neck.
> *(glances at the outfield)*
> Now what are they doing?

The three outfielders are doing their best to stay out of the game and hoping the ball won't come to them.

> NORMAN
> *(in centerfield)*
> Please don't come to me. Please don't come to me. Please....

> BRIAN
> *(in deep left)*
> I don't give a damn. It's his perfect game.
> Who's he to me or me to him?

Meanwhile, Joseph sets himself, winds up and throws. Polonsky fails to swing and—

> UMPIRE
> Strike one!

> MITCH
> *(spits and calls)*
> Come on, Polonsky, swing at something!

Polonsky bites his lip and concentrates. Joseph prepares his next pitch and Jim watches. The wind up, the pitch, Polonsky steps forward powerfully and swings but—misses. The catcher, Tim, just barely gets control of the ball.

> UMPIRE
> Strike two!

Mitch stands and grabs his batting helmet. Jim shakes his head.

> JIM
> Was that a wild pitch or is he just messing
> with the poor kid's mind?

> RICHARD
> He knows what he's doing. I think.

Out on the mound—

> JOSEPH
> Scare him off. Make him worry. Polonsky's
> okay. Best grade in science last year. High
> and inside but not too fast.

Mitch joins the on-deck batter, Mario, and nods towards Joseph.

> MITCH
> See that? He talks to himself.

Meanwhile, Polonsky waits at bat. Joseph focuses and watches Tim's signals. The outfielders are hiding behind their gloves.

> JOSEPH
> *(of signs)*
> No way. High and inside but not too fast.
> Deal with it.

He pauses, winds up and throws. Polonsky falls back, swings desperately and misses by a mile.

> UMPIRE
> Strike three!

Jim cracks up. He looks around for his other sons and sees Billy making time with some pretty high school girl higher up on the bleachers. But Richard has spotted trouble. Marie is driving by and slows to a crawl beside the playing field.

> RICHARD
> Uh oh! Aunt Marie's here.

> JIM
> *(ducks down)*
> Jesus Christ Almighty.

> RICHARD
> She's got Natalie with her.

> JIM
> Get her out of here.
> *(to Barrows)*
> Pete, can I borrow your hat?

He whips off Barrow's baseball cap and sits on the lowest bleacher. Richard runs over to Marie's car.

> RICHARD
> Hi!

> MARIE
> How's he doing?

> RICHARD
> Who?

> MARIE
> Joseph. Your uncle Tom said he's doing pretty good with the baseball.

Relieved, Richard continues—

> RICHARD
> Oh, yeah, well... He's good. Boring game though. No reason to stick around.

But Natalie climbs out the car's window and into his arms.

                    RICHARD
            Hey there, beautiful!

Marie switches off the ignition and lights a cigarette. Richard panics, seeing she wants to relax and chat. Back on the field, Mario approaches the plate.

                    JOSEPH
            *(mutters to himself)*
            Gotta let them hit some.

                    JIM
            *(likewise, nods)*
            He's gotta let them hit something.

                    BILLY
            Are you serious?

                    JIM
            They're gonna figure him out! The sequence
            of pitches.

                    JOSEPH
            *(meanwhile)*
            Yeah. Let him hit it.

Jim reaches behind himself and grabs Billy's ankle, forcing him over to the right, between himself and Marie's car, explaining—

                    JIM
            Not a base hit. Just a foul ball or an error.

                    BILLY
            *(of hand on ankle)*
            What are you doing?

                    JIM
            Sit between me and your aunt. Call your
            friend over here and block me.

Billy sees Marie and understands. He waves the girl over to sit with him. Meanwhile—

> BARROWS
> *(seriously engaged now)*
> He's got no help out there on the field. Those boys are terrified.

Mario approaches the plate and Joseph considers the situation. Having decided on a plan, he loosens up and looks straight at the shortstop, Charlie. Realizing he's been chosen, Charlie looks worried. He looks back and forth between the second and third basemen who both back off and look away, renouncing all responsibility. Joseph nods to Charlie. The kid adjusts his cap and gets ready. Joseph turns back to prepare his pitch. He studies Tim's signals and shakes his head no. Tim, behind the plate, sighs. He lifts his mask and looks for help from Coach Barrows. Barrows just shrugs and lights another cigarette.

> TIM
> Shit.

Tim puts his mask back on and gets ready. Mario is confident and alert. He taps his cleats with the bat and takes up position. Joseph winds up and throws. Mario steps into it gracefully and connects, sending a hard grounder to Charlie at shortstop that almost knocks him on his ass. The opposition's dugout goes wild. But Charlie keeps hold of the ball and throws Mario out at first. Mario runs it out and curses as he returns to the dugout, passing Mitch who is approaching the plate. Jim and Coach Barrows shake their heads in amazement. Billy is busy flirting.

> BARROWS
> This is a real kinda situation!
> *(looks around)*
> Where's Richard?
> *(then)*
> Jim, maybe you should go talk to him. To Joseph.

> JIM
> No.

BARROWS
He's got a perfect game going and Mitch
Jaralski is the only kid who knows how to
hit against him!

JIM
*(shrugs)*
Gotta let them play the game, Pete. Make
their own mistakes.

Barrows takes a hit from his hip flask and offers it to Jim. Jim just shakes his head and casts a glance back over his shoulder to check on Marie. Out at the curb, beside the car, Richard listens as—

MARIE
And how's your father doing? How was he
on Sunday?

RICHARD
Oh, he's doing fine.

MARIE
I mean, I guess this is what they call tough
love, Richard, but I really think it's the best
thing for him.

RICHARD
*(nods)*
Yeah. Yeah. You're right.

She enjoys the evening breeze and smokes.

MARIE
It's a shame he's missing Joseph's first
game, though. I know how he loves this stuff,
though I have no idea what any of you guys
see in it. But I remember how thrilled he was
when you played your first game of Little
League! You remember that?

Richard relaxes. He remembers this fondly.

**RICHARD**
Yeah, I do.

**MARIE**
And you had that baseball mitt you used to sleep with.

**RICHARD**
Joseph's using it right now.

**MARIE**
He bought that at Ebbets Field in Brooklyn before you were even born.

**RICHARD**
And got it signed somehow by Jackie Robinson!

**MARIE**
That's right! The first black man I *ever* heard addressed as Sir. Don't be surprised, it was a big thing back then. But your father was in awe. "Sir," he said, "can you please sign this for my son who I think will be born in August." Ha!
*(smokes)*
That was great. And your mother standing there not knowing exactly how pregnant she was anyway!

**RICHARD**
*(figuring the years)*
But, then...

**MARIE**
Between me and you, Richard, they were still ten days away from getting married! So...

**RICHARD**
*(amazed)*
Wait a minute. You mean...

Marie waves away premarital sex as insignificant. Then—

>                    MARIE
>           It was your uncle Ned who got him into
>           baseball in the first place.

Out on the field, Mitch takes the plate. Both dugouts and all the onlookers become quiet. Joseph prepares his pitch.

>                    JOSEPH
>           He won't swing at the first pitch.

>                    JIM
>           He won't swing at the first pitch. He wants to
>           see how tired Joseph is, find his weak spot.

Mitch waits. Joseph throws. Mitch doesn't swing and the ball is right down the middle for a strike.

>                    UMPIRE
>           Strike one!

Mitch is unruffled. Joseph gets the ball back from Tim and paces around the mound.

>                    JOSEPH
>           Now he's expecting a change-up.

>                    BARROWS
>                  *(curious, to Jim)*
>           Low and outside, probably, like with Polonsky?

>                    JIM
>           No! Mitch is on to him. He knows every pitch
>           Joseph can throw by now, right? He won't fall
>           for that.

Joseph throws again. Mitch steps back and holds his swing.

>                    UMPIRE
>           Ball one! High and inside!

                    JIM
　　Whoa.

                  BARROWS
                  *(worried)*
　　What do you think he's doing?

                    JIM
　　No idea.

Joseph gets the ball back, takes the mound, and waits for Mitch to get into the batter's box. But Mitch takes his time; takes a few practice swings, decides to relace his cleats.

                    JIM
                 *(chuckles)*
　　He's bleeding him. Messing with his
　　momentum.

Joseph waits patiently, focusing on home plate. Mitch finally reenters the box and lifts his bat. Joseph throws immediately. Mitch swings, connects badly, and the ball pops up back over the fence into the street—a foul ball.

                   UMPIRE
　　Strike two!

                    BILLY
　　Way to go, Joseph! I think he might have a
　　plan, Dad.

Joseph watches Tim's signals and shakes his head no. Tim thinks a moment, then tries new signals. But Joseph refuses them too. Tim hesitates, then gives yet a new set of signals. Joseph nods and Tim lifts his mask, studying Joseph in disbelief. But Joseph just nods again. So Tim replaces his mask and gets ready. Mitch steps back up to the plate. Joseph winds up and throws hard, a wild pitch way outside the box and Tim has to jump to get it.

                   UMPIRE
　　Ball two!

MITCH
Ha! You won't get me fishing for that shit,
Joseph!

Jim hangs his head, grinning. Joseph resets. Mitch waits. When the pitch comes, he checks his swing and Tim receives the ball right where it's expected.

UMPIRE
Ball three!

Tim knocks back his mask and looks up at the umpire.

TIM
Are you kiddin' me!

UMPIRE
*(relights his cigarette)*
Hey, who's the umpire here, you or me!

Mitch steps out of the batter's box, rattled. He glances out at Joseph. His coach, Mister Cassal, shouts from the dugout—

CASSAL
Way to go, Mitch! Good eyes! Good eyes!

Jim stands up and clings to the chain-link fence, impressed.

JIM
This kid Mitch is good.

BARROWS
Full count. He's either got to strike him out,
walk him, or let him hit the ball.

Joseph catches the ball thrown back to him and considers his team spread out across the field. He quotes Homer—

JOSEPH
"There is strength in the union even of very
sorry men."

                    *(returns to the mound)*
              Book thirteen, line two-thirty-seven.

Mitch steps back into the batter's box. Joseph studies the plate, winds up, and throws a blistering fast ball straight down the pike. Mitch is ready, steps into it and swings with a vengeance only to—WHOOSH!!!—miss. Joseph's teammates jump up as one and cheer.

                              UMPIRE
              Strike three!

                               JIM
                        *(stands, impressed)*
              There you go!

                              MARIE
                          *(looks over)*
              Oh my, I guess someone hit a home run or
              something.

Jim remembers himself and drops back down, fast, onto the bleachers. Richard hands his little sister back in through the car window to block whatever Marie might be able to see.

                             RICHARD
              Okay, here you go. I gotta go get Joseph. See
              you later, Aunt Marie.

                              MARIE
              Love you. I'll see you tomorrow!

The boys run in off the field to their mothers. Mitch cannot believe it. He stares at his cleats. Joseph wanders over to Jim, relieved.

                             BARROWS
              Excellent game, Joseph! Congratulations!

                             JOSEPH
              Sure. Thanks.

He reaches his father and unburdens himself of his mitt. Jim holds it and studies Jackie Robinson's signature, still faintly visible. Richard comes running back. Marie is driving away in the background.

> RICHARD
>
> What happened?

> BILLY
>
> He did it. Perfect game.

> RICHARD
>
> *(crushed)*
>
> And I missed it!

> JIM
>
> *(to Joseph)*
>
> Go shake hands with that kid. The pitcher.

> JOSEPH
>
> *(confused)*
>
> Mitch?

> JIM
>
> Go congratulate him on a well-played game.

Joseph looks to his brothers for help. They just shrug.

> JOSEPH
>
> *(to Jim)*
>
> He hates my guts.

> JIM
>
> Yeah, well, that's his problem.

Joseph huffs and puffs dramatically but does as he's told and crosses over to the other team's dugout. The other team sees him coming and stop packing their gear, alarmed. Mitch is up front, still at the edge of the field, still furious and stunned. He waits. Joseph reaches him and holds out his hand. Mitch backs off, offended. Cassal smacks him in the back of the head.

                        CASSAL
    Knock it off, wise guy!

                        JOSEPH
    Congratulations.

The opposing team looks at him like he's crazy. Cassal shoves Mitch forward and the boy grudgingly puts out his hand. They shake.

                        JOSEPH
    Good game.
            *(to all)*
    See ya!

Mitch and the others watch him go.

                        MITCH
    That kid is weird.

                        CASSAL
    Come on! Let's get this gear in the car! It's
    getting late!

07. INTERIOR, REHAB DETENTION—NIGHT

Amy is making the rounds with a young, tough, male orderly named Ike. She comes up a hallway, stops at an open door, knocks politely on the frame and looks in at Robert.

                        AMY
    Everything okay, Robert?

                        ROBERT
    I guess so. Maybe. Sometimes.

                        AMY
    Okay. Lights out. Good night.

She rolls her eyes in hopelessness as Ike locks Robert's door. She checks off a box on her clipboard, leads the way to the following door and repeats the protocol.

> AMY
> Everything okay, Mister Kushner?

08. EXTERIOR, HIGHWAY, JIM'S CAR—NIGHT

Richard speeds along. Jim is anxiously looking at his wristwatch. Billy and Joseph are in the backseat, Joseph hanging out the window, firing shots with his fingers at their imagined pursuers.

> JIM
> Joseph, sit down!

> BILLY
> *(grabs him by his shirt)*
> Get in here, cowboy!

> JIM
> So, when's the wedding?

> RICHARD
> When you get out.

> JIM
> That's over a month from now. She might have the baby by then.

> RICHARD
> We don't think so.

> JOSEPH
> Richard, what's wrong with having the baby before the wedding?

> RICHARD
> Joseph, not now.

> JIM
> Good question, Joseph. The answer is this: appearances.

JOSEPH
You mean like...

JIM
Yeah, like what people think.

BILLY
*(impatient)*
But, Dad, everyone thinks Richard's a stand-up guy for marrying Catherine when she's pregnant.

RICHARD
*(frustrated)*
I'm not marrying her <u>because</u> she's pregnant! I would've married her anyway eventually. It's just... It's just...

JOSEPH
*(tries to help)*
Shit happens.

RICHARD
Exactly. Thanks, pal.

JIM
*(back to Billy)*
Now, who's teaching him to have a mouth like this?

BILLY
What are you looking at me for?

JIM
*(to Joseph)*
Your brother's doing the right thing.

Proud of him, Joseph punches Richard in the arm.

RICHARD
Joseph, don't hit me while I'm driving.

                    JIM
But it's possible to do the right thing in the
wrong way.

                    BILLY
But what's the point in arguing about this
now, Dad!

                    JIM
Hey, shut up, you.

                    RICHARD
What's done is done. I mean, look, Mom was
pregnant with me before you were married.

Jim is stunned. Billy's mouth falls open in shock. Joseph looks from one to the other, confused. Finally—

                    JIM
Pull over.

The car skids to a stop on the highway's shoulder.

09. INTERIOR, REHAB DETENTION—NIGHT

Amy and Ike come down the stairs to the lower floor and begin their routine at the first door they come to.

                    AMY
Everything okay, Mister Hallahan?

                    HALLAHAN
Leave me alone, you fucking bitch!

                    AMY
             *(moving on)*
Excellent. Sleep well, Mister Hallahan.

                    HALLAHAN
             *(yells)*
I ain't afraid of you people!

                              AMY
                   *(checks him off her list)*
                    Always good to know.

Ike locks Hallahan in and they head up the hall.

10. EXTERIOR, HIGHWAY STORE—NIGHT

Jim kicks his way out the passenger side door and the boys follow apprehensively. They are in front of a small grocery store.

                              JIM
                    You two got any money? Billy, go in there and
                    get a carton of Marlboros.

                             BILLY
                   *(takes cash from Richard)*
                    You smokin' again?

                              JIM
                    No, it's for a friend.
                         *(of Joseph)*
                    Take him with you.

Billy drags Joseph with him into the store. Once they are alone, Jim leads Richard aside and stops.

                              JIM
                    Your aunt Marie was just a kid and she liked
                    gossip. She talked too much and liked butting
                    into everybody else's business. Just like now.

                            RICHARD
                    Look, Dad, it makes no difference to me if you
                    and Mom were pregnant before you got married.

                              JIM
                    It should, though.

                            RICHARD
                    Why?

                    JIM
            Because people judge you. Even when they're
            being nice and they're congratulating you on
            your marriage or the new baby or the whatever
            —some good job. They judge you. They know
            you might have done the right thing, but you
            didn't do it the right way. They think less of you.

                    RICHARD
            But that's crazy, Dad.

                    JIM
            Hey! I didn't invent the world! I just live in it.
                    *(sighs and starts again)*
            Listen, it was like this...

Joseph lingers in the store's doorway, listening.

## 11. INTERIOR, REHAB DETENTION—NIGHT

Amy stops at a door and frowns, disappointed.

                    AMY
            Mister Morris, you know you can't smoke
            in here.

In this room is a scholarly man in his fifties sitting at the edge of his bed, smoking.

                    MORRIS
                    *(philosophically)*
            Nurse Amy, given the circumstances, how
            might we define the nature of the current crisis?

Amy steps aside and allows Ike into the room. He takes the cigarette away from Morris. It becomes a wrestling match. Amy drops her clipboard and runs in to assist.

## 12. EXTERIOR, REHAB DETENTION—NIGHT

Jim is sprinting across the grounds with the carton of Marlboros.

13. INTERIOR, REHAB DETENTION—NIGHT

Ike and Amy manage to take away Morris's cigarettes. She rights her cap and retrieves her clipboard. Morris reaches out and tries to caress her ass but Ike shoves him back onto his bed. Just then, out in the hallway, Jim slips around the far corner and ducks into his room. Amy soldiers on—

> AMY
> Mister Morris, I'm going to have to write this up, I'm afraid.

She leaves the room and Ike locks the door. She heads up the hall and stops outside Jim's room.

> AMY
> I think Jim's asleep already.

Ike steps forward and opens the door quietly. Jim is, indeed, in bed and pretending to sleep. Ike leans back out and nods, closing the door and locking it. They move on. Inside, though, Jim rolls over on his back and whistles a sigh of relief.

14. INTERIOR, BROOKLYN CHURCH HALL, 1949—NIGHT

Jim dances with his sister, Nell. But he's only got eyes for Audrey who is dancing with an unknown man nearby.

> NELL
> But isn't there work on the fishing boats here in Brooklyn?

> JIM
> Oh, no, not really. The work's out of New Bedford, mostly.

> NELL
> *(teasing)*
> Who are you so fascinated by, Jim!

Caught and embarrassed, Jim smiles. The song ends.

                    JIM
          Let's sit this one out, okay?

                    NELL
          I have to go to the ladies'.

He comes out into the lobby and waits as Nell moves off to the ladies' room. He crosses to a long bench along the opposite wall and sits. Troubled by his emotion, he hangs his head and looks at the floor. After a moment, a shadow falls across his shoe and he looks up. Audrey is standing there looking at him. Ruthy, just fourteen at this point, is a few steps behind her. Jim straightens up, amazed, not knowing what to do or to say. But she takes a step forward and stops, shyly imperious.

                    AUDREY
          You're sitting on my coat.

Ruthy drifts back towards the dance floor and leaves them alone.

15. INTERIOR, MIKE FULTON'S HOME—NIGHT

Ruthy continues to tell the tale to Richard and Billy as Joseph and Brian eat a late supper, still in their baseball uniforms.

                    RUTHY
          And those was the first words she ever did say
          to him: "You're sitting on my coat." And your
          father, he went as white as a sheet!

                    BILLY
          Ha! I bet he did!

                    JOSEPH
          Did he ask her to dance?

                    RUTHY
          Now, what do you think?

                    JOSEPH
          He must've.

                         RUTHY
                        *(nods)*
                  That's right. He must've.

16. INTERIOR, DWYER HOME, BROOKLYN, 1949—DAY

Paddy Dwyer is trying to have his breakfast as his three daughters and wife buzz around him.

                         MARIE
                      *(to Cecile)*
              They danced five dances in a row, Ma.

                        ELEANOR
              And he walked us all the way home, right up
              here to the front steps.

Audrey is quiet and embarrassed. She glances at her dad.

                         PADDY
                  Fulton, you say now?

Audrey is about to answer but Marie eagerly cuts in—

                         MARIE
                     Jim. Jim Fulton.

Paddy grabs Marie by the wrist, sits her down in the closest chair and glares at her. She shuts up. He returns his attention to Audrey.

                         PADDY
                    From back home?

                        AUDREY
                     Placentia Bay.

Paddy nods. He sips his coffee.

                         PADDY
                      *(to Cecile)*
              That would be a son of John Fulton.

CECILE
You know of him?

PADDY
He has a fleet of fishing boats.

AUDREY
That's what he's working at here. He's fishing out of New Bedford with his brother, Mike.

MARIE
Is he a rich man, Dad, this Captain Fulton?

PADDY
*(amused)*
Marie, pull yourself together. There's nothing but poor men in Newfoundland. Why do you think I'm here in Brooklyn? But...
*(to Audrey)*
As poor men go, he's gentry. Farms a piece of the valley there in Placentia, too. He owns his land.

He takes his empty cup to the sink. Marie wanders away dreamily and Audrey is alone with Eleanor.

AUDREY
And what about you, my dear? I saw Sam Logan danced with you a hundred times at least!

ELEANOR
He's asked me to marry him. He'll come talk to Pa today.

Audrey is astonished: happy but also troubled.

17. EXTERIOR, BROOKLYN TAVERN, 1949—DAY

Still troubled, Audrey waits outside the crowded bar as Jim finishes a call on a payphone just inside the door.

JIM
Yeah. Okay. I'll be there.

He hangs up and joins Audrey.

AUDREY
Is it on?

JIM
Yes. I can get on a boat if I can get to New Bedford by tomorrow at six in the evening. Now...

AUDREY
I'm sorry, Jim.

JIM
Don't worry. Just... Explain this to me slowly.

AUDREY
I can't get married yet.

JIM
Why not?

AUDREY
Because Sam Logan has asked Eleanor to marry him.

JIM
So? That's wonderful. Right?

AUDREY
I can't get married before Eleanor.

JIM
Why not?

AUDREY
Because, Jim—pay attention: she's my older sister.

JIM
I don't understand. Sorry. I mean, if Eleanor wasn't married, you and I would have to wait until she was? And what would happen if she never got married?

AUDREY
No, that would be easy. If she were not engaged and we were—and we're *not*—then we could just go ahead.

He understands and sees where he screwed up. He looks at his shoes.

JIM
I was waiting to get engaged until I had the money for the ring and everything—to put the down payment on the hall and all that.

AUDREY
*(comforts him)*
I know. It's bad luck. But I can't get married before Eleanor. For now, the time has to be all for Eleanor, everything leading up to her special day. I can't interfere with that.

JIM
*(steps aside to think)*
Have they set a date?

AUDREY
Yes.

JIM
When?

AUDREY
In January.

JIM
I've got to go with the Army in November.

Crushed, Audrey sits on someone's front stoop and buries her face in her hands. Jim comes and tries to console her.

      AUDREY
I love her so much and, Jim, if you only knew how little we had growing up and how she sacrificed so much for me—back home in... in... Argentina.

18. INTERIOR, MIKE FULTON'S HOME—NIGHT

      RUTHY
Argentina?

      JOSEPH
     *(to Richard)*
Ain't that what he said?

      RICHARD
     *(corrects him)*
Argentia, Newfoundland. And you weren't supposed to be listening to us.

      JOSEPH
You guys were talking so loud! What was I supposed to do?

      RUTHY
     *(understands)*
Argentia! Yeah, that's where your mom and me is from and she ain't kidding. It was poor as dirt back there.

      BILLY
So, Richard, you're the result of a little going away present before Dad did his basic training!

      RUTHY
     *(dead serious)*
She was scared to death he'd be killed over there in wherever it was.

19. EXTERIOR, DWYER HOME, BROOKLYN, 1949—DAY

Ned and Paddy Dwyer usher all the women, a few kids, and a dog out of the house and into two cars parked at the curb.

>NED
>Let's go, folks! Next stop, Coney Island!

>MARIE
>*(petulant)*
>But it's November, Ned! The rides won't even be running!

>NED
>Yes, but the boardwalk and the sea in the rain and the wind is a beautiful sight to see! World famous! Right, Cecile?

>CECILE
>These girls all need some color in their cheeks. Eleanor, you go with Ned. I'll drive with Mister Dwyer and these two ruffians.

Cecile helps Ned's two little boys into the car. Then she glances up and winks at Audrey who is standing in the doorway leading out to the second-floor balcony.

>MARIE
>And why ain't Audrey coming?

>CECILE
>She's feeling poorly.

>PADDY
>Okay, let's get a move on.

Everyone gets in, the doors are closed and the cars drive off.

20. EXTERIOR, BROOKLYN TAVERN, 1949—DAY

Jim is at the end of the bar near the window. The two Dwyer cars come up the street and turn the corner in front of the tavern. Ned slows down, looks out over the dashboard and into the bar, tooting his horn. Jim tosses back his whiskey, waves to Ned, pays up and heads out. The Dwyers drive off as he walks back the way they've come.

21. INTERIOR, REHAB DETENTION—NIGHT

Jim jimmies the lock on his door and steps out into the hallway with the carton of Marlboros. He pauses to make sure the coast is clear then steps down to Morris's door. He sees there's a light on inside and so, using an unfolded paper clip, jimmies this door as well. Morris is waiting for him and Jim steps in. He offers the carton of cigarettes to his fellow inmate.

>                    JIM
> Thanks.
>
>                    MORRIS
> You're welcome, Jim. How did it go?
>
>                    JIM
>              *(sits, quietly excited)*
> A perfect game!
>
>                    MORRIS
> Perfect, how?
>
>                    JIM
> Oh.
>
>                    MORRIS
> Sorry. I don't follow sports.
>
>                    JIM
> Yeah, right. It's just... It was perfect. No one got on base.
>
>                    MORRIS
>              *(uncertain, but)*
> I see.

#### JIM
I mean, he's only nine years old and the other
kids too, but it's an impressive thing.

#### MORRIS
This is the liar?

#### JIM
Right, Joseph. But, you see, this is the thing:
it's very hard to lie in baseball. The rules are
there for everyone to see at the same time.
You can't fake anything—unless you're the
pitcher!

Morris is catching on.

#### MORRIS
And Joseph's the pitcher?

#### JIM
Yeah. If you're the pitcher you can—how do
I say this? You can tell a story to the batter
he's got to try to make sense of. And then,
while he's trying to understand that, you throw
the ball right past him and strike him out!

Morris ponders this, then looks at the door.

#### MORRIS
How do you do it with the doors?

#### JIM
Oh, they're badly hung. They're heavy duty,
but there's a little give in the hinges. So, if
you grab the knob and lift the whole door
even just a fraction of an inch you can pull
the lock mechanism away from the plate and
push back the bolt with... well, anything
small—like this paper clip.
  *(it occurs to him)*
I don't suppose this place was built as a

prison. Probably a school or a hospital at one time.
> *(sizes up Morris)*
What are you in for, Morris?

MORRIS
> *(smokes, exhales)*
Sexual deviancy.

This gives Jim pause. He tries hard not to look disgusted or alarmed. Morris sees this.

MORRIS
> *(offers him a cigarette)*
Don't worry, Jim, I don't like men.

Jim is visibly relieved. He accepts a smoke. Morris gives him a light.

MORRIS
I made myself unpleasant with a few ladies at work and then, once, in a parking lot outside a bowling alley.

Jim smokes. Then—

JIM
What line of work are you in?

MORRIS
Education. A teacher of philosophy at the university.

JIM
I thought you must be an educated man.

MORRIS
And you?

JIM
How do you mean?

MORRIS
Were you educated?

JIM
Oh, a little, here and there as I grew up. The
nuns in the parish had a school and taught us
kids to read when the weather was too bad
for going to sea or there was no farming to do.

MORRIS
*(arches an eyebrow)*
Did these barbarians who raised you send little
kids out to sea?

JIM
No, but us kids and the women we had to take
care of the piers and the crops while the men
were out fishing. There wasn't always time to
go down to the parish and learn something.
They taught me some math too. And that helped
me out when I joined the Army. Fast-tracked
me into the corps of engineers because, you
see—because of the math.

Morris indicates Jim's wedding ring.

MORRIS
How long has it been, Jim, since your wife
passed on?

JIM
Almost six months now. October 29 this last.

MORRIS
And now you're about to be a grandfather!
At what?

JIM
Forty-six!

They laugh silently and shake their heads in amazement.

                        JIM
    This poor girl, Catherine, she's not yet
    sixteen and as big as a house with child. The
    sisters down the parish won't even let her
    come to school no more.

22. INTERIOR, MIKE FULTON'S HOME—DAY

Catherine sits pouting in Ruthy's kitchen while Maggie Dwyer experiments with the girl's hair, deciding how to style it. Bobby, Ruthy's 17-year-old incipiently gay son, is comparing fabrics and holding them up to Catherine's shoulder. Catherine's mother, Trish, is smoking hard as Marie paces and rants—

                        MARIE
    They can't do that! Trish, listen to me, you and
    Paul have been paying tuition for three kids up
    there at the school for five or six years now.

                        TRISH
    Seven.

                        MARIE
    Just think: what if you took them all out of there
    and put them in public school!

                        TRISH
                    *(terrified)*
    But we've already spent all this money on
    their uniforms.

                        MARIE
    I know, but it's just a threat.

                        RUTHY
    The parish don't want to lose students and the
    money their parents pay.

                        CATHERINE
                    *(morose)*
    I don't want to go to public school.

                    TRISH
          Don't worry. We'll think of something.

                    RUTHY
               *(sighs)*
          I wish Audrey was here. She never let those
          nuns boss her around. She'd know what to do.

This gives Marie an idea. She sits, accepts a smoke from Trish, lights up, then—

                    MARIE
          Audrey would go talk to the pastor.

                    RUTHY
               *(tickled)*
          Oh, Father Russell had a crush on Audrey
          as plain as the nose on your face.

                    TRISH
               *(worried)*
          I don't want this to get, you know,
          political. If the mother superior heard we
          went over her head to the pastor, she'd be
          furious.

                    MARIE
          We'll go see him for another reason.
               *(stands)*
          Ruthy, can I use your phone? I'll call and
          make an appointment.

                    RUTHY
          Sure. Go on.

Bobby holds up white fabric samples and shows them to Trish—two different shades of white.

                    BOBBY
          What do you think, Missus Fiore? This or
          this?

                              TRISH
                         *(smokes, then)*
                Well, Bobby, it can't be white, of course.

Catherine breaks down in tears and wails tragically.

23. EXTERIOR, MIKE FULTON'S HOME—DAY

In amongst the steel skeleton of Mike's unbuilt ship, Richard, hearing Catherine cry, hangs his head and covers his ears. He's surrounded by his cousins, John and Edward, and his own two brothers. Bobby leans out the screen door, all business—

                              BOBBY
                             *(calls)*
                    Richard, what are you wearing?

                             RICHARD
                        *(looks up, confused)*
                          What do you mean?

                              BOBBY
                        When you get married.

Richard just looks at Billy.

                              BILLY
                       *(answers for Richard)*
                      We hadn't got that far yet, Bob.

                              BOBBY
        Think beige.

                              BILLY
        Beige.

                              JOHN
        Why beige?

                              BOBBY
                    Because that's what Catherine's wearing.

And he heads back inside. Billy points at Richard—

> BILLY
>
> Beige.

> RICHARD
>
> So, I gotta buy a new suit?

> BILLY
>
> We might need to become drug dealers again.

> EDWARD
>
> You think Bobby's a faggot?

This startles Richard. He looks to Billy, who looks to Joseph, who gives up his imaginary sword fight on deck and looks on, totally intrigued.

> BILLY
> *(hands boy empty can)*
> Joseph, here, go get me another beer from the cooler in the garage.

Joseph starts to protest but a look from Richard changes his mind. He jumps down and trudges off.

> RICHARD
> *(finally, to Edward)*
> What, because he knows how to dress?

> EDWARD
>
> That, yeah. But he likes to cook too. And he knows stuff about, like—furniture and decorating and shit. It's weird.

Richard and Billy don't have an opinion about this but just look at their older cousin, John.

> JOHN
> *(shrugs)*
> He cooks pretty good, though.

24. EXTERIOR, MAIN STREET—DAY

Marie leads Ruthy and Trish from her car to the church. They stop at the traffic light and doll themselves up a little with a compact, lipstick and eyeliner. While Ruthy touches herself up, Marie notices the movie theater.

> MARIE
> *(curious)*
> I read about that movie in Cosmo.

> TRISH
> *(reads marquee)*
> "Summer of 42."

> RUTHY
> *(hands back compact)*
> You read Cosmopolitan?

> MARIE
> At the hairdresser. I don't want to keep magazines like that around the house and give the girls ideas! There'd be no end to it!

They move on when the light changes.

> RUTHY
> You got the envelope, Marie?

> MARIE
> Right here.

> TRISH
> *(of movie)*
> It's supposed to be provocative.

> RUTHY
> Supposed to be what?

> TRISH
> Racy.

RUTHY

Ha! There ain't much can shock a girl who's already got six sons, believe you me!

25. INTERIOR, CHURCH OFFICES—DAY

Marie, Ruthy and Trish enter as the parish priest, Father Russell rises from his desk.

RUSSELL

How are you, Missus Dolan!

MARIE

Fine, thank you, Father. You know Missus Fulton, of course.

RUSSELL

Of course. How do you do? And how are all those fine young men of yours?

RUTHY
*(happy and innocent)*
Oh, they're all up to no good, I'm sure, Father, God bless 'em.

The priest is a little derailed by this, but passes over it in his good-natured way.

RUSSELL

Yes, well, ah...

MARIE
*(continues)*
And this is Missus Fiore, Paul Fiore's wife.

RUSSELL

Oh! Nice to meet you! Paul is a great help to us as vice chairman of the Holy Name Society.

TRISH

Thank you, Father. He loves his work there.

> RUSSELL
> Now, Missus Dolan, I understand you would
> like to request a special Mass.

Marie places the envelope on the desk and slides it towards him.

> MARIE
> Yes, for my dearly departed sister, Audrey.

A short spasm of sadness convulses Father Russell and the ladies see it, discreetly glancing aside.

> RUSSELL
> God have mercy on her soul.

> MARIE
> *(and posse)*
> Amen.

> RUSSELL
> Such a beautiful woman.
> *(corrects himself)*
> I mean, such a wonderful and devoted mother.
> Such good kids with a decent and upright
> husband...
> *(then)*
> But, correct me if I'm wrong: am I to
> understand he's had a little run-in with the
> law?

> MARIE
> Well, yes, he's had a little—it's been a
> difficult time.

> RUTHY
> And, you know, Father, Jesus himself had a
> few run-ins with the law too and we love
> him all the same no matter what.

Marie closes her eyes and bites her lip. Trish stares at the floor and grips Ruthy's wrist, squeezing tightly. Ruthy sits back and keeps quiet. Finally, Father Russell forces a smile and continues.

> RUSSELL
> Well, let's see. When can we schedule this?

> MARIE
> It would be best if it could be before Audrey's oldest boy, Richard, my godson, gets married.

> RUSSELL
> Richard's getting married?

> MARIE
> To Missus Fiore's second daughter, Catherine.

> RUSSELL
> Well, that's just terrific. But how did I miss that!
> *(checks his desk calendar)*
> I didn't see it on the schedule.

> TRISH
> *(carefully)*
> Well, Father, it can't be a church wedding.

Father Russell sits back, understanding.

> RUSSELL
> I see.

> TRISH
> She's pregnant.

> RUSSELL
> But they're going ahead and starting a proper family.

> TRISH
> Well, that's how I like to think of it.

Father Russell stands and looks out the window.

RUSSELL
Yes, the church remains a little old-fashioned about all this.
*(frustrated)*
But, for crying out loud, Richard was an alter boy here! He coached the special education kids in softball! I suppose time is of the essence. When is she due?

TRISH
April.

RUSSELL
Oh my. I would go to bat with the diocese for Richard and Catherine but the church machinery doesn't move that fast.

TRISH
I understand. But...

RUSSELL
*(sees her hesitate)*
Yes?

TRISH
It would be a big help if Catherine could graduate the tenth grade.

RUSSELL
*(nonplussed, darkening)*
The tenth grade?

TRISH
Yes, Father.

RUSSELL
How old *is* Catherine?

TRISH
*(bravely)*
Almost sixteen.

Father Russell looks to Marie.

>                    MARIE
> She's a very mature and intelligent young
> lady.

>                    RUTHY
>              *(can't help it)*
> And cute as a button!

26. INTERIOR, FIORE HOME—DAY

Returning from work, Paul Fiore, fifty-three, comes in the back door of his home up the street from the Fulton's. But his way into the house is blocked by the washing machine that Richard is fixing.

>                    PAUL
> What happened?

>                    RICHARD
> The drain hose got twisted up and sprung a
> leak. I taped it tight again and got it clear.
> But we'll see. Here, let me move this back.

Richard drags the machine back into place so Paul can continue on into his kitchen. This home is always in a state of mild chaos. Paul is a floor manager at an industrial printing works. He tosses his jacket aside and finds his two littlest girls, Maria (6) and Lizzy (8) at the table doing their homework and dancing to music on the radio. He kisses them both on the head, fixes himself a scotch and soda, then moves into the living room. There, he finds his other daughters, Karen (18) and Diane (12), buzzing around Bobby as he builds Catherine's wedding dress on the girl herself while she stands on a chair in the center of the room.

>                    CATHERINE
> What do you think, Dad?

>                    PAUL
> You know, sweetheart, some chicks can just

wear any old thing and make it work. Lovely.
*(kisses Karen)*
Your mom not back from work yet?

### KAREN
She had a meeting at the church, I think.

### PAUL
*(kisses Diane)*
I hope she ain't planning my funeral or something.

### CATHERINE
*(disapproves)*
Daddy!

Someone is knocking at the front door. Paul moves to answer it.

### PAUL
That would be the undertaker now, I suppose.

Opening the door, cocktail in hand, he is surprised to find Sister Ann-Margaret.

### PAUL
Sister Ann-Margaret! Good evening!

### ANN-MARGARET
Peace be with you, Mister Fiore. Can I have a word with Catherine?

### PAUL
Come on in.

### CATHERINE
Sister!

### ANN-MARGARET
Well, look at you!

### CATHERINE
Bobby designed it.

ANN-MARGARET
Well done, Bobby. Though, I am no expert.
*(moving on)*
Here, Catherine, you need to take this test.

CATHERINE
Now?

ANN-MARGARET
As soon as possible. Grades need to be submitted by tomorrow afternoon.
*(checks the time)*
Why not now? You'll pass this test confidently and complete the tenth grade as planned. And then we can organize for next year. However, I do need to be present when you take it. And I'm expected back at the convent to lead evening prayers at nine o'clock.

She looks to Paul. Paul looks to Catherine.

PAUL
*(shrugs)*
What do you say?

CATHERINE
Okay. Sure.

Everyone goes into action. Bobby whisks away the piles of fabric. Karen carries a table in from another room. Diane leads the little girls out into the backyard. Finally, the cluttered living room is turned into a spare and clean study hall. Sister Ann-Margaret places the test on the desk and moves aside to wait on the couch.

ANN-MARGARET
It's arithmetic, English, science and history. You'll have ninety minutes.
*(checks her wristwatch)*
And: begin.

Catherine opens the test booklet and lifts her pencil.

                    PAUL
              *(leans in from kitchen)*
        Sister, you want a highball or something?

                ANN-MARGARET
        What's that you have?

                    PAUL
        This is a Seven and Seven. But I can fix you
        a Rum and Coke too.

                ANN-MARGARET
        That would be delightful. Thank you.

Meanwhile, Catherine, in her wedding gown, concentrates on her test.

27. EXTERIOR, FIORE HOME—DAY

Paul comes out the back door, stands on the stoop and looks around the neighborhood for Trish. He sees Bobby opening the barbecue.

                    PAUL
        Good instincts, Bob.
              *(comes down to the yard)*
        Where is the mother of my children? Maria,
        come here. Where's your other shoe?

                    MARIA
        I gotta pee.

                    PAUL
        Lizzy, take her to the little girl's room, will ya.
        And try to be quiet in there. Find her shoe.

He sees Richard studying the front end of his car.

                  RICHARD
              *(concerned)*
        I think you're leaking antifreeze, Mister Fiore.

PAUL
Is that what that is?

RICHARD
Probably just a loose fitting. Or a cracked hose.

PAUL
*(hands him money)*
Leave it for now. Here, go get some hotdogs and hamburgers and whatever you boys drink to dull your nerves these days.

BOBBY
Mister Fiore, you got any vegetables?

PAUL
*(alarmed)*
Vegetables?

BOBBY
In the fridge?

PAUL
Bobby, I ain't been in the fridge for a decade unless I'm going for fresh ice cubes. But go ahead. Knock yourself out. See what we got.

Richard moves off just as his uncle Tom Dolan arrives.

PAUL
Tom!

TOM
Marie over here?

PAUL
No. My wife's missing too. I thought she might be over your place.

TOM
Nope. My place is deserted.

                    PAUL
Hang around. I just sent my new son-in-law
up to the deli to get some grub.

                    TOM
Ha! Don't hold your breath there, pal. There's
still time for Richard to cut and run!

                    PAUL
Oh! That's rude!
          *(drinks, then)*
Yeah, I was just telling Trish yesterday: of all
the deadbeat, scumbag, two-bit pricks to knock
up my 15-year-old number two daughter, I'm
glad, after all, that it was Richard.

Then Mike arrives.

                    TOM
          *(cracks open a beer)*
Evening, Mike!

                    PAUL
You looking for Ruthy?

                    MIKE
She here?

                    PAUL
Goddamn! All our brides are gone AWOL!

Bobby comes out from the house with a pile of vegetables.

                    MIKE
          *(to Bobby)*
You seen your mother?

                    BOBBY
Not since lunchtime.

Karen follows Bobby out with plates and silverware.

                    KAREN
Dad, I told you, they went to a meeting at
the church.

                    TOM
          *(slaps his leg)*
I knew it: They're planning our funerals!

                    PAUL
That's what I said.

                    MIKE
          *(of grill)*
What you got in mind there, Bobby?

                    BOBBY
Hotdogs, hamburgers. I can make a kind of
grilled chicken salad, I think. Karen, you got
olive oil in there?

                    KAREN
          *(goes to check)*
I'm sure.

                    MIKE
Well, that'll do.
          *(of cooler)*
Got another beer in here, Paul?

                    PAUL
Probably. Take a look.

Tom sits back and wonders aloud—

                    TOM
Now, where can these dames all be?

28. INTERIOR, MOVIE THEATER—DAY

Marie, Ruthy and Trish are riveted, amazed, and terrified by the afternoon matinee of *Summer of '42*.

MARIE
Is she...

TRISH
She is.

MARIE
My God. That's unbelievable.

TRISH
She's lonely, Marie.

RUTHY
Her man's gone off to the war.

MARIE
But this kid's not even handsome.
*(then)*
Oh, wow, look at that underwear.

RUTHY
I had a bra just like that.

TRISH
That's all Christian Dior like they have at Bloomingdale's.

MARIE
*(impatient)*
Look, he doesn't even know how to kiss!

TRISH
Well, I think that's the...

STRANGER
*(off)*
SHHHH!!!!!

The ladies quiet themselves and watch the film.

# Episode Four

01. INTERIOR, REHAB DETENTION—DAY

Jim packs his one suitcase and prepares to be released. He washes his hands at the sink and inspects his freshly-shaven jaw in the mirror. He tosses his shaving gear in the suitcase and closes it. Just then, there's a knock at the door.

                  IKE
    *(off)*
Jim, you decent?

                  JIM
Come on in, Ike.

Ike opens the door wide as Jim slips into his jacket.

                  IKE
Congratulations, Jim.

                  JIM
Thanks.

                  IKE
Good luck.

                  JIM
You too.

Ike moves off into another corridor and Jim makes his way down past the neighboring cells. Morris is standing in the doorway of his own, waiting.

                  MORRIS
Is it Saturday already?

                  JIM
    *(shoots his cuffs)*
Once every week.

                  MORRIS
Good luck, Jim

JIM
*(shakes his hand)*
You too, Morris. You stay out of trouble now, alright.

MORRIS
I'll try.

Jim continues on, moving past Hallahan's cell.

JIM
Take it easy, Hallahan.

HALLAHAN
Fuck off, Fulton!

JIM
*(not surprised)*
Yeah, that's always an option, I suppose.

Jim stops at Robert's cell. The nervous young man is seated on the edge of his bed looking worried and confused, as usual.

JIM
Robert, it's gonna be okay.

ROBERT
*(looks up)*
Yeah?

JIM
*(lies)*
There's nothing to worry about.

ROBERT
*(not comforted)*
Okay.

Jim moves on, shaking his head, not hopeful. At the end of the hall he meets Nurse Amy, clutching her clipboard and beaming. She's dolled herself up a little and is trying to control her feelings.

This is not lost on Jim.

AMY

Well done, Jim.

JIM

Well, I wish I didn't have to do it in the first place. But, now that it's done—well, it's done.

AMY

I'll show you out.

Together, they walk out from the ward.

JIM

You look all brand new.

AMY
*(bashful)*
Oh, well, it's Saturday, you know. And, well...

He helps her out by changing the subject.

JIM

My son's getting married today. If I'm lucky I'll get back home with time enough to change into a new shirt.

AMY

Oh, yes! Yes. You must be so proud!

JIM

Worried is more like it.

They reach the front desk and main entrance. They have trouble negotiating this parting. Finally, Jim pauses and turns.

JIM
*(clears his throat)*
Listen, ah... Amy, do you like to dance?

## 02. EXTERIOR, MIKE FULTON'S HOME—DAY

Mike is working on his ship in the backyard, welding the hull's ribs into place, assisted mostly by his son, Edward. Brian and Joseph are there to help as well but are just daydreaming and playing quietly on their own.

> MIKE
> Brian! Don't touch that! I told you. Sit still till I need you.

Mike and Edward move to the next spot to be welded. Joseph is seated on the edge of the partially completed deck, looking around.

> JOSEPH
> Uncle Mike, why does a ship need a captain?

> MIKE
> You still here? Come down and hold this angle iron in place. Brian, you too.

The two nine-year-olds clamber over. Edward makes them hold a five-foot-long piece of one-inch-thick iron at a specific place in relation to a mark on a taut rope suspended from the deck ten feet above and anchored to a nail on the grid of wooden planks that make up the floor extending the length of the ship.

> MIKE
> Lower on the right, Brian.

> EDWARD
> Joseph, up an inch.

Edward holds another piece of iron of the same gauge. Once he's sure the boys have their piece in the right spot, he positions his own. Mike knocks down the lenses of his goggles and moves in to weld.

> MIKE
> Look away you two!

JOSEPH

But...

Too late. The white-hot arc of the weld is underway. Brian and Joseph are frozen in place, terrified. Done, Mike leans back, flips up his goggles, and inspects his work.

MIKE

That'll do. Edward, secure the join beneath with that two-by-four there.
*(then)*
Don't you two let go yet!

BRIAN

The iron's hot, Dad!

MIKE

Where are your work gloves?

BRIAN

You ain't gave me none.

MIKE

Hey, your tools are not management's responsibility.
*(then)*
Edward?

EDWARD

*(of two-by-four)*

Set.

MIKE

Okay, you two, stand down till further notice.

The boys wander aside, half blinded. But Joseph is still anxious to know—

JOSEPH

*(rubs his eyes)*
But why *does* a ship need a captain?

MIKE
Because if no one's in charge, everyone's in charge.

JOSEPH
*(plays with a heavy clamp)*
And that's bad?

MIKE
Usually. That's why it's important to choose a good captain. Otherwise there's confusion.
*(then)*
Stop fooling with that, Joseph. It's not a toy! Put it back where it was.

Joseph puts aside the clamp. Mike and Edward resume their work but the kid interrupts them again.

JOSEPH
Is that what they call a mutiny?

EDWARD
*(losing patience)*
Don't they need you next door? Uncle Jim's getting home today, right?

JOSEPH
Not till later.

But Mike is amused.

MIKE
Now, what have you been reading?

Joseph drags a paperback out from his pocket and hands it over.

MIKE
*Mutiny on the Bounty.* This any good?

JOSEPH
It ain't *Moby-Dick*.

Mike sets his goggles far back on his head and extinguishes his acetylene torch. He feels like talking.

>                         MIKE
> You know, my father—your grandfather—
> he made my older brother Leonard captain
> of six of his twelve boats for one trip. This
> was—let me think—must have been 1935
> or so. Before the war. I wasn't much older
> than you two, cabin boy on my father's craft.

03. EXTERIOR, JOHN FULTON'S BOAT, 1935—DAY

Mike at age twelve watches his dad, John Fulton, on the bridge of his large well-worn commercial fishing vessel. The sky is dark and the North Atlantic is threatening. John is watching the storm approach. His crew are watching him. There are five other boats in the vicinity. He steps into the pilot's cabin and lifts the radio.

>                         JOHN
> Len?

>                         LEONARD
>                     *(off, over radio)*
> Da.

>                         JOHN
> Where are you?

04. EXTERIOR, LEONARD FULTON'S BOAT, 1935—DAY

*(Intercut with previous scene)* On the bridge of his own lead boat, Leonard is watched by his own crew. He replies—

>                         LEONARD
> Due south of you. We're making for land.

>                         JOHN
> Len, I think we stand a better chance moving
> farther out to sea. The storm will catch us closer
> to shore and smash our boats to pieces.

Leonard silently curses himself, having considered this as well. But he studies the sky and the water. He's convinced.

> LEONARD
> Da, we should all head in. I think the storm will head out to sea as it comes further south.

John, too, considers this as he studies the waves and the sky, the faces of his crew. He is not convinced.

> JOHN
> Len, bear in mind we've got most of the men of the town with us.

> LEONARD
> I will. And I'll get them home. But we've got to move now.

> JOHN
> I can't do it, Len. I've got the Grand Banks between here and there and if the storm catches us as we're crossing it, we're done for.

> LEONARD
> Then bear east, Da, out to sea, and hurry. I'll make for Cape May.

> JOHN
> Godspeed, Len.

> LEONARD
> Godspeed, Da.

05. EXTERIOR, MIKE FULTON'S HOME—DAY

> JOSEPH
> And they were all lost at sea! No, that can't be because...

> MIKE
> Settle down.

                        JOSEPH
                    *(jumps up)*
            Pirates! They met German pirates in submarines!

                         MIKE
            Are you gonna shut up and let me tell this story
            or not!

                        JOSEPH
                        *(sits)*
            Sorry.

06. EXTERIOR, PLACENTIA, 1935—NIGHT

The storm is raging on land as well. John's forty-year-old wife, Louisa, makes her way across the harbor front, assisted by Jim, who's just nine. The two of them nearly get blown down in the wind.

07. INTERIOR, HARBOR STATION, 1935—NIGHT

Three men in a high office with reinforced windows looking out on to the harbor and the sea beyond. Louisa enters with the boy. The men wait as the woman knocks aside her heavy oilskin coat.

                        WALLACE
            Missus Fulton.

                        LOUISA
            Mister Wallace.
                    *(then, to the others)*
            Jeremy. Tom.

They murmur their respects as they fiddle with radio knobs.

                        WALLACE
            No word yet. We lost touch with Len's boats
            about two hours ago.

                        LOUISA
            And my husband?

>           WALLACE
> No signal since midday.

She just nods, then—

>           LOUISA
> Jeremy, any news of your brother and his crew?

>           JEREMY
> They made landfall at Torbay this afternoon. The boat's in bad shape but no men lost.

>           LOUISA
> Thank God for that.

Louisa starts to raise her hood again, but—

>           TOM
>       *(of the boy)*
> Who's this one, now?

>           LOUISA
> This is Jim, my youngest.
>       *(to Jim)*
> Say hello to Mister Tobin. This is your friend, Althea's, pa.

>           JIM
> Good evening, Mister Tobin.

>           TOM
> Likewise.

>           LOUISA
>       *(leaving)*
> Thank you for your time, gentlemen.

>           WALLACE
> We'll send word if we hear anything at all, Missus Fulton.

LOUISA
    Thank you.

As she steps back out onto the staircase—

                    TOM
                *(calls quietly)*
    Jim.

                    JIM
                *(stops, turns in)*
    Yes sir?

                    TOM
    You look after your mother and your sisters
    now.

Jim just looks from Tom to Jeremy and then to Wallace. All of them regard him sternly.

08. EXTERIOR, FULTON PIERS, 1935—DAY

Three long piers are built out over a wide, deep inlet at the bottom of a steep valley. The storm has passed and Jim finishes coiling a length of rope, prepping the piers for the eventual return of the boats. But as he tries to look around the tall cliff blocking his view of the harbor, he sees nothing but debris floating by in the water: broken boats, parts of houses. He looks towards the Fulton house way up above the piers where the road cuts through the small town. There are about twenty women with small children gathered in the road, talking nervously and quietly to one another. Jim turns back out to the water. Louisa appears behind him with Nell and May (both young teenagers).

                    LOUISA
    Jim, they'll not be returning. It's the four
    of us now.

Jim nods slowly, accepting this. Then he turns back and, looking past Louisa, his face lights up. Louisa turns to follow his gaze. Leonard and his crew are being carried into town on the back of open bed pickup trucks from over the hill above. The women on the road see this too and start moving towards them. Up above, Leonard jumps off the lead truck, stops and waves at his mother. Louisa passes out. Startled, Leonard starts to run down the slope towards her but stops when he sees, from the higher ground, over the cliff, the masts of his father's boats drifting down the inlet. Jim turns back to the water just in time to see the boats rounding the cliff and coming into view.

09. EXTERIOR, FULTON PIERS, 1935—DAY

Later, John's six busted up boats are docking and Leonard's crew are throwing ropes and setting to work.

> JOHN
> *(seeing Leonard)*
> What'd you do with my boats!

> LEONARD
> We sold them as fire wood to pay the men who drove us back here!

> JOHN
> *(jumps to pier)*
> Jesus Christ Almighty. That's a hell of a setback. Lose anyone?

> LEONARD
> Franklin's in a hospital in Cape May with two fractured knees. Axel Riley met a girl in a bar and we'll never hear from him again. How about you?

Just then, Nell comes up to her father with a bottle of whiskey. He takes it, kisses her head and drinks. Then, seeing Louisa—

> JOHN
> Is that your mother?

> NELL
> She fainted.

JOHN
*(answers Leonard)*
We're whole. We almost lost Mike.

They watch Mike climb down off the boat, shaky and pale, fairly traumatized.

JOHN
Got sided bad by an evil swell and almost rolled. Threw Mike in the drink but he got tangled up in some ropes so we could pull him back out again.
*(to Mike)*
Mike, hold your hand out flat.

Mike does this, though he's clearly unsteady.

JOHN
Look at that! Steady as a rock!

LEONARD
*(plays along)*
You're made for the sea, Mike! You surely are!

Leonard pats Mike on the back and sends him away. He looks at his father, skeptical. The older man moves off.

JOHN
*(of Mike)*
He'll be alright.

Leonard then sees Jim coiling rope.

LEONARD
Goddamn it, Jim! Who taught you how to coil rope!

JIM
*(defensive)*
You did.

                    LEONARD
            Did I? Alright, then: look, it's got to lead
            from the center, see...

Meanwhile, John comes to Louisa. The girls make way.

                    JOHN
                *(sits down beside her)*
            Missus Fulton, what are doing asleep on my
            pier?

                    LOUISA
                *(won't even look at him)*
            Don't you Missus Fulton me. Have you lost any
            of my sons?

                    JOHN
                *(hands her the bottle)*
            Not a one, dear. Not a one. How are the crops?

Louisa drinks and winces. She takes his hand and doesn't answer.

10. EXTERIOR, JIM FULTON'S HOME—DAY

Billy drives the car up into the driveway and kills the engine.

                    BILLY
            Welcome home.

                    JIM
            Well, you didn't burn the house down. That's
            a start.

                    BILLY
            We tried our best but we didn't have it in us.

Jim grins and stands out of the car.

11. INTERIOR, JIM FULTON'S HOME—DAY

Entering, Jim finds Joseph busy at the kitchen counter. He is immediately suspicious.

> JIM
> Now, what are you up to?

> JOSEPH
> Coffee.

> JIM
> *(sits at table)*
> Where's Natalie?

> BILLY
> Up at the Fiore's. She's part of the wedding.

> JIM
> *(checks the time)*
> Oh, Jesus, we should get a move on.
> *(stands)*
> Joseph, you got anything to wear?

> JOSEPH
> *(brings coffee)*
> What's wrong with what I'm wearing?

> JIM
> You can't go to a wedding in sneakers.

> JOSEPH
> But it's in a driveway.

> JIM
> *(sips coffee, then, wincing)*
> What is this?

> JOSEPH
> *(excited)*
> It's got cinnamon in it.

> JIM
> You put cinnamon in my coffee?

                    JOSEPH
        I heard on the radio it's a cool thing to do.

Jim looks at Billy.

                    BILLY
        You got a tie I can borrow?

                    JIM
              *(hands back coffee)*
        In my closet. Don't take the blue one. I want
        to wear the blue one.
              *(to Joseph)*
        Make me another cup of coffee—without
        cinnamon.

                    JOSEPH
        Really?

                    JIM
        Yeah.

                    JOSEPH
        You sure?

                    JIM
        Yeah, I'm sure.

                    JOSEPH
              *(bewildered)*
        Okay.

                    JIM
        And let's find you some proper shoes to wear.

12. EXTERIOR, FIORE HOME—DAY

The front door opens to reveal Catherine, resplendent in her gown and pregnant as hell. Her sisters and Natalie all tumble out with her, down the stoop and into the front yard. There, her dad is waiting for her with scotch and soda in hand. She takes his arm and Paul hands his drink to Maggie Dolan, who places it in the mailbox for safekeeping. Paul and Catherine are guided across the small lawn to the end of the driveway. Family, friends and the neighbors are crowded against one another up against the houses on either side. Up top, before the garage at the back of the yard is Father Russell with Richard and his best man, Billy. On a sign from Sister Ann-Margaret, Bobby places the needle on a record: *A Whiter Shade of Pale*, by Procol Harum. Catherine's little sisters and Natalie start up the driveway, tossing flower petals around. Paul then escorts Catherine forward. Jim catches Billy's eye and gestures to Richard. Billy looks over and sees his brother's tie is askew. He rights it just in time for Catherine's arrival. She hugs her dad and he moves off to join Trish who hands him her highball and wipes away her tears.

RUSSELL
*(waits for quiet, then)*
Richard and Catherine, have you come here freely and without reservation to give yourselves to each other in marriage?

RICHARD & CATHERINE
Yes.

RUSSELL
Will you honor each other as man and wife for the rest of your lives?

RICHARD & CATHERINE
Yes.

RUSSELL
Will you accept children lovingly from God and bring them up according to the law of Christ and his church?

Richard and Catherine are a little overwhelmed at the largeness of these questions. They answer uncertainly.

RICHARD & CATHERINE
Well. Yeah. Yes.

**RUSSELL**
Repeat after me: I, Richard, take you, Catherine to be my wife.

**RICHARD**
I, Richard, take you, Catherine to be my wife.

**RUSSELL**
I promise to be true to you in good times and bad...

**RICHARD**
I promise to be true to you in good times and bad...

**RUSSELL**
In sickness and in health...

**RICHARD**
In sickness and in health...

**RUSSELL**
And I will love you and honor you all the days of my life.

**RICHARD**
And I will love you and honor you all the days of my life.

Father Russell now turns to Catherine.

**RUSSELL**
I, Catherine, take you, Richard, for my lawful husband...

**CATHERINE**
I, Catherine, take you, Richard, for my lawful husband...

**RUSSELL**
To have and to hold, from this day forward...

CATHERINE
To have and to hold, from this day forward...

RUSSELL
For better, for worse...

CATHERINE
For better, for worse...

RUSSELL
For richer, for poorer...

CATHERINE
For richer, for poorer...

RUSSELL
In sickness and in health...

CATHERINE
In sickness and in health...

RUSSELL
Until death do us part.

CATHERINE
Until death do us part.

The two young people are practically swaying with fatigue.

13. EXTERIOR, FIORE HOME—DAY

Later in the day, the party is going strong. Paul falls into a lawn chair between Jim and Ruthy.

PAUL
Well, that's one. Four more girls to go and I can retire!

MARIA
*(his 6-year-old)*
Can I get married next, Dad?

PAUL
Well, beautiful, today's a special occasion, but from now on we've got some ground rules around here.

RUTHY
*(skeptical)*
Oh! And what would those be, Mister Fiore?

PAUL
First of all, you've got to be eighteen.

MARIA
Eighteen! That's like forever!

RUTHY
Oh, phooey. I was fifteen when I married Dad and it's a good thing I did or he'd have taken up with Magda Chenowski from over the next parish!

PAUL
*(to Jim)*
This true?

JIM
Mike only had eyes for you, Ruthy. I swear to God.

RUTHY
You can never be too sure. Sometimes a girl is got to put her foot down on the gasoline.

PAUL
*(nods)*
Pedal to the metal.

RUTHY
Right, like he says.
*(to child)*
Come on, Maria, let's go dance.

PAUL
*(carefully)*
You gonna be okay with these newlyweds
as tenants?

JIM
Well, we've got the room right now while
Joseph and Natalie are still with their aunts.
Billy will be moving out before long. And it
will be good to have someone taking care
of the house.

PAUL
*(stands to go mingle)*
Well, go easy on 'em. Catherine's not exactly
the Suzy Homemaker type.

JIM
*(resigned)*
Who is at her age?

Paul moves off and Jim crosses to Paddy Dwyer.

JIM

Paddy.

PADDY
Welcome back, son.

JIM
*(shaking hands)*
Thanks. How you holding up?

PADDY
Can't complain.
*(sits)*
Still not over it, though. That was a hard
knock losing Audrey.

Jim sits beside the older man. They sit in silence a moment, then
Paddy lays a hand on Jim's arm.

#### PADDY
I went off the rails a bit myself when Audrey's mother passed away.

Jim sits back. This is news to him.

#### PADDY
Drinking, fighting... I sent Audrey and Eleanor back to Newfoundland to be raised by relatives. They were only... I don't know how old they were.
*(holds his hand out)*
About that high maybe. Didn't see them again until they were young ladies come to live with Cecile and me there in Brooklyn. By then we'd had Marie. It's like some smart aleck in the bible says: "This too shall pass."

They watch the young people dancing joyously around Richard and Catherine.

#### JIM
It terrifies me to look at them: so young and...
*(sits back and grins)*
But I was that stupid when I asked you if I could marry Audrey.

#### PADDY
That you were. You were as green as they come. So what are you afraid of? They'll learn. What, do you think you're smarter than Richard?

#### JIM
I might be.

#### PADDY
Yeah, well you've had time to make some mistakes and learn a little.

#### JIM
The world's tougher than he knows.

PADDY
Yeah, he's a nice decent young man, it's true.
And, believe it or not, that's your doing.

JIM
*(considers this)*
I think it was Audrey's doing.

PADDY
He's got it in him, though: the grit.
*(slaps his knee, laughing)*
You should've seen him when us lot made
him sign you into the nut house!

The old man turns away, beside himself with silent laughter. Jim just grins ruefully—the memory of this still stings.

JIM
*(standing)*
You need anything, Paddy?

PADDY
No, son, thanks. But, listen: the likes of you
and me might be tougher than Richard, but
we're no match for this little girl he's
married, Kathleen.

JIM
Catherine.

PADDY
*(startled)*
Catherine? Her name's not Kathleen?

JIM
It's Catherine.

PADDY
Jesus Christ.
*(lets it go)*
Okay. But anyway, that girl is tough as nails

and she's going to get Richard through this world whether he likes it or not.

Jim practically staggers away from this encounter with his father-in-law. He meets his brother, Mike, bent over the plastic beer cooler.

>                    MIKE
> Welcome home, Jim.
>
>                    JIM
> Thanks. There a 7-Up or something in there?
>
>                    MIKE
> Yeah. Hold on.
>          *(finds one and hands it over)*
> When did you get in?
>
>                    JIM
> Couple of hours ago. Billy came got me.
>
>                    MIKE
>            *(with difficulty)*
> Sorry we had to go through all this, Jim. But they said it was for the best.
>
>                    JIM
> Forget it. Thanks for taking care of the mortgage for me.
>
>                    MIKE
> You should call Len back home. He took care of most of the mortgage.
>
>                    JIM
>              *(stung)*
> No.
>
>                    MIKE
>            *(reluctantly)*
> Yeah.

JIM
He take money out of his savings?

MIKE
Maybe. I don't know. He wanted to do it.

JIM
Damn.

MIKE
Call him.

JIM
I will.

Starting on his way to do so, Jim comes face to face with Marie, who grins coquettishly.

MARIE
Hey there, stranger!

JIM
Hello, Marie.

They hug uneasily. Then—

JIM
Look, Marie, I'm sorry.

MARIE
Oh? About what?

JIM
Listen, don't give me a hard time.

MARIE
Jim, come on, loosen up.

JIM
I was out of line last time we met. That's all I wanted to say.

MARIE
You were. And I appreciate you admitting it.

Now, he'd like to tell her off but—

JIM
*(controls himself)*
I gotta... I gotta go call my brother, Len, back home.

MARIE
*(calls after him)*
You tell Len I'll never forgive him for not coming down here for Richard's wedding! And give my love to Angela!

As Jim comes out into the front yard, shaking his head free of Marie, he finds Joseph holding open the Fiore's mailbox, looking in at the forgotten cocktail.

JIM
What are you doing? Tuck your shirt in.

JOSEPH
Dad, there's a drink in the mailbox.

JIM
*(takes it, sniffs)*
That's Mister Fiore's.

JOSEPH
What's it doing in there?

JIM
*(replaces drink in box)*
He must've put it there for some reason. Come away. What are you doing opening other people's mailboxes?

JOSEPH
We going home now?

                    JIM
            No, I have to go back and call your uncle Len.
            Did you eat? Go back inside and get someone
            to give you a hotdog. I'll be back later.

Joseph watches his dad walk down the street, then glances around the neighborhood, disquieted.

                    JOSEPH
            Mighty strange. Could be anything in any of
            these mailboxes. Who knows what goes on?

                    MAGGIE
                *(comes around house)*
            What are you doing out here, you little
            delinquent?

                    JOSEPH
            Can I have a hotdog?

                    MAGGIE
            Yeah, they just put some on. Git!

He runs off. She opens the mailbox, looks around cautiously, then takes the drink and knocks it back. Returning the empty glass to the mailbox, she hurries back to the party.

14. EXTERIOR, JIM FULTON'S HOME—DAY

Jim comes down the middle of the street and sees a strange man standing in his front yard.

                    JIM
                *(suspicious)*
            Can I help you?

                    GIORDANO
            James Fulton?

                    JIM
            Who's asking?

GIORDANO
*(shows his badge)*
Constantine Giordano. I'm your parole officer.

JIM
Oh. I see.

GIORDANO
I was in the area so just came by to introduce myself.

They shake hands. Giordano puts away his badge and takes out a little notebook and pen.

GIORDANO
So, how are things so far?

Jim looks around at the neighboring homes, self-conscious.

JIM
So far? I just got out about three and a half hours ago.

GIORDANO
Those could be tough hours, believe me. Where you coming from?

JIM
My son just got married up the street.

GIORDANO
Is that so? Congratulations, I hope.

JIM
So, how does this work? You and me? You come once a week or something?

GIORDANO
*(evasive)*
I come by when I can, every once in a while, just to see how things are going.

                    JIM
              *(irritated)*
         You mean I'm under surveillance.

                  GIORDANO
              *(shrugs)*
         Well, in a manner of speaking maybe. Anyway,
         I gotta shove off. See you next time, Jim.

Giordano pockets his notepad, gets in his car, and drives off. Jim heads inside.

                    JIM
         Shit.

15. INTERIOR, JIM FULTON'S HOME—DAWN

It is still dark. Billy is sleeping upstairs. Jim is in the kitchen buttoning his shirt. He pours a cup of coffee then comes to the foot of the stairs and calls—

                    JIM
         Billy.

Billy's head rises from the pillow.

                   BILLY
         Huh.

                    JIM
         Let's go. Get up.

Billy hesitates, dazed, then steps from the bed. Jim waits at the foot of the stairs. He listens, hears movement, is satisfied and returns to the kitchen where he sips his coffee and laces up his work boots. Billy makes his way downstairs and towards the bathroom, grabbing a towel from the hall closet.

                    JIM
         No time for a shower. You ain't going
         nowhere you need to be clean for.

Billy stops, half asleep, and let's this sink in as Jim glances out the window above the kitchen sink at the dawn light on the horizon.

>JIM
>Gonna be a hot day.

He places his coffee mug in the sink and grabs his car keys.

>JIM
>Let's go.

16. EXTERIOR, JIM FULTON'S HOME—DAWN

Billy stumbles out the front door of the house, still half dressed. Jim is waiting beside the car on the passenger side.

>JIM
>That door locked?

Billy turns back, locks the door and continues on, but—

>JIM
>Check it.

Billy goes back, checks the door. It is in fact not locked. He locks it again, closes it a second time and finally confirms it is locked.

>BILLY
>It's okay.

>JIM
>Come on, we gotta go.

>BILLY
>*(waking up)*
>Why don't we just get a new lock?

>JIM
>There's nothing wrong with that lock. It's just the way you lot use it.

He throws the keys and Billy catches them. Buttoning his shirt, he gets in behind the wheel and yawns.

> JIM
> What are you waiting for? We've got seven minutes till the train pulls in.

Billy puts the car in gear and backs out of the driveway.

17. EXTERIOR, TRAIN STATION—DAWN

Moments later, they pull up and Billy parks at the roadside. They get out.

> JIM
> *(looks back)*
> That door locked?

Billy goes back, opens the car, pushes down the lock and slams the door again. He hurries after Jim across the lightly trafficked road to the station where dozens of workingmen are arriving to take the train into the city. Billy is still just waking up. Jim notices this as he himself gets in line to buy a coffee from the drive-up coffee stand. Billy follows along, going wherever his father goes.

> JIM
> *(orders)*
> Black no sugar.

Billy is fascinated to watch the speed and efficiency with which the coffeeman manufactures steaming hot styrofoam cups of coffee and makes change for the steady stream of workingmen passing by him. It is Billy's turn. He takes a moment to compose his thoughts. The whole process comes to a halt. The coffeeman looks at him and then just calls to the next guy.

> COFFEEMAN
> Yeah?

> NEXT GUY
> Two regular. One no sugar.

The whole process continues as if Billy didn't exist. He is shunted aside and looks for Jim who is already climbing the stairs to the elevated platform, talking with Mike. The train is pulling into the station.

>                    MIKE
> You going down the hall?
>
>                    JIM
> No, they sent me out on Friday boltin' up on
> the Turner job at William and Wall Street.
> How about you?
>
>                    MIKE
> Still on the Manhattan Bridge. Most likely be
> there through the summer. That Billy?
>
>                    JIM
> God help us all.

Billy runs up, trips on the stairs and makes the train just in time.

18. INTERIOR, TRAIN—DAY

Jim finishes his coffee and looks back over his shoulder to check on Billy. He's sound asleep a few rows back, crowding the space of the man next to him who closes his *New York Post* and nudges the kid forcefully. Billy wakes with a start and sits up straight.

19. INTERIOR, NEW YORK, PENN STATION—DAY

Billy hustles along following his dad as Jim, making no attempt to help, just plows along on his routine way to work: out the train, up some steps, down a long passage with thousands of commuters, down another set of steps, through a subway turnstile...

>                    BILLY
>               *(panicked)*
> Dad! Dad!

Jim turns back, understands, and returns with a frown, handing

Billy a subway token and a ten-dollar bill.

> JIM
> Buy yourself some tokens on the way home.

He moves off. Billy watches other people and learns how to drop the token in and move on through the turnstile.

20. INTERIOR, SUBWAY TRAIN—DAY

Jim glances over and sees Billy hanging from a strap, yawning.

21. EXTERIOR, NEW YORK STREET—DAY

Daylight is glaring sideways down all the streets as Billy follows Jim up out of the subway and across the sidewalk. They cross the street and enter a diner.

22. INTERIOR, NEW YORK DINER—DAY

Jim enters, passing some men he knows from work.

> DIZZY
> Morning, Jim.

> JIM
> Dizzy.

> CLARENCE
> Jim, you taking the raising gang?

> JIM
> What? No. Montgomery's got the raising gang.

> DIZZY
> We heard they might change him out.

> JIM
> *(not interested)*
> This is my son, Billy.

                         DIZZY
    Billy.

                         CLARENCE
    Glad to know ya.

Billy nods and mumbles. The waitress arrives.

                         ELAINE
    Who's this?

                         JIM
    My son, Billy.

                         ELAINE
    Mornin' sunshine! Can you use a little
    coffee?

She's already pouring it and Billy nods appreciatively. She chucks her chin at some men leaving.

                         ELAINE
    See you later, guys.
              *(to Jim)*
    The usual?

                         JIM
    Yeah.

                         ELAINE
    And him?

                         JIM
    Tell the girl what you want.

                         BILLY
    Ah, hmmm...

                         ELAINE
              *(to Jim)*
    The same?

Jim nods, yes.

23. EXTERIOR, JOB SITE—DAY

Still wolfing down a slice of toast, Billy hurries after Jim as he crosses the street from the diner and enters the job site. He pauses at the rough-hewn wooden gate leading onto the site as a huge cement truck rumbles in past him. He looks up at the thirty-three-story structure: all straight lines of iron against the sky.

>JIM
>
>Hey!

Billy looks over and sees Jim waiting impatiently outside the door of a debris covered cargo container—the Shanty.

24. INTERIOR, JOB SITE, SHANTY—DAY

Billy enters as Jim steps into his work clothes.

>JIM
>Find a hook and put your stuff there.

>BILLY
>
>What stuff?

>JIM
>You ain't brought no work clothes?

>BILLY
>
>I got boots.

Jim just shakes his head and turns away, changing out of his street shirt and into a soiled standard-issue work shirt. Dizzy looks on from down the shanty, giggling.

>DIZZY
>Ain't no girl gonna sit nowhere near you on
>the train home, son.

Jim grins and shakes his head as he steps outside. He hands Billy a pair of sturdy canvas work gloves.

> JIM
> Here, you'll need these.
> *(then)*
> Clarence, I think he's with you today.

> CLARENCE
> Right. Hey, Jim!

> JIM
> *(turns back)*
> Yeah?

> CLARENCE
> Shop steward was asking for you.

> JIM
> *(heads out)*
> Thanks.

Billy stands there, not knowing what to do. Clarence finishes lacing up his boots, grabs his hardhat and stands.

> CLARENCE
> Grab a helmet.
> *(points under a bench)*
> Under there, maybe.

Clarence passes by on his way out as Billy rummages amongst a pile of discarded hardhats under a raw wooden bench built into the wall.

25. EXTERIOR, JOB SITE, YARD—DAY

Jim crosses the yard to a younger man, Kevin, the union shop steward for the job.

> KEVIN
> *(seeing him)*
> Jim!

JIM

Kevin.

They shake hands.

KEVIN

You think you can see yourself clear to taking the raising gang?

JIM

What's up with Gene Montgomery?

KEVIN

He's not moving fast enough for the contractor.

JIM
*(annoyed)*
The contractor ought to be told there's no point in rushing with work this heavy. Gene knows what he's doing.

KEVIN

There's been mistakes. Some accidents.

JIM

Up top?

KEVIN

Up top. Down in the street. Bear got sent to the hospital with his finger amputated last week.

Jim considers all this.

JIM

Let me talk to him.

KEVIN

Kind of a waste having you just boltin' up, Jim. I don't mean to pressure you. But there'd be a fair shake more in your envelope at the end of the week if you took the derrick.

                        JIM
            Let me talk it over with Gene.

                       KEVIN
    Sure.

Jim follows Kevin's gaze to Billy stepping uncertainly across the yard with his hardhat under his arm. He trips over some scrap metal and just manages to catch his hardhat as it falls. He straightens up just in time to miss being hit by some wooden planks being carried by. Jim hangs his head and rubs his eyes.

                       KEVIN
            This Richard?

                        JIM
    Billy.

                       KEVIN
            He with Clarence today?

                        JIM
    Yeah.

                       KEVIN
    Don't worry.

                        JIM
            About what, exactly?

                       KEVIN
                  *(grins, moving off)*
            See about Gene. We'll talk later.

Jim checks his watch and heads for the elevator, passing Billy.

                        JIM
                  *(tapping his hardhat)*
            Put on your cover!

Startled, Billy puts on his hardhat and waits for further instructions from somebody. Clarence passes by.

CLARENCE

Okay, let's do it.

Billy follows everyone towards the elevator. An older guy, Cully, assigned to be elevator operator, sits on an upturned box. There's a cigarette dangling from his lip and he already has a can of beer on the floor by his foot. Ten or twelve men crowd into this six-by-ten-foot cage at the outside edge of the structure. Cully closes the gate and pulls a lever. The cage jolts into gear and rattles upward. Billy is pressed against the perimeter, looking out at the city as they climb steadily higher. He's amazed at the view. Dizzy sees this and nudges Jim.

DIZZY

This one the scholar?

Jim looks over, grins and modestly concedes—

JIM

He's not as dumb as he looks.

The cage rattles and squeaks as it makes its way higher and higher. Billy takes in the sharply dressed people already busy in the offices of the skyscrapers around them. But they rise up over some lower buildings and he's stunned, suddenly, to see the entire Brooklyn Bridge spanning the East River.

BILLY
*(awed, to Clarence)*
What is that?

CLARENCE

That's a bridge.
*(then)*
What, Jim, you never let this genius out of the house or what?

The cage jolts to a stop and Billy goes white with panic. But the other men are mildly startled too.

                    JIM
Jesus, Mary and Joseph.

                  CLARENCE
That's what we like about you, Cully: your light
touch.

                   CULLY
Thirtieth floor. Power Tools, Housewares and
Ladies Lingerie. Please watch your step exiting.

He drags open the gate and the men all file out onto the thirtieth floor. Billy looks around for direction and catches Jim's eye as he moves off. Jim gestures to Clarence.

                  CLARENCE
This way, Young Fulton!

26. EXTERIOR, JOB SITE, 30TH FLOOR—DAY

A little later, Clarence is explaining to Billy—

                  CLARENCE
Okay, so I'm in charge of the Bolt List. Each
one of these men boltin' up—your old man
included—needs 36 bolts per point.

                   BILLY
A point being?

                  CLARENCE
Excellent question! Where one or more beams
meets a column—that's a point.

                   BILLY
Got it.

                  CLARENCE
         *(indicates barrels of bolts)*
24 three and five-eighths and 8 five and
three-quarter.

>                    *(demonstrates)*
> Two of the right washers. Look, see? And
> a nut for each. That's them here. And here.

                    BILLY
Okay.

                    CLARENCE
We make up these baskets for each point.

He grabs a rugged steel mesh basket and drops it at his feet. Billy watches as Clarence deftly "makes" a bolt: taking a five-eighths-inch bolt, throwing on two of the right washers and then fitting on the appropriate nut. He drops this into the basket.

                    CLARENCE
*Voila!* It's not rocket science but it helps
make the world safe for democracy. Here,
get started with the five and three-quarters.

The two of them set to work making bolts.

27. EXTERIOR, JOB SITE, 30TH FLOOR—DAY

Later, Jim is bolting up. He finishes with one point and walks along a beam, trailing the heavy pneumatic impact wrench. He looks off and sees Billy moving across a beam 16 feet up from the lower floor's aluminum decking but close to the perimeter. He steps extra carefully, balancing a basket of bolts in either hand. He stops, preoccupied by the cavernous drop down into the street. Clarence is waiting for these bolts and watching Billy.

                    CLARENCE
Just look at your feet.

                    BILLY
Yeah?

                    CLARENCE
Just look at your feet and never mind the
scenery.

Billy considers this. He looks at his feet and moves across the beam with confidence. Jim, relieved, relaxes and resumes his own work. Billy sits on the opposite beam from Clarence, on the other side of the column, and prepares to bolt up this point with him.

> BILLY
> You ever seen any one, you know—fall?

> CLARENCE
> No. Most guys get hurt, even killed, tripping over a plank and splitting their skull open on some random piece of iron.
> *(of the bolt in Billy's hand)*
> That's not right.

> BILLY
> *(compares and realizes)*
> Oh, yeah.

> CLARENCE
> That's not three and five-eighths or five and three-quarters.
> *(takes bolt)*
> There are sometimes mistakes in the Bolt List. It's the right diameter, though.

> BILLY
> What do you do if it's the right diameter but the wrong length.

> CLARENCE
> *(hands over folding rule)*
> There's a formula. If you didn't know what the Bolt List called for, you could figure it out. Thickness of metal plus diameter of the bolt plus a quarter inch, then the thickness of the washer, if used. That'll be the right length.

Billy opens the folding rule and sets about making the measurements of the iron.

                    BILLY
          Thickness, diameter, plus a quarter inch—
          washer.
                *(measures bolt)*
          Three and five-eighths.

                    CLARENCE
          That's your man.

Billy leans over and studies the flange of the beam where it meets the corresponding flange of the column. Four bolts are needed here. One loosely fitting bolt is already in one of the four holes temporarily holding the two pieces of iron together. The remaining three bolt holes are askew. The bolts can't get through.

                    BILLY
          The holes don't line up.

                    CLARENCE
          That's what your drift pin is for.

Billy sits up, wondering if he's being toyed with.

                    BILLY
          Seriously?

                    CLARENCE
          Yes, son, this is how we barbarians bring
          into being contemporary architecture. By
          brute force. Gimme your drift pin.

Billy moves aside so Clarence can demonstrate and hands him a drift pin from the canvas bag on his work belt. It's a five-inch-long steal bar with ends that taper to blunt points of about half an inch. Otherwise, it's as wide as the appropriate bolt. Clarence fits one of the tapered ends into one of the eclipsed bolt holes. There's enough purchase for him to leave it there. He stands back.

                    CLARENCE
          Now take your beater and set that shit straight,
          William!

Billy straddles the beam, aims, and swings his four-pound sledge hammer too softly and nothing happens. Then the pin drops out and falls harmlessly to the deck. Clarence laughs at him.

> CLARENCE
> No way you'll save the world for democracy swinging your beater in so sissified a manner, soldier!

Challenged, Billy sets a new drift pin and positions himself to take a long, manly swing. Clarence steps back and watches warily from behind the column. Billy swings but connects badly and the drift pin shoots off at an angle, fired like a bullet down at the aluminum decking, which it cuts cleanly through, lodging itself in the freshly poured concrete of the floor below, inches away from an Italian mason who doesn't even notice. Back upstairs, Clarence and Billy change places.

> CLARENCE
> Look, you stand there so you can get a good swing at this son of a bitch. Use the sixteen-pound sledge with the long handle.

Billy takes hold of the long-handled hammer, but hesitates when Clarence grips the drift pin and holds it in place, glancing up at Billy.

> CLARENCE
> Go on. Set your feet where you need them and plan your blow.

> BILLY
> *(hesitates)*
> If I miss, I'll take your hand off.

> CLARENCE
> Miss? Who said anything about missing? This is a union job. Hang the full sixteen pounds of that beast from your outstretched arms and golf this thing into plum. It's almost lunch.

Billy finally does as he's told. He sets his feet, holds the beater far down it's handle, traces his line of swing back from the tip of the drift pin, then—WHOOSH! BANG! He connects. Clarence whips his hand away and falls back.

                    BILLY
               *(startled)*
     You okay?

                    CLARENCE
     Yeah, we're blood brothers now. I think we
     got it started. Hand me the four-pounder.

Billy hands him the smaller hammer and Clarence continues driving in the drift pin. The bolt holes are brought into alignment.

                    BILLY
               *(watching closely)*
     I think it's good.

                    CLARENCE
     Make that bolt.

Billy climbs down and fits one of the bolts through the now aligned holes in the flanges.

                    BILLY
               *(victorious)*
     In!

                    CLARENCE
     We called that *made*, Professor.

                    BILLY
     Made!

28. EXTERIOR, JOB SITE, 30TH FLOOR—DAY

Elsewhere, Jim is hearing too much dangerous banging around and cursing up top. He looks over at another man who notices the same. Jim sets aside his tools, walks across the beam and climbs a ladder leading up top. Up top, things are out of control. Jim almost gets hit by a dangling iron beam, but ducks as it hits a set column instead. A couple of men grab hold of it. Jim glances up to a younger man standing on a beam above him, Chet, who seems to be pleading for Jim to intercede. Jim finds the man in charge, the raising gang foreman, Gene Montgomery, who is about his own age and throwing his helmet to the floor repeatedly, cursing in frustration. Jim signals to Chet and Chet signals to the others to take a break.

                    JIM
              *(respectfully)*
    Hey Gene, everything all right up here?


                   GENE
    Fucking morons they send over from the hall.
              *(drinks from hip flask, then)*
    You?


                    JIM
    No. Listen, Gene, they're asking me if I'd
    take the derrick.


                   GENE
    They are?


                    JIM
    I said no.


                   GENE
    Really?


                    JIM
    You're okay up here, aren't you?


                   GENE
    They want it done too fast, Jim. Truckloads
    of steel arriving too quick.


                    JIM
    Yeah, I know.

                    GENE
          I can't hardly set it before they're screaming
          there's more coming and the city's fining
          them for having trucks in the street.

Two younger guys are fooling around and snapping short lengths of rope at one another.

                    JIM
          Hey, knock it off!

They knock it off.

                    GENE
          Would you?

                    JIM
          Take the derrick?

                    GENE
          I don't mind. I can't... It's the stress.

Jim scratches his head and sighs. He's already studying the situation and the men.

                    JIM
          Who's that, Tom Kelly's boy?

                    GENE
          Yeah. Worthless. And there's Jackie-Neal
          tying on and Bear connecting with Chet.

Jim looks up to see Bear, an Oneida Indian, following the conversation up on a beam above them.

                    JIM
          Bear, how's your finger?

                    BEAR
          The doc sewed the fuckin' thing right back
          on. Look.

He removes his glove and wiggles his finger back and forth.

>                    JIM
> Does it work?

>                    BEAR
> Stiff. Gets a little numb is all.

>                    JIM
> You can connect with a hand like that?

>                    BEAR
> Usually.

Jim is dismayed. He sees Montgomery is now off talking to the shop steward and he decides to take over.

>                    JIM
>                 *(up to Bear)*
> How about you take care of signaling?

>                    BEAR
> Glad to do it.

>                    JIM
> Good.
>                 *(to Chet)*
> Chet, who you want up there with you?

>                    CHET
> Jackie-Neal.

Jackie-Neal is a Canadian Cree Indian and is already approaching, stopping to grab the rolled-up building plans from Kevin and hand them to Jim.

>                    JIM
> Jackie-Neal, how's the new wife?

>                 JACKIE-NEAL
> Expensive.

                       JIM
        You want to go connecting with this maniac
        up there?

Jackie-Neal glances up at Chet who turns his helmet back to front and assumes a boxer's stance.

                   JACKIE-NEAL
        Oh, I suppose I can manage him.

29. INTERIOR, NYC DELI—DAY

Amid the lunchtime rush, Billy and Clarence pay for their sandwiches and drinks and head out for the sidewalk. Billy glances back in as they exit.

                      BILLY
        There's some tables back there.

                    CLARENCE
                  *(keeps moving)*
        Best to stay close to the job. You get used to
        your own sweat but the noncombatants take
        offense.

30. EXTERIOR, NYC DELI & JOB SITE—DAY

As he steps outside, Billy glances at himself in the plate glass window, suddenly aware of his body odor. He sees his shirt and face are stained with sweat and oil and rust. He follows Clarence around the corner to the job. Crossing the street, he sees Jim appraising the three truckloads of iron beams and columns parked at the curb. There's a young ironworker named Daniel standing up on the back of the truck.

                       JIM
        You've done this before?

                     DANIEL
                  *(nods, confident)*
        Past few years, always.

Billy sits on some lumber and takes in the busy life of the city street. He's knocked out by the sophisticated and pretty women passing by. He forgets to eat. Clarence sees this.

                    CLARENCE
        Billy, eat. The girls will always be there to ogle.

                    BILLY
                *(unwraps sandwich)*
        Was I ogling?

                    CLARENCE
        Like a peasant come to the big city!

Billy eats and looks on as some of the other tradesman catcall the girls walking by, making explicitly obscene gestures. They terrify an attractive secretary—

                    DIZZY
        Oh, come to daddy, baby!

                    WALLY
        Ouch!

                    BEAR
        Shake that booty, bitch!

                    WALLY
        Spank it! Spank it!

The secretary runs this gauntlet, disgusted and terrified. Clarence looks at Billy and sees he's unsettled.

                    CLARENCE
        Where you hope to go to college?

                    BILLY
        Wow, that was... wow. Excuse me?

                    CLARENCE
        Where you hope to go to college?

BILLY
Not sure yet. You go to college?

CLARENCE
A few semesters. Then I went and took some time off just in time to get myself drafted. I fell into this line of work after I was discharged.

He stands to throw his trash away and intercepts a pretty teenaged black girl, Julia, unknowingly about to run the gauntlet as well. He catches her eye and—

CLARENCE
Trust me, miss, there's a nicer view from the opposite sidewalk.

Julia registers the situation. She glances at Billy who nods and chucks his chin at the far side of the street.

JULIA
Thank you.

She crosses the street and Dizzy hits Billy's arm with his newspaper.

DIZZY
Yeah, you see, niggers will look out for each other that way. It's a proven fact.

Clarence pays no attention to this, but Billy is stunned.

CLARENCE
*(checks his watch)*
Okay. We're back in.

They head back to work.

31. EXTERIOR, JOB SITE, 33RD FLOOR—DAY

Later that afternoon, Jim is pushing the derrick, gripping the building plans at his side. Order and efficiency are evident. He calls to Bear—

> JIM
> Let's shake this all out. All these intermediaries, north to south along the side here!

Bear conveys instructions into the walkie. Billy and Clarence are making bolts one floor below and can watch all the action up top.

> BILLY
> So who's Bear talking to on the walkie?

> CLARENCE
> The engineer who operates the winch.

> BILLY
> Where's he at?

> CLARENCE
> In the hole—the basement.

Billy steps aside and studies the action of the derrick, following the route of the cables running up from the hook at the end of the boom, then down the length of the boom and into the base of the derrick. He steps over and watches these cables whizzing up and down the shaft created for them to where all is lost in darkness thirty-three stories below.

Down in the "hole" (the basement of the building) the engineer, Artie, operates the winch. Following instructions he receives from Bear over headphones, he draws in and lets out cable by pulling different levers.

Out in the street, Daniel fastens a thick eight-foot length of cable around an enormous I-beam that sits waiting on the truck's flatbed. He "chokes" the I-beam with the cable and hooks the "eye" of this "choker" into the hook at the end of the cable stretching down from the boom way up above. Once it's secure, he speaks into his walkie and signals up to Bear.

Watching over the side of the building, Bear speaks into his walkie and gives the signal to Artie. Artie receives Bear's signal and pulls a lever. The I-beam is lifted off the truck and rises slowly skyward. Up top, it rises up over the edge of the building. Two men push against a ten-foot-long "bullstick" and pivot the derrick so that the I-beam comes where it is needed—an open place between two standing columns. Chet and Jackie-Neal are waiting at the top of either column. As the I-beam is positioned close to where they want it, Chet grabs one end of it and guides it into place, bringing the flange of the I-beam and the flange of the column into alignment. He uses a two-foot-long tapered iron rod ("sleever bar") to connect the two massive pieces of iron temporarily. Once he has it, Jackie-Neal does the same on his end. Once that's done, these two "connectors" connect the I-beam with temporary bolts from the canvas bags on their belts, retrieving their sleever bars. One of them shimmies out to the center of the I-beam and unhooks the choker. They move on and start the process all over again elsewhere. Clarence sees Billy is enthralled.

> CLARENCE
> That's how it's supposed to be done.

> BILLY
> It's so quiet.

> CLARENCE
> As it should be.

> BILLY
> Man, that's got to be a blast, huh?

> CLARENCE
> Connecting?

> BILLY
> Yeah. Wow.

> CLARENCE
> It ain't boring. But it's no picnic either.
> Especially in bad weather.

Billy comes back over and continues making bolts.

                         BILLY
            You ever been up there?

                        CLARENCE
            Yeah. I was connecting for your dad two
            winters ago. Just a week. They were short of
            men down at the hall.

Billy hesitates before mentioning it but, finally—

                         BILLY
            I can't help but notice you're the only black
            guy up here.

                        CLARENCE
            Shhh! Don't go starting no rumors, now!

They grin ruefully and continue working.

32. INTERIOR, PENN STATION—DAY

Coming off the subway and making his way towards the suburban commuter train, Billy trails along behind Jim. The boy is dazzled by the dense crowd.

33. INTERIOR, TRAIN—DAY

The train rattles its way out of the tunnels and into the daylight of Queens, heading east. Jim studies the sports page of his *Daily News*. He glances over to see Billy sound asleep in a seat across the aisle.

34. EXTERIOR, TRAIN STATION—DAY

Jim and Billy come down to the street with dozens of other men and women returning from work. Billy is just waking up. He pauses and stretches, yawning.

                          JIM
                      *(skeptical)*
            You okay to drive?

                              BILLY
        Yeah. Sure.

                               JIM
        Don't get us killed, now.

                              BILLY
        Dad, it's only five and half blocks away.

                               JIM
        Plenty of room to get into trouble, trust me.

They get in and drive off.

35. EXTERIOR, JIM FULTON'S HOME—DAY

They pull into the driveway and Billy cuts the engine. Handing the keys back to Jim, he sees his father pausing before getting out of the car.

                              BILLY
        What?

                               JIM
        What kind of grub do you think Catherine's
        made for us to eat?

                              BILLY
        Oh, well, you know they're half Italian up
        the street, Dad. There might be tomato sauce
        involved.

                               JIM
        Goddamn it.

They head inside.

36. INTERIOR, JIM FULTON'S HOME—DAY

Billy bangs out of the bathroom wearing just a towel and drying his hair with another, continuing a conversation with Richard who is setting the kitchen table.

>           DILLY
> And then you ride up the side of the building
> in this rickety little elevator contraption.

Jim comes up the hallway from his room in a fresh shirt, glances in at the bathroom and frowns.

>           JIM
> Jesus, Mary and Joseph, Billy! Do you gotta
> leave a puddle across the goddamn floor in
> here every time! Jesus.

But he enters anyway and slams the door behind him.

>           CATHERINE
>         *(rattled, at stove)*
> He always like this?

>           BILLY
>         *(heads upstairs)*
> No, he's not always this funny!

Catherine looks at Richard, worried, as she sets down a pot of food on the table.

>           RICHARD
>         *(reassures her)*
> Don't worry.

37. INTERIOR, JIM FULTON'S HOME—DAY

Later: they're all around the table, eating. Jim is staring at the food on Richard's plate.

>           JIM
> What is that?

>           CATHERINE
> Eggplant.

JIM

Eggplant.

JOSEPH

It's vegetarian!

CATHERINE

No, it's a vegetable.
*(to Jim)*
That's meat sauce and mozzarella cheese on top.

JIM

*(very skeptical)*
Oh, well, that makes all the difference, I suppose.

RICHARD

There's a piece of steak there too.

JIM

*(lightens up)*

Oh?

CATHERINE

*(disappointed)*
And potatoes.

JIM

Terrific. Don't get up. I'll get it.

And he moves to the stove with his plate.

BILLY

*(nudges Catherine)*
This is great. You want some bread?

CATHERINE

Yeah. Thanks.

Jim comes back to the table with a plate of steak and potatoes.

JIM
So what's the new job then?

RICHARD
Well, it's still the loading dock. But I'd be manager of the loading dock.

JIM
Trafficking.

RICHARD
Right. Trafficking and expediting they call it.

JIM
There a raise?

RICHARD
Forty dollars more a week.

Jim sips his coffee and shrugs, encouraged.

CATHERINE
*(to Joseph)*
Stop playing with your food.

JIM
Joseph, knock it off and eat your eggplant.
*(then, to Richard)*
It's good. It means they trust you. I don't suppose there's anything like a union over there, though, huh?

RICHARD
*(shakes his head)*
No, I'm sure there's not.

There's a knock on the front door.

PAUL
*(off)*
Hello!

CATHERINE
*(relieved)*
Daddy!

Paul lets himself in and comes to the kitchen. Billy stands and offers his seat.

BILLY
Here, Mister Fiore. I'm just done.

PAUL
*(sitting, to Jim)*
Mister Fulton.

JIM
Mister Fiore.

PAUL
I hear they do a killer eggplant over here at the Fulton place.

Catherine is already making him a plate.

JIM
Trish not feeding you anymore?

PAUL
Her, Marie and Ruthy have started some cockamamie movie club. Every Monday evening, now, they go see whatever the *Long Island Newsday* declares a likely cultural event.
*(to Catherine of plate)*
Thanks, sweetheart.

And he sets into his meal.

38. INTERIOR, JIM FULTON'S HOME—DAWN

The next morning, the routine starts again with Jim calling from the bottom of the stairs.

                        JIM
    Billy.

Billy bolts upright in bed, amazed it's time to get up already. Hearing Billy is on the move, Jim returns to the kitchen and pours boiling water on his instant coffee. Billy comes down and goes into the bathroom. Jim sips his coffee and looks curiously at a gym bag sitting on the floor near the back porch. One sip of his coffee is enough and, disgusted, he pours it down the sink. Then Billy comes in, neatly but casually dressed, and grabs the gym bag. He's ready.

                        BILLY
    Got the keys?

                        JIM
                    *(tosses him the keys)*
    What's in the bag?

                        BILLY
    My work clothes.

                        JIM
    You gonna carry that in and out of the city
    every day?

                        BILLY
    Why not?

### 39. EXTERIOR, JIM FULTON'S HOME—DAWN

Coming out of the house—

                        JIM
    I just bring my work clothes back on Friday
    and carry a clean set in on Monday.
                    *(stops)*
    That door locked?

Billy turns back and checks the door. It's unlocked. He locks it. He waves to his uncle Mike and cousins as they, too, head out for the station. Jim is already in the car when Billy gets in behind the wheel.

>BILLY
>They don't even lock that shanty overnight.

>JIM
>Who's gonna steal a bunch of dirty work
>clothes from the shanty? I mean, you shouldn't
>leave your watch in there.

Billy backs the car out into the street. Jim studies the gym bag.

>JIM
>Is this Richard's old bag?

>BILLY
>Yeah.

Billy drives away.

>JIM
>The Little League gave him that. The whole
>team got one for winning the pennant.

They turn the corner and head for the station.

# Episode Five

## 01. EXTERIOR, JOB SITE, 37TH FLOOR—DAY

Another day on the job. Billy hustles well, making bolts with Clarence and carrying them to the men who need them, tying knots, hoisting baskets, and making points himself. He and Clarence are an efficient and well-coordinated duo.

Jim and his gang, likewise, are setting steel like a well-oiled machine. A load of iron is set down on the decking as Bear relays directions into his walkie.

But the engineer down below, Artie, accidentally knocks over his coffee while receiving Bear's directions. Jumping back from the spill, his shirt sleeve catches one of the levers and draws in a cable at high speed.

Back up top, Bear and everyone else turns and looks, startled, as the huge hook and four-ton iron ball at the end of the cable draws up way too fast towards the boom.

Artie jumps for the lever and rights it but—BANG!!!! It's too late.

Jim and his gang have ducked for cover, holding their breath. The overhauling ball is at the top of the derrick's boom, which is still extended, the sheave block jammed into the tight space at the top of the boom. The whole derrick is listing dangerously. The cable guys securing the derrick at several points along the perimeter are straining.

                        JIM
                      *(shouts)*
       Bear, get him to draw up! Draw up!

                      BEAR
                  *(into walkie)*
           Draw up! Draw up!

Down below, Artie is back in control and pulls the right levers. Up top, the boom draws up till it bangs noisily up against the mast. The derrick gradually steadies.

                         JIM

    Goddamn it!

The men all stand back. This is serious. Billy looks on. Clarence joins him and looks to the nearest cable guy secured about ten feet away to their right. They see it strain and give a little, the cable slipping in the turnbuckle that fastens it. Billy looks from this to his dad. Jim is doing the same, watching the various cable guys for signs of giving, his hardhat tossed aside and his arm raised, warning the men to stay back where they are. Satisfied that the derrick has steadied, he gestures for Bear to hand him the walkie. Bear jumps over and stands beside him as Jim controls his fury and prepares to speak.

                         JIM
                      *(to Bear)*
                What's his name?

                         BEAR
    Artie.

                         JIM
                     *(into walkie)*
                Artie...

                        ARTIE
    Jim, I'm sorry, man...

                         JIM
    Artie, shut the fuck up.

Artie is sweating. He wipes his brow with a handkerchief.

                         JIM
    Pay out and draw in fast—once.

Artie prepares to do so, then—

                        ARTIE
                      *(worried)*
                Everyone okay up there?

JIM

Pay out, goddamn it!

Artie pulls a lever and pays out, but it's pointless. Right there before him, he sees the cable just loll out onto the floor. Jim, too, sees the cable running through the boom simply slacken. The overhauling ball is stuck. Then Artie draws in. The cable rolls up on to its spindle again and, up top, the cable goes taut through the boom and the derrick just shivers with the tug. This is all Jim needs to see.

JIM

Jesus, Mary and Joseph.

He hands the walkie back to Bear.

BEAR

Jim, me and Jackie-Neal can run up there
and get it unstuck.

JIM

Your finger's not nearly whole yet. No.
Forget it.

Clarence is already assembling the tools needed and hanging them from his work belt, approaching Jim.

JIM

Those for me?

Clarence stops. He grins and nods, resigned, and undoes the work belt. He helps Jim set it on himself.

CLARENCE

Let me go up, Jim. I've done this before.
You know that.

JIM

And you've got a seven-month-old little
girl at home somewhere. I know that too.
Hand me that length of rope.

As Clarence coils the rope, Jim glances over at Billy.

CLARENCE
There's Jackie-Neal, then.

JIM
He just got married.
*(fastens the belt)*
Suit Billy up.

Clarence pauses, raises an eyebrow, skeptical.

CLARENCE
You sure?

JIM
What do you think?

Clarence sizes Billy up, thinks and turns back. He nods, confident in Jim's decision.

JIM
Billy, work with Clarence!

Hearing this, Bear tilts back his helmet and shakes his head. He looks up at Jackie-Neal who just shrugs and looks across to Chet. Chet lights a cigarette and turns away to look out over the city. Meanwhile, Clarence sets Billy up with what he'll need.

CLARENCE
Here, eight-pound sledge, wrecking bar,
spud wrench. Put this body harness on.

BILLY
*(putting it on)*
What do I do when...

CLARENCE
Just do what he tells you. Don't look down.
Tie off every four or five steps. Gimme those
gloves. Take these. Better grip on 'em.

BILLY
*(catching on)*
I mean, are we going...

CLARENCE
That's right, Professor. You're on your way
to the top! Go get 'em.

Jim is waiting for Billy at the bottom of the derrick as the kid practically staggers over, heavy tools hanging from his belt.

JIM
Retie your boot lace.

Billy looks down and does so as Jim climbs up onto the base of the derrick. Billy follows.

JIM
You on that side. Now just climb, stop,
tie off an arm's length above you, climb
again and repeat—until we get there.
Secure that beater.

Jim starts climbing, grabbing hold of the mast's crosshatching steel struts, finding a foothold as he can, and moving slowly and carefully up, step by step. Billy, breathless but excited, secures his sledgehammer and prepares to follow.

BILLY
*(whistles gamely)*
Okay.

Likewise, Billy grabs hold of a strut, finds purchase for his foot and climbs. After four or five steps, he reaches up and ties off by clipping to a higher strut the safety hook at the end of the six-foot-long lanyard attached to his harness. Then he continues. He overtakes Jim.

JIM
*(winded)*
Slow down! We're not in a race here.

As they slowly and methodically progress, it gets quieter and quieter. The noise of the job site, and even the city, falls away. There is nothing around them. They're three, then four stories above the top of the job, higher than any of the nearest buildings and the view, when Billy manages a quick glance, is for a hundred miles in any direction. The derrick sways and Billy pauses. Jim stops too and, seeing Billy's expression—

> JIM
> That's normal. From down below, you wouldn't even notice, but the derrick's always swaying a little in the wind.

Down on the deck, Kevin, the shop steward, approaches and stands beside Clarence.

> KEVIN
> Where's Billy Fulton?

> CLARENCE
> Up top.

> KEVIN
> *(looks up)*
> Holy fuck. What happened?

> CLARENCE
> The ball got stuck.

> KEVIN
> Is that Jim up there?

> CLARENCE
> Yeah.

Jim and Billy finally reach the top of the mast and tie off there. Jim stands up, higher than the stuck ball, with his hand on it, and inspects the problem.

> JIM
> Damn, it's in there fast.

He reaches back and draws a spud wrench from his belt. This is a two-foot-long iron bar, tapering at one end to a point, with a standard wrench jaw at the other end. He tries to find a place between the ball and the top edge of the boom to insert the pointed end. He finds something promising.

> JIM
> Okay. You tied off? Get yourself up here
> and drive a drift pin in beneath the ball right...
> > *(searches, then)*
> ...there.

Billy positions himself up higher. He reaches back into the bag on his belt for a drift pin. He's stunned by the view: all of New York Harbor, Staten Island in the distance, the dense city far below. Jim sees he's overwhelmed.

> JIM
> Forget the view! Look at your hands.
> > *(as Billy steadies himself)*
> Now hand the drift pin to me.

Billy does so. Then he reaches for the sledgehammer hanging heavily from his belt.

> JIM
> Hold on. You know how to make a slip
> knot?

Jim removes the coil of rope from off his shoulder.

> BILLY
> You mean a bowline hitch?

> JIM
> Now don't you go fucking showing off up
> here with me! Yeah, a bowline hitch—
> whatever. On the handle of the beater. Put
> it here.

Billy sets the head of the eight-pound long-handled "beater" on the flat metal at the top of the mast. Jim holds it there while Billy makes the knot, pausing once or twice to remember how. Jim watches and sees the mistakes Billy's almost about to make but, in the end, doesn't need to correct him. Billy tries the knot and checks its hold. It works. He looks at Jim.

> BILLY

Right?

Jim nods and ties off the rope's other end.

> JIM

That's a slip knot.

> BILLY

The apprentice manual calls it a bowline hitch.

> JIM
> *(repositions himself)*

Thank you very much, Professor. Now, get that drift pin in under here as I pry at this.

> BILLY
> *(in disbelief)*

Are you kidding me?

> JIM
> *(furious)*

Oh yeah, I come up here all the time just to tell jokes, Bill!

> BILLY

I mean, Dad...

> JIM

Don't call me Dad on the job!

> BILLY

I'm just saying, this ball is—what—a couple of tons?

                        JIM
            Four tons, to be exact! And if it drops from
            this boom more than a few inches at once it'll
            tear this whole derrick off this job and send
            us crashing into those buildings across the way!
                    *(this sobers Billy up)*
            Now: the drift pin right there as I jimmy this
            thing.

Billy readies himself with the drift pin, gets it into place, lifts the hammer and twists back to get a good swing.

                        BILLY
            Ready?

                        JIM
            Yeah. Go!

Jim pushes and tugs at the spud wrench, trying to lever the ball a little as Billy hits at the drift pin ineffectually.

                        JIM
            Just keep trying! Don't wait! Just keep at it!

Jim keeps pushing back and forth with the spud wrench. Billy keeps pounding at the drift pin. Their work, the jimmying of the four-ton ball, is swaying the derrick now. Clarence and Bear look over at the straining cable guys. Billy works with greater force, swinging harder and faster until, to his amazement, the ball does give a tiny bit and the drift pin finds some purchase.

                        JIM
                    *(falls back)*
            Ho! Ho! Okay!

Winded from the exertion, Billy leans back. But his foot slips and he falls, jerking to a stop six feet below, caught by the body harness. Jim looks down at him, too paralyzed to scream. Down below, all the men but Clarence turn away. The sledgehammer is swinging free at the end of the rope, clanking against the boom. Billy laughs as he tries to swing back and grab hold of the mast.

                    BILLY
              *(once secure, of hammer)*
         Call it what you will, but that's a good knot
         to know, huh!

Jim starts breathing again, deeply shook as Billy climbs back up and reels in the hammer.

                    JIM
         You done fucking around? Can we get back
         to work here?

                    BILLY
              *(straightens up quick)*
         Yeah, I'm good.

                    JIM
         Thank you. Thank you very much.

Jim turns back and makes a signal down to Bear. Bear sees it, nods, and speaks into his walkie—

                    BEAR
         Artie.

                    ARTIE
         Bear.

                    BEAR
         He's ready.

Artie and his gang have secured a half-inch-thick steel cable to the brake lever, tying off its other end to a massive steel column a few yards away.

                    ARTIE
         We got the brake tied off.

Up top, Jim has the sledgehammer now. He positions himself even higher, his boots in the struts almost at the top of the mast. He's tied off, so he can lean back out from the mast and make the best swing possible. He measures his swing from the tip of the drift pin. Then—

                    JIM
    Billy, get over here on the mast side!

Billy fearlessly allows himself to swing free and over to the mast side. He re-hooks his harness in place and waits, looking up at Jim.

                    JIM
    Okay, hold tight! When this thing comes
    undone we're gonna move!

                  BILLY
    Right!

Jim makes the sign of the cross, lifts the hammer, steadies himself, winds back and prepares to swing. Down below, the men wait. Jim swings, connects, and the pin barely moves. He resets, swings, connects and the whole rig jolts. Down in the hole, Artie sees the cable pay out an inch and go taut. Up top, Clarence watches the cable guys. They're straining hard. Jim lets the rig steady. He glances down at Billy.

                  JIM
    Get down a little lower in case I lose
    control of this beater.

Billy unhooks, climbs down a few feet and ties off again. Jim studies how the sheave block is positioned, considers the weight of the ball, the tautness of the cable, the placement of the drift pin. He gets back up in position, measures his swing, and reins back.

                CLARENCE
    This is the one.

Jim swings, connects, and the ball gives an inch. The sheave block slips out a bit. Down in the hole: the cable on the brake lever is straining mightily, slipping in the turnbuckles. Up top, Jim is angry that this last swing didn't do it. Now, he swings the hammer at the four-ton ball itself and that does it. The sheave block slips free. But that few inches of release jolts the derrick dangerously. Jim drops down and is caught with the body harness. He steadies himself by locking the hammer's head in the struts of the mast. Clarence sees the cable guys slipping.

> BEAR
> Fuck.
> *(into walkie)*
> Lock it up!

In the hole, Artie takes the winch out of neutral.

> ARTIE
> Okay, we're back in gear!
> *(of cables on brake)*
> Undo those!

The other men down in the hole start unfastening the cable holding the brake lever. Up top, Jim and Billy wait out the rocking of the rig. Once it settles, Jim leans out and signals to Bear.

> BEAR
> *(into walkie)*
> Pay out slow.

Artie pays out a little cable. Up top, the sheave comes unstuck and the ball descends a few feet, normally. Jim sighs, relieved, and rests his head against the mast. He waves a signal at Bear.

> BEAR
> *(into walkie)*
> They're coming down.

Jim and Billy secure their tools and start back down. Billy is energized and excited.

> JIM
> *(still rattled)*
> What are you grinning at, wise guy! Watch your footing!

Chastened, Billy conceals his grin and concentrates on his footing. They climb down.

02. INTERIOR, NYC BAR—DAY

Clarence and Bear drag Billy in after work. They gather at the bar.

> BEAR
> *(to bartender)*
> Sir, whatever this criminal needs is on us.

> BILLY
> *(ordering)*
> A beer—draft. Thanks.

He looks to Clarence.

> CLARENCE
> You all right?

> BILLY
> *(still buzzed)*
> That was amazing!

> CLARENCE
> *(laughs)*
> Well, I'm not letting them take you away from the Bolt List!

They get their beers and toast, drink, then—

> BEAR
> That was fucking well done, Billy.

> BILLY
> *(down plays it)*
> Oh, I'm not afraid of heights, I guess.

> BEAR
> Fuck that! Neither are we. But your old man's temper is another thing altogether!

CLARENCE
*(shakes his head)*
We could hear him yelling at you from
down on the floor! What, were you trying
to teach him something about weights and
measures!

Billy laughs too, but is then perfectly excited about the engineering involved. He puts down his beer.

BILLY
I had no idea the ball was four tons. I suddenly
understood the math of the whole thing and, like...

He's speechless.

BEAR
*(nods)*
Yup.

CLARENCE
Yeah. It's about as dangerous a thing as can
happen.

BILLY
Why the hell did he take me up there with him?
All you guys know this stuff better than me.

The older guys trade a knowing look and Bear indicates Clarence should field this.

CLARENCE
Well, I guess he thought that if he was going to
take a man up and risk getting him killed—well,
then, that man ought to be his own flesh and blood.

Billy sips his beer, thinks, and sets his glass on the bar again.

BILLY
*(sober, to Bear)*
It was that likely we'd be killed?

Bear doesn't answer. He shrugs and looks away. Billy then looks to Clarence.

> CLARENCE
> It's happened to him before.

> BILLY
> To my dad?

> CLARENCE
> He lost a derrick in 1965.

> BEAR
> The Esso Building on Ninth Avenue and 47th Street.

> CLARENCE
> Not the same thing that happened today. But the derrick went over—twenty stories above the street. Bear was on the job.

Billy looks to Bear.

> BEAR
> I was in the boltin' up gang. From what I know the load down on the truck wasn't choked right and the iron settled while they were raising it up out of the street.

> BILLY
> Oh, Jesus...

They can all see this in their heads: five I-beams, each weighing half a ton, choked together too loosely, rising high above the street. Suddenly, they shift and settle, collapsing into a tighter bundle, creating a massive tug on the cable lifting them.

> CLARENCE
> *(voice over)*
> That jolt was enough to tear the derrick off the building and into the street.

03. EXTERIOR, THE FULTON HOMES, 1965—DAY

Audrey and Ruthy are at the fence between their yards, busy with little children and chores. But they're worried and anxious, conversing in whispers. Mike and some of his older boys are gutting fish in the driveway, cleaning their boat after a day on the water.

                      BEAR
                *(voice over)*
Men were killed.

                    CLARENCE
                *(voice over)*
Others crippled.

Mike looks up from his work and sees Paddy Dwyer stepping out of his car and approaching Jim and Audrey's house. Audrey moves to her father and he hugs her, whispering consolation. She steps aside and lets Paddy go up into the house. Mike's son, Edward (9) points out—

                    EDWARD
Dad, look Mister Dwyer's here!

                    MIKE
Yeah, I see. Come on over here, Edward,
and hose down the driveway.
            *(then)*
John, take these guts over to Missus Smith.
She wants 'em as fertilizer for those trees she's
planting.

But Mike is watching Jim's house too, concerned.

04. INTERIOR, JIM FULTON'S HOME, 1965—DAY

Paddy comes through the living room, passing Joseph (4), who is on the floor playing with crayons. Paddy then turns into the hallway and walks down to Jim and Audrey's bedroom. Jim is sitting at the edge of the bed, haggard, unshaven and drawn. He lifts his head and sees his father-in-law in the doorway, then just looks back down at the floor. Paddy comes in and sits beside him. Joseph has followed at a safe distance and looks on.

> PADDY
> It wasn't your fault, Jim.

> JIM
> But it was my responsibility.

Paddy can't answer this. He just squeezes the younger man's shoulder for strength and looks over at the little boy.

05. EXTERIOR, PADDY DWYER'S HOME—DAY

It's evening. Billy is sitting in the backyard with Paddy drinking a can of beer. The old man remembers and nods, sadly.

> PADDY
> It's what you risk in taking charge.
> *(drinks, sizes up Billy)*
> A man doesn't forget that kind of thing, son. He's lucky he got over it. But your dad put a bad thing to good use. He got good enough and, yes, mean enough, so that other people's mistakes couldn't fault his responsibility. He's hard, certainly—in some ways. Maybe because he's soft in others. He hates being a boss. But his skill at what he does makes him one.
> *(drinks, considers, then)*
> He's not a hard man to work for, though, if you're ready to work hard.

06. INTERIOR, JIM FULTON'S HOME—NIGHT

Billy comes in the back door and lays his gym bag aside. He finds Jim at the kitchen table paying his bills; all his accounting in a shoebox.

> JIM
> What train you get?

BILLY
6:32. You get a ride home from the station?

JIM
Yeah. Your uncle Mike was on the same train. You put gas in the car?

BILLY
Yeah. I stopped over to see Grandpa.

JIM
We've got to replace that line of pipe over in his basement before long.

BILLY
*(wincing)*
Yeah, I told him we'd be over.

Jim sees he's in some kind of pain.

JIM
What's up?

BILLY
Got a bad cavity, I think. Tooth's killing me.

JIM
Go see a dentist. You're under my union health plan till you're eighteen.

BILLY
Okay.

But Jim sees he's really in pain.

JIM
Douse the bad tooth in whiskey.

BILLY
*(uncertain)*
Yeah?

                    JIM
It's there under the sink. Help you get some
sleep at least.

Billy reaches under the sink and gets the bottle. He pours a shot and swishes it around in his mouth. He hates it.

                    BILLY
Goddamn! This is what whiskey tastes like!

                    JIM
You can get used to it. Be careful.

Billy returns the bottle to its place and coughs.

                    BILLY
Tastes like some kind of horrible candy or
something.

                    JIM
Yeah, that's how it starts. Tastes like candy
and the next thing you know you can't go a
day without it.

                    BILLY
            *(asleep on his feet)*
I'm going to bed. Goodnight.

                    JIM
See you in the morning.

Billy goes to the hallway and opens the door to the cellar. He comes down to the half-finished basement where his bed now is. Richard is transferring laundry from the dryer to a hamper.

                    BILLY
Hey.

                    RICHARD
            *(looks over)*
Hey. How was your day?

BILLY
Wow. I'll tell you tomorrow. I can hardly keep my eyes open.

RICHARD
Sorry you got to sleep down here.

BILLY
No problem. How's Catherine making out?

RICHARD
She's fine. Just going crazy waiting.

BILLY
She's due, like—when?

RICHARD
Yesterday.

BILLY
Oh, man. Well, we got a full tank of gas in the car.

RICHARD
We got a suitcase packed.

BILLY
Okay. Let the boss lady say when!

He falls back on his bed and passes out immediately. Richard heads back upstairs and Jim looks up from his accounting.

JIM
How we fixed for detergent down there?

RICHARD
I didn't notice.

JIM
You'll need twice more of everything once the baby comes.

Richard removes cash from his wallet.

> RICHARD
> This is for the month.

> JIM
> Thanks.

Jim puts it in the shoebox with his checkbook, spiral notepad and pen. He sips his coffee.

> JIM
> Catherine okay going up and down the stairs?

> RICHARD
> Her mom says it's good. It'll make the baby come faster.

> JIM
> *(shrugs)*
> I guess she knows what she's talking about.
> *(then)*
> Listen, make the baby's room the one over here above the kitchen. Not that one over there above my bed.

> RICHARD
> Sure. Catherine just liked that room better.

> JIM
> Well, when she has a house of her own, she can decide what she wants. But I can't be kept up all night by a wailing child.
> *(stands)*
> I gotta get some shut eye. Goodnight.

> RICHARD
> Goodnight.

Richard goes upstairs with the laundry. He turns into the room on the right—above the kitchen—where Catherine is lying in bed, reading. She watches Richard study the far room which already has a crib in it.

                    CATHERINE
    What is it?

                    RICHARD
                *(joins her)*
    He wants us to make this the baby's room
    and for us to sleep over there.

                    CATHERINE
    Why?

                    RICHARD
    That's how he wants it.

                    CATHERINE
    But that'll make a better nursery.

                    RICHARD
    He gets up at five in the morning every day.
    He doesn't want a screaming baby above him
    all night.

                    CATHERINE
    Richard, our baby isn't going to be crying all
    the time.

Amused, he starts folding the laundry.

                    RICHARD
    Oh, no?

                    CATHERINE
    Of course not.

                    RICHARD
    How do you know that?

She sets aside her book.

CATHERINE
You're not a big mouth. I'm pretty quiet. Our child is bound to be the same.

RICHARD
*(kisses her)*
All babies cry, Catherine. No one takes it personal.

CATHERINE
Your father seems to.

RICHARD
Well, it's his home.

CATHERINE
We're paying rent.

RICHARD
A little, at least.

CATHERINE
And we take care of the house all day.

07. INTERIOR, MIKE FULTON'S HOME—NIGHT

Joseph is at the kitchen table with his unfinished supper before him. He sees the kitchen lights go out in his own home across the fence. Mike is smoking his pipe and playing solitaire at the head of the table. A chair has been upended and stuck on the banquette at the foot of the table, making it impossible for Joseph to slip out that way.

MIKE
*(studies the cards)*
Trust me, Joseph, you'll not get out from behind this table till you finish what's on your plate.

JOSEPH
It's cold.

MIKE
And who's fault is that?

Mike catches the kid glancing at the clock above the stove.

MIKE
Don't be looking at the clock. I know what time it is and I have all the time in the world.

JOSEPH
You have to get up early for work in the morning.

MIKE
Never you mind that. Now who is this kid giving you trouble at school?

JOSEPH
Mitch. He says I'm illegitimate.

Mike is confused, offended, alarmed.

MIKE
Now where's he get off saying such a thing?

JOSEPH
He says everyone knows my dad threw me and Natalie out of the house because we're somebody else's kids.

The pipe practically falls out of Mike's mouth. He sets it aside.

MIKE
Now, these are fighting words, son. You've got to organize yourself and do this felon some damage.

JOSEPH
He's bigger than I am and I beat him at baseball so he hates my guts. And he's got all these unhappy and violent friends.

MIKE
*(shrugs, planning)*
He's got a gang. So be it. You've got a gang too. There's a small army of Fulton's here. There's Marie Dolan's boys. Even the Gosse kids. How old are they now, I wonder? And can they fight? You see, that's the thing...

JOSEPH
*(moving on)*
But why am I living here anyway now that my dad's home?

This brings Mike back to earth. He lifts his pipe and returns to his cards.

MIKE
There's no room over there now that Richard and Catherine are expecting the baby.

JOSEPH
But it's my home.

MIKE
It's Richard's home too. And he's older than you. He's got seniority. It's like here—
*(gestures to the table)*
The older boys eat first and finish everything on their plate. Then they're gone and we let you littler punks in.

Ruthy enters in her bathrobe, annoyed.

RUTHY
Now, what are you two doing up at this hour of the night! Dad, you ought to have been in bed half an hour ago!

JOSEPH
*(victorious, points)*
Ha!

                    MIKE
There's some lout at school telling him he's...
What's the word?

                    JOSEPH
Illegitimate.

                    RUTHY
            *(shocked)*
Now what kind of language is that to be
coming from the mouth of a nine-year-old boy!
I won't have it in my house, Joseph! I won't!
Now get out from behind there and get up to
bed!

Joseph slides down off the banquette, crawls out under the table and flees. Ruthy removes the upended chair from the foot of the table.

                    RUTHY
Dad, you're as bad as they are, I tell ya.

                    MIKE
            *(of Joseph)*
That one is the very devil himself.

08. EXTERIOR, JOB SITE, YARD—DAY

The start of another day. Jim, Billy and Clarence step out of the shanty, punching their arms into their work shirts, donning their hard hats and tightening their belts. Jim studies the sky.

                    JIM
There's cold weather moving in already.

                    CLARENCE
How many floors we got left?

                    JIM
Twenty-three. We'll be back down the hall by
Christmas, I suspect.

He moves off to the elevator and the shop steward, Kevin, walks up to Billy.

                    KEVIN

Billy!

                    BILLY
                 *(turns back)*

Hey, Kevin.

                    KEVIN

Listen, you'll take the coffee order from now on.

He hands Billy a small notepad and a pen. Billy looks up from it, to Kevin and then to Clarence. Clarence is aggravated and looks away.

                    KEVIN
                 *(sees this)*

Sorry, Clarence.

                  CLARENCE
          *(hands Billy some change)*

Coffee, black no sugar.

Clarence moves off and gets on the elevator with Jim. Billy looks to Kevin for an explanation.

                    BILLY

I fuck up somehow?

                    KEVIN

No. We just got apprentices down the hall who need their time on the job. You'll never be a journeyman. You'll be off to college a few months from now. It's not fair to the membership.

                    BILLY

Yeah, I suppose.

KEVIN
The Arab deli there on the corner has everything you need. And then there's the liquor store just around the corner this way. Come up top with the order at ten in the morning and two-thirty in the afternoon.

BILLY
Right.

Kevin moves off and men start towards the elevator.

DIZZY
You got the order today?

BILLY
Yeah.

DIZZY
Scrambled egg and bacon on a roll with butter, hot tea, plain, no lemon and a nip of Jim Beam.

Dizzy moves on before Billy can ask for a translation. He looks to Wally who is now handing him cash too.

WALLY
What, you don't know what a bacon and egg sandwich is?

BILLY
What's a nip?

WALLY
It's one of those, you know, one of those airline size bottles.

BILLY
Right. Okay. And Jim what?

WALLY
Beam. Whiskey.

                    BILLY
          Got it. What'll it be?

                    WALLY
          A nip of vodka. Smirnoff. Regular coffee,
          sugar on the side and a toasted bialy.

Wally moves on and Billy takes everyone else's order.

09. INTERIOR, NYC DELI—DAY

Billy studies the wall of international newspapers and magazines as two Palestinian men, Rashid and Yosef, assemble the coffee order behind the counter.

                    RASHID
          Excuse me young man.

                    BILLY
          Yeah?

Rashid holds up a page torn out of Billy's notebook with the order scribbled on it.

                    RASHID
          Is this toasted bialy with no butter?

                    BILLY
          He didn't ask for butter. Said just toasted.

                    RASHID
          Where's the other guy?

                    BILLY
          What other guy?

                    YOSEF
          Stan. He always does the order.

                    BILLY
          They need him up there. I'm the new guy.

YOSEF

You got a box?

BILLY

A box?

Yosef finds him an empty cardboard box and grabs a black magic marker.

YOSEF

What's your name?

BILLY

Billy.

YOSEF
*(writes name on box)*

Billy.
*(then)*
Okay. This is your box. You leave it here by the pornographic magazines when you come in with the order, you give the order to Rashid or myself, Yosef, and we take care of it all.

BILLY

Sounds like a good system.

RASHID

You gotta have a system. Gotta.

Billy watches as Rashid works preparing all the hot liquids; coffee with milk, black, tea with milk, lemon, or plain, snapping on the lids, notating on top what each is, putting them in the box.

YOSEF

Take a seat. You need something?

BILLY

I'm okay, thanks. I gotta go around the corner. Be back in ten.

                    YOSEF
　　Do so.

10. INTERIOR, NYC LIQUOR STORE—DAY

Billy lines up a collection of nips of various liquors. The cashier is a sexed-up forty-year-old lady who flirts with him outrageously.

                    CANDICE
　　You're not gonna drink all this yourself?

                    BILLY
　　No. Afraid not.

                    CANDICE
　　And you're not going to be operating any
　　heavy machinery, I suppose.

                    BILLY
　　Not me, personally, no.

She starts ringing them up, batting her lashes at him as he pays.

                    CANDICE
　　Won't be driving an automobile?

                    BILLY
　　Don't even own one.

                    CANDICE
　　Oh, that's a shame. Should I ask you for your ID?

                    BILLY
                *(adds five dollars)*
　　Probably not.

                    CANDICE
              *(pockets five dollars)*
　　Yeah, you're probably right.

Billy looks aside, enjoying himself.

11. INTERIOR, JIM FULTON'S HOME—DAY

Catherine and her sister, Karen, are at the kitchen table studying different insurance policies.

> KAREN
> What do they mean by the deductible?

> CATHERINE
> I think that's what we pay for our medical
> bills before the insurance company starts to
> pay us. And...
> *(lifts another page)*
> And the premium is what we pay each month.

> KAREN
> The higher the premium, the lower the deductible.

> CATHERINE
> Yeah, that seems to be how it...

She stops. There's the sound of water splashing to the floor. She looks down at her lap. Karen stands, panicked.

> KAREN
> Oh shit!

> CATHERINE
> *(fascinated)*
> My water broke.

Karen hurries over to the kitchen sink and calls out the window across the fence to Ruthy.

> KAREN
> Aunt Ruthy!

12. INTERIOR, MIKE FULTON'S HOME—DAY

Ruthy is mopping the kitchen floor as she wrangles a crowd of little kids around the table.

                    RUTHY
          *(to one)*
     Hey! Give that back to him.
          *(to another)*
     Eat that.
          *(out the window)*
     Karen?

                    KAREN
     It's happening!

                    RUTHY
     Catherine?

                    KAREN
     Yeah!

                    RUTHY
     Oh, my.
          *(then calls)*
     Okay, I'll be right over! Call Aunt Marie
     for the car!

Ruthy holds open the back door and cocks her thumb outside.

                    RUTHY
     Everyone out. Brian, take them to the beach
     or something. Bobby, come with me.

13. EXTERIOR, DOLAN HOME—DAY

Marie can't get the car started. She grinds the ignition but no luck. Her daughter, Anna (13), is loitering listlessly in the front yard.

                    MARIE
     I told your father a hundred times the
     alternator needed to be replaced in this thing!

                    ANNA
          *(whines)*
     Mom, can I go to the mall?

MARIE
*(stands out of car)*
No. Run over to Grandpa's house and tell him to drive over to Uncle Jim's with his car. The baby's due.

ANNA
What baby?

MARIE
Catherine's baby.
*(walking away)*
Now, hurry! Go!

Marie starts out around the corner for Jim's place. Sulking, Anna walks off in the opposite direction.

14. INTERIOR, JIM FULTON'S HOME—DAY

Marie arrives and lets herself in. She throws aside her bag and comes through the house.

MARIE
I sent Anna over to get my father's car because...
*(stops, startled)*
Oh, good God! Ruthy.

Catherine is laid out on the kitchen table with Karen holding her hand. The birth is already underway.

RUTHY
This child's on the way, Marie. We can't wait for the car.

MARIE
Catherine?

CATHERINE
*(amazed)*
It's coming.

                    MARIE
            Hold on. Hold on...
                *(aside to Ruthy)*
            You've done this before?

                    RUTHY
                *(worried but game)*
            Catherine will do it all. But, yes, two of
            my lot were delivered at home. So...

                    MARIE
                *(not reassured)*
            Jesus, I'm calling an ambulance.

She goes to the phone.

                    RUTHY
            They'll never get here in time.
                *(to Bobby)*
            Okay. Boil my good scissors there in that
            pot on the stove.
                *(then)*
            Karen, hold her head still. Catherine, where
            are the towels?

                    CATHERINE
            In the hall closet.

## 15. EXTERIOR, PADDY DWYER'S HOME—DAY

Anna is knocking dully on the front door but can't get a response from Paddy. She leans over and looks in a window and sees his hand resting on the arm of his chair. She hears the TV.

                    ANNA
                *(bored and impatient)*
            Grandpa! Grandpa, wake up!

No response. She goes down the steps and around the back of the house. She tries the kitchen door but it's locked too. She goes to one of the windows, finds it open and climbs in.

16. INTERIOR, JIM FULTON'S HOME—DAY

Marie is on the phone in the hall with the police as Catherine screams in the kitchen. Bobby runs into the bathroom and pukes.

> RUTHY
> Okay! Okay. There now, Catherine. Push.
> Karen hold her. Bobby, don't you dare pass
> out on me! Where is he? Hand me that towel.

> MARIE
> *(into phone)*
> Yes, four twenty-three...

> DISPATCHER
> *(on phone)*
> Four twenty-three, South Dunville Avenue.

> MARIE
> That's right. Just south of Hoffman Avenue
> off Delaware.

And suddenly it's quiet. Marie gasps and waits. She turns back to the kitchen. A smack is heard and an infant cries out.

> MARIE
> Oh, sweet mother of God.

> DISPATCHER
> Excuse me, ma'am?

> MARIE
> It's...

17. INTERIOR, PADDY DWYER'S HOME—DAY

Anna stands in the kitchen at the phone, crying, getting a busy signal at Jim's house. She is looking on at Paddy Dwyer, dead in his favorite chair, a spent cigarette in the fingers of his left hand and his right lightly poised around a shot of whiskey on the table beside him. She gives up on the call. She hangs up and removes the cigarette from Paddy's lifeless fingers. She places it in the ashtray. Then she grabs his car keys and lets herself out the back door. Unheeded, the television continues to play. There is late-breaking news:

> NEWS ANCHOR
> Four students at Kent State University are dead, shot by members of the Ohio National Guard as they protested the US war in Vietnam and President Nixon's authorization, now, to invade Cambodia, a neutral country to the west of Vietnam...

18. EXTERIOR, PADDY DWYER'S HOME—DAY

Anna climbs in behind the wheel of Paddy's car.

19. INTERIOR, FACTORY FLOOR—DAY

A woman from the front office, Meg, is waving down Richard, trying to shout over the noise of the factory floor. Richard is busy checking a truckload of deliveries and only sees Meg when someone hits him in the arm and points her out. He knows immediately what's up.

20. INTERIOR, FACTORY OFFICE—DAY

Richard runs in and grabs the phone Meg holds out to him.

> RICHARD
> Hello, this is Richard.

21. INTERIOR, JIM FULTON'S HOME—DAY

*(Intercut with previous scene)* Marie is back on the phone in the hallway. They're cleaning up in the kitchen. The newborn is heard crying.

> MARIE
> *(matter of fact)*
> Richard, it's your Aunt Marie. Catherine has had her baby.

                    RICHARD
            Is she alright?

                     MARIE
            She's fine. So is the baby girl.

Richard stands back with a smile and a sigh of relief. Meg and the others in the office relax as well.

                    RICHARD
                 *(back into phone)*
            Are you still at the hospital?

                     MARIE
            No, we're here at your father's house. Your
            aunt Ruthy delivered the baby here on the
            kitchen table.

Richard goes pale and has to sit. He stumbles back into a chair. The others assist him.

                    RICHARD
            What happened!

                     MARIE
            My car's alternator is shot like I've been
            telling your uncle Tom for months but he
            didn't listen to a goddamn word I said. And
            now, of course...

Richard is too dazed to follow. He hangs up and announces—

                    RICHARD
            It's a girl. Everyone's good.

His co-workers applaud. Richard looks behind him at his loading dock staff—all older, tougher dudes than himself.

                    RICHARD
            I have to go home. Hector, you got the
            manifests for those two trucks?

                HECTOR
             *(laid back)*
        Yeah. I can handle it.

                RICHARD
        Good. Thanks. I'll be back in the morning.

                HECTOR
        Richard, let someone drive you.
             *(looks around)*
        Kirk?

                KIRK
        Sure! Come on, Richard!

22. EXTERIOR, STREETS—DAY

Kirk chauffeurs Richard home on his Harley-Davidson chopper.

23. EXTERIOR, JIM FULTON'S HOME—DAY

There's an ambulance in front of the house. Anna drives down the street, badly, hardly able to see above the dashboard, and crashes lightly into the garbage cans as she stops. She steps out of the car and stands there, crying. Marie bangs out the front door, about to scream at the girl, but then realizes.

                MARIE
        Where's Grandpa?

Anna runs to her mom and Marie embraces her—stunned.

                MARIE
        Oh, boy.

Just then, the Paramedic and the EMT come out of the house.

                PARAMEDIC
        The girl and the baby are doing just fine,
        Missus Dolan. There's no need to go to the
        hospital, I think, unless...

                    MARIE
    No. No, of course.

                    PARAMEDIC
    Everything okay?

                    MARIE
    We've had... a death in the family.

A moment later, Richard arrives on Kirk's chopper. He gets off the bike and runs up the steps. He pauses before entering, looking off to Marie out near the ambulance with the EMT.

                    RICHARD
    You leaving?

                    MARIE
    Go see your daughter. Come see me later.

24. INTERIOR, JIM FULTON'S HOME—DAY

Richard comes in and finds his aunt just leaning back out of the refrigerator with a cold can of beer. She hikes her thumb at the ceiling.

                    RUTHY
    Upstairs, young fella.

Richard bounds up the stairs to Catherine. Ruthy pops open the beer, takes a swig and brings the can to Bobby who is lying on the couch.

                    RUTHY
    Good work, Bobby. Here, have some of
    this. I don't think Uncle Jim keeps anything
    stronger in the house.

Bobby sits up, pale and ill. He takes the beer and drinks.

                    BOBBY
    Mom, that was gross.

                    RUTHY
              *(still high)*
        Yeah, well, nothing comes from nothing.
        We're here and then we're not. Get used to it.

                    BOBBY
              *(bewildered)*
What?

                    RUTHY
              *(sees the time)*
        Oh, I gotta get back and start supper. Dad'll
        be on his way home soon. Boil my scissors
        again and bring 'em back with ya. And get
        all those towels washed and dried. Throw
        out the ones that are, you know, too soiled.
              *(calls up the stairs)*
        Catherine, I'll come back after supper and
        see how you're making out! Richard, don't
        go crowding her! Karen, call your mom at work!
              *(exiting)*
        Now, where's Aunt Marie run off too?

Upstairs, Richard sits on the edge of the bed and looks at the baby in Catherine's arms. Karen is buzzing around, making her sister comfortable.

                    CATHERINE
        We'll name her after your mother.

                    RICHARD
Sure.

25. EXTERIOR, CHURCH—DAY

Paddy's funeral. Marie stands aside and watches as the pallbearers carry the casket to the hearse.

26. INTERIOR, STATION CAFE—DAY

Marie leads the crowd in and finds four or five retired policemen waiting with a table full of sandwiches.

> CORRIGAN
> My condolences, Missus Dolan, on your loss.

> MARIE
> Thank you, Officer Corrigan.

> HOPKINS
> The fellas over at the precinct and us, we chipped in and got some food and stuff.

> MARIE
> *(sits at a table)*
> That's very considerate of you, Officer Hopkins. Thank you.

The bartender, Schmidt, shakes Tom's hand.

> TOM
> Morning, Schmidt. A beer for me and a highball for Marie.

Joseph follows Billy to the bar and interrogates the cops.

> JOSEPH
> So, you arrested my grandpa?

> CORRIGAN
> Oh, a number of times, surely.

> HOPKINS
> That man ran us ragged all over town for a couple of years there.

> CORRIGAN
> He was a worthy adversary he was, though. Give him that.

> JOSEPH
> Did he rob banks and stuff?

CORRIGAN
No, he was a...
*(aside to Hopkins)*
What the hell did we call 'em back then?
*(then, to Joseph)*
Oh! He was a union agitator.

HOPKINS
That's it! Union agitator!

Officer Corrigan leans in close to the kid and repeats slowly and ominously—

CORRIGAN
Union *agitator*.

HOPKINS
No disrespect to the family but the man was
a total godless communist if ever I did see one.

CORRIGAN
Kept a picture of FDR in his goddamn wallet is
what I heard.

BILLY
*(collects some drinks from Schmidt)*
They were just trying to force rich corporations
to pay men a decent wage and secure health
benefits.

CORRIGAN
True enough, but that was against the law back
then.

BILLY
*(amazed)*
An honest day's pay for an honest day's work?

HOPKINS
And who's to say what an honest day's work is,
then, I ask you that! Huh?

Jim grabs Billy by the collar and pulls him away quick, smiling and waving amiably at the cops.

>JIM
>*(to Billy)*
>You'll be fighting the likes of these guys just like your grandfather if you're not careful.

>BILLY
>Is that true?

>JIM
>*(back at the table)*
>I don't remember Paddy keeping a picture of FDR in his wallet. Do you Tom?

>TOM
>Not to my knowledge, no.

>BILLY
>I mean: it was illegal to unionize?

>JIM
>I guess so. When I wanted to marry your mother, Paddy offered to get me work and get me into the union. I was new to the States and didn't know any better.
>*(laughs)*
>I asked him if that sort of thing was legal!

>RICHARD
>What'd he say?

>JIM
>He said: more or less!

They all laugh and Jim tries to recall the incident—

>JIM
>More or less! More and more these days! Something like that. Here's to him.

They bang their various drinks together. Then—

CORRIGAN

Hey! Jim Fulton!

JIM

Oh Jesus, Joseph's in tight with the cops. Here I am, Officer. Is he bothering you?

CORRIGAN

This is the kid what threw the no hitter a few months back?

JIM

That's him.

CORRIGAN

Jesus Christ Almighty, I thought he was having me on.

JIM
*(comes over)*
That's entirely possible too. But about this he's telling the truth.

SCHMIDT

My granddaughter tells me about him. He's the most famous liar in school, apparently.

JIM
*(considers Joseph)*
Yeah, well, you've gotta be good at something, I guess.

CORRIGAN

What are you drinking, kid?

JOSEPH

Coke.

Corrigan shoves his small stack of cash across the bar.

CORRIGAN
Schmidt, get this kid a Coke on me.

Trish, Marie and Ruthy all fuss over the new baby.

MARIE
She's the spittin' image of Richard when he was born.

RUTHY
Ain't it so!

TRISH
*(holds child)*
I'm thinking she might be a red head, though. Where's that come from?

CATHERINE
Dad's aunt Evy was a redhead, wasn't she?

TRISH
Oh, who knows. She was as white as snow when I first met her and all the pictures are in black and white.

Uncle Leo enters with his two sons and wife.

MARIE
Leo, where have you been!

LEO
Sorry we missed the funeral, Marie. We were at a wake for Mary's uncle in Brooklyn.

MARIE
Don't worry.
*(then, moving on)*
Mary...

MARY
Oh, Marie, I'm so sorry...

#### LEO
*(of infant)*
This the new recruit?

#### TRISH
*(displays baby)*
Leo, this is Audrey.

#### LEO
No kidding! Now, that's as it should be, it really is.

Across the room, Mike is drawing on a tablecloth while Bud, Jim and a few others look on.

#### MIKE
You see, I can take this part of the garage down and get her out into the street that way. I don't have to raise the masts until she's in the water.

#### TOM
But, Mike, how are you gonna get her through the streets?

#### JIM
Yeah, I mean, with the depth of the keel—right? Once she's on a truck she'll be as tall as a house. Taller.

#### MIKE
Yeah, I'm gonna have to have a talk with town hall about the telephone and power lines, I guess.

#### TOM
The county, more likely.

#### SCHMIDT
Mike, for crying out loud, what possessed you to build a ship in your backyard a mile and a half from the water!

LEO
*(comes to bar)*
In steel, mind you.

MIKE
It's not been done before, you know—a ship like this. Once I get her done, she'll be able to sail all the way back home to Newfoundland —in winter, if need be. Further! Even into the Arctic Ocean.

RUTHY
*(calls across room)*
You're not taking none of my boys on that ship in bad weather Dad!

MIKE
Anyway, Mister Gipetti hadn't built his house behind us when I started. That was an empty lot with a clear path out to Herbert Street and on up to Delaware Avenue.

MARIE
Leo, sing us a song.

Everyone likes this idea.

LEO
What should it be? You choose, Marie.

MARIE
Nothing about a funeral or dying, please!

MAGGIE
"Black Velvet Band!"

RUTHY
Oh, yes!

MARIE
Fine! Tragic romance. That'll do!

Joseph jumps up onto a chair in the middle of the room, stomps his foot, and announces—

JOSEPH

This is the story—that my uncle Leo is going to sing—this a story about a guy who falls in love with a pretty girl who turns out to be— a *crook*!

Everyone applauds. They attend eagerly and Joseph rises to the occasion by adding, theatrically—

JOSEPH

And this guy, this guy takes the blame for the girl's crime and goes to jail so—even though everyone knows he's innocent—he goes to jail so that the girl—this pretty criminal— he goes to jail so that she'll know he loves her!
*(to Leo)*
Right?

LEO

Close enough.

Applause. Marie shakes her head.

MARIE
*(to Trish)*
He'll talk the nation into making him president one day. Mark my word.

Meanwhile—

CORRIGAN
*(wistful)*
I like a good crime ballad now and then, if it's sung well.

LEO

I'll try my best, Officer. Joseph, hand me

my beer there. Thanks.
>*(then, to the infant)*
I used to sing this with your other grandmother,
may she rest in peace.
>*(drinks, then)*
You all know the chorus. Here goes.

Jim moves aside to the end of the bar, out of everyone's way. He looks down at his hands as—

>                    LEO
>              *(sings)*
> In a neat little town they call Belfast
> Apprentice to trade I was bound
> And many an hour's sweet happiness
> I spent in that neat little town
> As sad misfortune came o'er me
> Which caused me to stray from the land
> Far away from my friends and relations
> Betrayed by a black velvet band.
>
>                    ALL
>           *(join in for chorus)*
> Her eyes they shown just like diamonds
> I thought her the queen of the land
> And her hair hung over her shoulder
> Tied up with a black velvet band!

Jim looks back at the room again and sees Audrey seated near Leo, singing as they did years earlier, both of them younger but surrounded by everyone in the here and now.

>               LEO & AUDREY
> I took a stroll down to Broadway
> Meaning not long for to stay
> When who should I meet but this pretty fair maid
> Come traipsing along the highway
> Now she was both fair and so handsome
> Her neck it was just like a swan
> And her hair hung over her shoulder
> Tied up with a black velvet band.

                   ALL
              *(more raucous)*
        Her eyes they shown just like diamonds
        I thought her the queen of the land
        And her hair hung over her shoulder
        Tied up with a black velvet band!

Having the time of her life, Audrey looks across the room and right at Jim, smiling—in love. Jim stands back, looks aside and, while everyone is singing, slips out the backdoor unnoticed.

27. EXTERIOR, STATION CAFE—DAY

Coming out to the little dirt parking lot behind the bar, Jim meets Father Russell on his way in.

                   RUSSELL
    Jim!

                   JIM
    Father.

                   RUSSELL
        Sorry, I'm late. We had another funeral
        after your father-in-law. Missus Battaglia.

                   JIM
        Oh, God, that's a mercy, though. She was in
        a lot of pain for so long.

                   RUSSELL
        Yeah. Poor woman. Ninety-six years old.

                   JIM
    Really?

                   RUSSELL
        Saw it on the documents.

                   JIM
        Listen, I was just on my way over to see you.

RUSSELL
Everything alright?

JIM
I want to make confession. But I guess it can wait till...

RUSSELL
Let's do it here.

JIM
Yeah? Here? In the parking lot?

RUSSELL
Why not?

JIM
I mean, we don't need to be in the—you know, in the...

RUSSELL
In the confessional? No. But if it would make you feel better, we can go back to the church. I got time.

JIM
No, I don't want to bother you. I know Marie wants to talk with you.

RUSSELL
Nonsense! This is what I do. I'm a priest. Here. This phone booth. Sit in there.

Jim does so and Russell sits on an old crate just beside it.

JIM
Bless me, Father, for I have sinned. My last confession was six weeks ago.

RUSSELL
I remember. What's troubling you, Jim?

JIM

It's about my wife, Audrey, and me.

He lights a cigarette and offers one to the priest, who accepts.

JIM

I suppose I loved her more than I ever loved anyone. But she could make me angrier than anybody I ever knew. She was smart, Father. Not in a, you know, educated way. Just quick like. She made me feel stupid sometimes. Not on purpose. I just... couldn't keep up. And I'd get angry. You see, that's the thing: I got a temper. But maybe she wasn't as smart as she thought she was either.
*(shakes his head clear)*
I don't know. I sometimes said things. Things I didn't mean.
*(smokes, rushes to qualify)*
I also said things I did mean. Because she needed to hear it. I don't regret that. Sometimes she just needed to be talked back to in no uncertain terms. She could be a little out of line herself sometimes.
*(clears his head)*
But I couldn't help myself and I sometimes said things I didn't mean. Just to be as hurtful as possible. That's the plain fact of the matter. Pride, I guess. Right? Pride's a sin.

He looks to the priest for confirmation. Father Russell would rather ease Jim's conscience but is forced to nod and agree.

RUSSELL

Yeah. It is.

JIM

Yeah, I thought so.
*(smokes, then)*

> I'm just afraid if those things I said, things
> I didn't mean, things meant to hurt, might've
> been in her mind when she passed over.
> That's what kills me. And, so, I think that
> I've sinned.

Russell waits a moment, organizing his thoughts, challenged.

> RUSSELL
> Sins, Jim...
> *(changes his mind, starts again)*
> Look, first of all, Audrey is with God.
> None of these earthly hassles trouble her.
> She's free now. She's at peace. But you aren't.
> That's what sin does when you have a
> conscience. It grates. It's a thorn in your side.
> Yes, pride is a sin. But sins can be forgiven if
> your repentance is sincere. And I have no
> doubt yours is.

> JIM
> *(weighs this, then)*
> Is it wrong to be proud of my kids?

> RUSSELL
> Don't be proud of your children. Be grateful.

> JIM
> Oh, I am. I love 'em no end and that's the truth.
> But they got their heads in the clouds, Father.
> My four-year-old girl is the most sensible one
> out of the lot.

Father Russell laughs. He drops his cigarette and grinds it into the dirt with his heel.

> RUSSELL
> It's a changing world, Jim. We might learn
> from something. Sure, they'll make mistakes,
> but they'll have ideas too. Don't lose your
> temper. That's your penance. That and ten

Hail Mary's. Try to pass on to them what was passed on to you. Don't be afraid.

Jim sits back and pauses, almost insulted.

JIM

Afraid of what?

RUSSELL
*(stands)*

Change.

# Episode Six

01. EXTERIOR, JOB SITE, YARD—DAY

Billy is taking everyone's order as they drift towards the elevator.

>                    BEAR
> Coffee, milk, sugar on the side. On the side!
> Got it? Not like yesterday.
>
>                    BILLY
> That was my fuckup, Bear. I owe you a coffee.
> Keep your money.
>
>                    BEAR
> You're a gentleman, Bill. I don't care what
> Dizzy says about ya. You see the game last
> night?
>
>                    BILLY
> First four innings. Fell asleep. They'll bounce
> back. Don't worry. Dizzy! You want anything?
>
>                    DIZZY
> No, I'll be coming down myself.

This strikes Billy as odd and he turns to Chet.

>                    BILLY
> Dizzy makes his own hours now, I suppose.
>
>                    CHET
>            *(combing his hair)*
> We're gonna have a little field trip mid
> morning. Nothing for me neither.

And that's it. No one else places an order. Jim is hanging back, reading the newspaper. The headline reads: *Student Anti-War Protestors Dead in Ohio*. The shop steward, Kevin, approaches.

>                    KEVIN
> Jim, we just got word from Brennan over at the
> Building and Construction Trades Council.

JIM
*(looks up, preoccupied)*
Yeah. What?

KEVIN
*(of paper)*
It's about all that.

JIM
You read this?

KEVIN
Yeah. Yeah...

JIM
These kids were, like, eighteen years old. Billy's age.

KEVIN
Yeah, I know. It's awful. And there's a thousand more students coming in here this morning to Federal Hall around the corner to protest.

Jim folds up the paper, tosses it aside and heads towards the elevator.

JIM
Well, let them have their say, I guess.

KEVIN
Yeah, but the Building and Trades Commission wants our membership to go counterprotest and show support for the president's foreign policy supporting the war.

JIM
*(stops, turns back)*
What?

KEVIN
I know.

                    JIM
        Kevin, we've got two truckloads of iron in
        the street right now and another due here by
        one o'clock this afternoon.

                    KEVIN
        I agree. But it's...
                *(turns aside, frustrated)*
        It's a political thing.

                    JIM
        Not for me it isn't. I'm going to work.

Jim gets on the elevator and the gate closes with a crash.

02. INTERIOR, NYC DELI—DAY

Billy, too, is reading the various newspapers. It's slow, after the morning rush.

                    YOSEF
                *(of order)*
        Hey, Professor, this all you got for me this
        morning?

                    BILLY
        Yeah, I think the guys are knocking off early
        or something.

Billy wanders over to the seating area, still reading, and settles onto a stool at the window counter. Suddenly, he realizes he's sat too close to a young woman, Julia (18, black). He stands back.

                    BILLY
        Oh, God, sorry. Didn't see you there.

                    JULIA
                *(pleasantly)*
        No worries.

Untypically flustered, Billy removes his hardhat. Julia has a few books open before her on the narrow counter.

> BILLY
> *(of books)*
> That looks like biology.

> JULIA
> Correct.

> BILLY
> You go to school around here?

> JULIA
> No, I go to Columbia way uptown. But I have an internship at a laboratory down here two days a week. And there's this two-hour gap between shifts. So, I thought I'd come in here. It seems safe and pleasant.

> BILLY
> It is. The proprietors, my friends Rashid and Yosef, here, insist on safety and pleasantness in everything they do.
> *(then...)*
> I'm Bill.

> JULIA
> Bill.

> BILLY
> Or Billy. William. Hey you. I get that a lot these days around here.

> JULIA
> *(charmed)*
> You're not a real construction worker, I think.

> BILLY
> Oh, but I am! I am! Look, this is my hardhat.

And he displays it for her. She takes it, looks it over, knocks some dust off of it and then sets it aside.

>                    JULIA
> You don't remember me.

>                    BILLY
> No, I do. About a month ago my friend
> Clarence steered you clear of our job site
> before you were terrorized by our comrades
> on the sidewalk.

>                    JULIA
> Yes. That's me. I'm Julia.

They shake hands.

>                    BILLY
> Lovely to meet you.

But Billy is distracted by the activity on the street outside—many young people moving in the same direction.

>                    BILLY
> What's going on out there?

>                    JULIA
>         *(looks)*
> They must all be headed for the protest at
> Federal Hall.

>                    BILLY
> Oh, yeah! That's right down here, isn't it? I
> was just reading about all this. You want to
> go over and check it out?

>                    JULIA
> No. I don't really like crowds. That's why I
> wanted to stay here.

>                    BILLY
> Oh. Right. Cool.

JULIA
But you should go if you want.

BILLY
No.

JULIA
Don't let me...

BILLY
No. I'll read about it in the papers tomorrow. Right now, I'd rather be right here.

She smiles, flattered. They relax.

JULIA
I go to a lot of protests with my parents.

BILLY
*(interested)*
Oh yeah?

JULIA
Yes. My dad's very active in Black Power and civil rights stuff.

BILLY
Oh.

JULIA
You know, if you're a black person in America, there's a lot of things to protest about. It's kind of never ending.

BILLY
*(grins sheepishly)*
I guess so.

JULIA
*(amused)*
No black folk where you come from, huh?

                    BILLY
             *(no need to fake it)*
    Not a one!

They both laugh.

                    RASHID
    Billy, you okay over there? Maybe the
    young lady needs something? Huh?

                    BILLY
    Oh, yeah. You want anything? Maybe, ah...

                    JULIA
    I'll have another tea. Sure. Thank you.
             *(calls to Rashid)*
    Thank you!

03. EXTERIOR, JOB SITE, 41ST FLOOR—DAY

Billy goes up top with the coffee order. Kevin is in the elevator with him. The cage opens and they exit. Kevin just takes a few steps, stops and whistles. Men all across the floor down their tools and head excitedly to the elevator. Jim sees this and looks to Bear. Bear looks at his walkie and then to Jim, signally it's gone dead. Chet shimmies down a column and drops his belt, heading for the elevator.

                    JIM
    Listen up!

Chet stops. The rest of the men stop too.

                    JIM
    Any man who goes down off this building
    now might as well go down the hall afterwards
    because he's not working in my gang anymore.

                    CHET
             *(amazed, stutters)*
    Jim, those fucking students in Ohio had it

coming. These assholes down in the street
have it coming too.

                    JIM
I've said my bit. Do as you please.
          *(aside)*
Billy, you got my coffee?

Chet hesitates. He looks up at Jackie-Neal.

                    CHET
You staying?

                    JACKIE-NEAL
I got no beef with anyone down there.

                    CHET
          *(to Bear)*
You?

                    BEAR
I'm at work, Chet.
          *(to Billy)*
Hey you, Professor, gimme that coffee.

The other men want Chet with them. Dizzy comes closer.

                    DIZZY
Jim, these educated punk bastard students
just want to get outta defending their country!

This raises even Billy's ire and he opens his mouth to speak but—

                    JIM
Shut up, Bill. Look at the deck.

Billy does. But, anyway—

                    WALLY
          *(on a beam up above)*
Dizzy, you piece of shit! When was it you last

defended your country? You was never a
serviceman and ain't gone further away than
Jersey in your whole life!

> DIZZY

Fuck you.

Dizzy stomps off. Chet hangs back, watching Jim.

> CHET

> You for real?

> JIM

> If you're going—go.

Chet waits but then goes. The men leave and Kevin approaches.

> KEVIN

> You're short one connector now.

> JIM
> *(disregards this)*
> Clarence, you want to go connecting?

> CLARENCE

> Sure thing.

> KEVIN

> Jim, look, I know you're pissed off...

> JIM

> I'm not pissed off. I got two good connectors.
> We're ready to get back to work as soon as
> you assholes get your shit together.

> KEVIN
> *(of Clarence)*
> He's an apprentice. There's other guys here,
> with more time in. White guys.

Jim throws his coffee to the deck. Billy and Clarence look over.

JIM
This coffee sucks!
*(then, to Kevin)*
Look, he was a journeyman before you
assholes made him an apprentice to work
around some Affirmative Action regulation.
I don't care if he's black, white, red, yellow
or green. He's the best ironworker up here
besides, maybe, Jackie-Neal and me. You and
the AFL-CIO have just set me back at least
three days now with this work. These moron
contractors are gonna be up here, in my face,
trying to rush us along, mistakes will happen,
men will get hurt...

KEVIN
Okay! Okay. Got it. Fuck.

JIM
*(up to Jackie-Neal)*
Jackie-Neal, you okay with Clarence up there
with you!

JACKIE-NEAL
*(nods)*
Easy. Done.

JIM
Clarence?

CLARENCE
*(straps on Chet's belt)*
An honor and a privilege, as always.

JACKIE-NEAL
*(to Billy)*
Hey, shit-for-brains, where's my orange juice!

BILLY
*(remembers)*
Oh! Sorry...

He finds the carton of juice in his box and tosses it up to Jackie-Neal. Kevin goes away. The men just stand around. There's nothing to do.

>                    JIM
>               *(to Billy)*
>     Stay up here, you. At least till lunch.
>               *(calls to everyone)*
>     Stand down, guys. Nothing to do but wait.

Billy, carrying his box, joins Clarence at the perimeter. They're both looking down into the street.

>                    BILLY
>     See anything?

>                   CLARENCE
>     No. That building's in the way.
>               *(turns back, of Billy)*
>     Look at you! You're the cleanest ironworker
>     I've ever seen!

>                    BILLY
>     A good thing, too! Because I just met the
>     most lovely girl!

>                   CLARENCE
>     Don't tell me you're hookin' up with the chick
>     in the liquor store!

>                    BILLY
>     Oh! Can you imagine? But she won't have
>     nothing to do with a guy who don't own
>     his own automobile.

>                   CLARENCE
>               *(steps away)*
>     Well, a girl's got to have standards, son.

>                    BILLY
>     How are things with you?

CLARENCE
*(sits and opens his coffee)*
Pretty good. Your old man just kicked me up into a higher tax bracket.

But even this troubles Billy.

BILLY
Yeah, it's a good thing you're green, huh?

CLARENCE
Shhh!!! Us little green men gotta stick together.

They high-five without enthusiasm.

BILLY
This gonna be a problem?

CLARENCE
For me? No.

BILLY
Which one of these guys is going to be pissed a black man's connecting and getting a bit more in his envelope each week?

CLARENCE
Chet's the only one's really got a problem and he's gone. So... And it's not over yet. Your old man's right. We're gonna have to work three times as fast now to keep the contractor happy after all this wasted time.

BILLY
*(looks down to street again)*
What are they gonna do down there, you think?

CLARENCE
They're gonna beat up on some college students. When they're old, they'll tell their grandchildren they were patriots. Same old.

BILLY

How can someone consider themselves a patriot by supporting this war?

CLARENCE
*(laughs)*
Whoa! Professor, you sound all engaged and shit!

Billy pulls three different newspapers out of his cardboard box.

BILLY

I mean, you were over there in Nam. I'm not telling you anything. But this shit is insane. You been reading this?

CLARENCE
*(of papers, impressed)*
What, you just sit down in the deli reading newspapers all day?

BILLY

Pretty much. They've got newspapers in thirty-six different languages. Twenty in English alone. Anyway, Nixon is now saying that to end our war in Vietnam we have to invade another country—Cambodia!

CLARENCE

And this surprises you?

BILLY
*(embarrassed)*
I suppose it does.

Clarence watches him as he goes quiet and opens his paper.

CLARENCE

Don't go all ashamed on us, William! You're seventeen! What else they say in those newspapers today?

                          BILLY
            Here's an interesting item: "The Black Panthers
            invited to address a meeting of the Communist
            Vietnamese National Liberation Front."

Clarence gingerly takes the newspaper from Billy, folds it up and returns it to the box.

                          CLARENCE
            You know, Bill, I think today is not the day
            to be seen reading too much.

04. INTERIOR, PENN STATION—DAY

Billy comes running down the stairs to the platform.

05. INTERIOR, TRAIN—DAY

Billy makes his train and jumps in just as the doors close. There's standing room only. He looks around for his father and finds himself amidst a small crowd of construction workers. They hold cans of beer and look him over suspiciously.

                          GARSON
            What are you looking at asshole?

                          BILLY
                      *(disregards him)*
            I'm just...

                          JOHN
                          *(off)*
            Billy!

Billy's cousin, John, Ruthy and Mike's eldest son, calls from a few yards down the aisle. He works his way closer. He, too, has an open beer and is wearing his hardhat. He knows the other workers.

                          GARSON
            You know this kid?

JOHN
This is my cousin, Billy.

SERRA
(to Billy)
You one of those commie fag anti-war students?

JOHN
He's on the Turner job at Wall Street and William.

SERRA
(surprised)
Oh.

BILLY
You seen my dad?

JOHN
Down the next car.

GARSON
You're Jim Fulton's son?

BILLY
(moving on)
See you back home, John.

GARSON
(to John)
Looked like a commie fag student to me.

JOHN
(drinks, then)
He's alright.

06. INTERIOR, TRAIN—DAY

Billy comes into the next car and finds Jim standing in the crowded aisle.

JIM
Where the hell have you been?

BILLY
It was hard getting through the station. Lotta cops. Fights breaking out.

Having found a place to settle, Billy pulls a copy of *The Village Voice* out of his gym bag and starts to read.

JIM
Don't read that near me.

BILLY
What?

JIM
I know people on this train.

BILLY
Dad, it's just...

JIM
I know what it is. If you're gonna read that stuff stand somewhere else.

Billy folds the paper up and returns it to his bag.

07. INTERIOR, JIM FULTON'S HOME—DAY

Jim and Billy come down the street and pull up into the driveway. In the living room, Catherine, Karen, Bobby, and Richard are watching the news on TV, passing the crying baby back and forth between them.

NEWS ANCHOR
The riot started just before noon when more than 200 construction workers mobilized by the New York State AFL-CIO attacked about one thousand high school and college students and others protesting the recent Kent State

shootings and the American invasion of Cambodia. The riot then spread to City Hall. Thus far, more than seventy people have been injured, including four policemen...

JIM
*(enters)*
Turn that off.

RICHARD
You guys okay?

CATHERINE
What happened?

JIM
*(switches off TV)*
Quiet that child.

He moves off to his room. Billy tosses down his gym bag and takes the baby. The others look to him for more info, but—

BILLY
You probably know more than I do. We were up on the building all day. But it was spooky coming home.

KAREN
They went wild.

BOBBY
They were showing it on TV.

CATHERINE
They were beating up people in the street.

RICHARD
*(takes child)*
It's bad.

Billy moves to turn the TV back on. But—

                    CATHERINE
          Billy, no.
               *(of Jim)*
          He's in a bad enough mood as it is.

                    BILLY
               *(backs off)*
          Anything to eat?

                    CATHERINE
               *(returns to kitchen)*
          About twenty minutes.

                    KAREN
               *(of Billy's curiosity)*
          Go up to our house. My dad's probably got
          it on.

Billy nods and goes out the door.

08. INTERIOR, FIORE HOME—DAY

As usual, the Fiore house is easygoing pandemonium. The two little girls are running around making noise and twelve-year-old Diane is trying to cook pasta as Paul, cocktail in hand, watches a small TV set on top of the fridge. Billy knocks on the back door.

                    BILLY
          Mister Fiore?

                    PAUL
          Come on in, Billy.

                    BILLY
               *(enters)*
          Hey, Diane.
               *(lunges)*
          Whoa! Let me help you with that.

He saves a boiling pot of spaghetti from splashing on her and pours it into the waiting colander. He joins Paul at the TV.

PAUL
*(of news)*
You part of this madness?

BILLY
No, just trying to find out what happened.

PAUL
Ah, damn. They've moved on to the weather.
*(turns off TV, sits)*
From what I'm hearing, organized labor in New York supports the president's continued propagation of the war and doesn't like smart-aleck kids who read too much.

BILLY
Yeah, that's the impression I'm getting.

PAUL
Get yourself a beer there in the fridge.

BILLY
Thanks.

Billy does. Diane carries over the plate of spaghetti and places it before her dad.

PAUL
Thank you, dear. You got any parmesan in this fine establishment?

DIANE
Oh yeah!

PAUL
Don't run!

BILLY
*(returns from fridge)*
Missus Fiore doing the night shift at the department store?

PAUL
Yeah, for the rest of the week, apparently.
  *(to Diane, of parmesan)*
Thank you.

BILLY
You think he'll get away with it?

PAUL
Who?

BILLY
The president.

PAUL
Sure, he will.
  *(eats)*
They don't make you president if you can't lie through your teeth and if you get squeamish over a few thousand more dead soldiers.
  *(sets down fork)*
When do you turn eighteen?

BILLY
This coming October.

Paul just nods and looks away, troubled, sipping his drink.

PAUL
How long is Richard's deferment?

BILLY
I think he's got till next summer.

PAUL
Diane, go quiet your sisters down. Put 'em in front of the TV upstairs.

BILLY
You mind if I use your phone?

                         PAUL
                       *(eating)*
                  Sure. There in the hallway.

Billy gets up and finds the phone on the wall in the hallway. He removes a paper receipt from his wallet, dials and waits. Someone answers.

                         BILLY
                  *(stands to attention)*
               Oh, hello. May I speak to Julia, please?

09. INTERIOR, WILSON HOME—DAY

*(Intercut with previous scene)* Missus Wilson, Agnes (50, white), lowers the phone from her ear and calls down the hall of this tasteful and spacious city home.

                         AGNES
                  Julia! It's for you.

Julia sets aside her reading and comes up the hall, curious.

                         JULIA
                       *(whispers)*
            Who?

                         AGNES
                       *(grinning)*
                  A young man named Billy.

Julia makes a display of shy delight and takes the phone. Agnes moves back into her well-appointed kitchen. There, we see her husband, Eliot (55, black), also reading as he waits for supper at the table.

                         JULIA
            Hi.

                         BILLY
               Hey. Is this a bad time to call?

JULIA
No. No, we won't be eating for an hour yet.
Are you alright?

BILLY
Me? Yeah, sure, I'm good.

JULIA
That was terrifying today.

BILLY
I know, I'm just learning about it now.
I was up top on the building and couldn't
see what was happening. Were you okay?

JULIA
No. Yes! I mean, thank you. No. I stayed in
the deli with your friends, Rashid and Yosef,
till almost three in the afternoon. I didn't dare
go into the streets.

Billy can see it all in his head and is deeply disturbed.

BILLY
How are those guys? When I left work, I saw
they were closed.

JULIA
They locked up and turned off the lights when
things started getting loud. Me and a few other
customers just sat there in the dark with them
till the construction workers moved off and
things quieted down.

BILLY
Wow.

JULIA
*(tries to lighten up)*
I was pretty sure you weren't amongst them,
though.

                        BILLY
            No. No. But I feel bad about all this.

                        JULIA
            Yes, it must be confusing.

10. INTERIOR, JIM FULTON'S HOME—DAY

Supper's ready. Everyone's at the table waiting for Jim. But he comes out of his room in a clean shirt and a sports jacket.

                        JIM
                  *(shoots his cuffs)*
            Sorry, Catherine, I'm eating out tonight.

                        CATHERINE
            But there's steak! And potatoes.

                        JIM
            Enjoy it. I've got an appointment.

He grabs the car keys and goes out the front door. Catherine looks across at Richard. He stands, moves to the living room and watches as Jim backs his car out of the driveway and takes off.

                        CATHERINE
            If he gets pulled over for anything, that's
            violating his parole.
                  *(cuts her meat)*
            He'll do time for that—and not in a hospital.

Billy returns, coming in the back door.

                        BILLY
            You see that? Dad just drove away in the car.

                        CATHERINE
            There's extra steak and potatoes.

                        RICHARD
            Sit down. Eat.

                    BOBBY
I think he has a date.

                    CATHERINE
        *(sniffs)*
That aftershave?

                    KAREN
Think so.

                    BOBBY
That was a brand-new shirt. Still had the creases in it.

                    CATHERINE
I could've made lasagna.

                    BILLY
        *(eats, delighted)*
Wow, what a day! What a *day*!

The others pause and stare at him like he's out of his mind.

11. EXTERIOR, RESTAURANT—DAY

Jim parks his car behind the restaurant. He steps out, locks the door and looks around to make sure the coast is clear. He walks around to the front and waits handsomely. A moment later, Amy drives in and parks. Jim comes over and opens the door for her.

                    AMY
Have you been waiting long?

                    JIM
Just got here.

                    AMY
How?

                    JIM
Oh, it's not far.

                    AMY
              *(of restaurant)*
        I've wondered about this place.

                    JIM
              *(leads her in)*
        It's very good. You said you like seafood, right?

                    AMY
        Yes, very.

12. INTERIOR, RESTAURANT—NIGHT

Jim and Amy are seated.

                   WAITER
        Anything to drink, Miss?

                    AMY
        I'm going to have a glass of wine, Jim, okay?

                    JIM
        Of course, not a problem.
              *(then, to Waiter)*
        I'm okay with the water.

                    AMY
        The Chablis. Thanks.
              *(sets aside menu, joking)*
        So, what's all this I hear about you
        construction workers terrorizing the city
        today?

                    JIM
              *(holds up hands)*
        It wasn't all of us.
              *(then, frustrated)*
        It's politics, I guess. That's what they tell me.
        I don't understand half of it. The whole thing
        made a mess of my day. The rest of the week
        is going to be all ass-backwards.

                    AMY
Oh, I'm sorry.

                    JIM
How are things with you?

                    AMY
Good. I have an interview for a job at Nassau
County General Hospital—in administration.
A desk job.

                    JIM
You'd leave the nuthouse?

                    AMY
          *(frowns, amused)*
It's not a nuthouse.
          *(then)*
But, yes. Apart from nice experiences like,
for instance, meeting you, it gets hard to be
down in the trenches with the patients for
too long. It's just too sad.

                    JIM
I can imagine.

                    AMY
I mean in the other wings—not where you were:
a lot of them just aren't going to get better. It's
one thing to know this in your head. But to go to
work each day and look that reality in the face
again and again—it's too much after a while.

Jim lays his hand on hers. Her wine arrives.

                    JIM
You're a good soldier. You deserve time off
the line.

                    AMY
You're a veteran, aren't you?

                    JIM
A veteran? Oh, that's a fancy word for the
soldiering I did. I spent two and half years on
a base in Germany somewhere loading and
unloading trucks.

                    AMY
Well, every little bit helps, I suppose.

                    JIM
I guess. I never had any idea what it was we
were supposed to be trying to help, though.
But they did give me courses in civil
engineering. And that helped me in the work
I do now.

She sips her wine and studies the menu.

                    AMY
What are you going to have?

                    JIM
I think I'll have the steak and potatoes.

                    AMY
Really, while you're here at a fine seafood
restaurant?

                    JIM
I'm not a big fan of seafood. I just knew
you liked it.

Amy smiles, flattered.

13. INTERIOR, PADDY DWYER'S HOME—NIGHT

Marie appears at the top of the basement stairs and looks down into the darkness. She takes a few steps down and listens.

                    MARIE
Joseph, what are you doing down there?

JOSEPH

Nothing.

MARIE

Like hell nothing.
*(comes down)*
You're up to no good, I bet. You always are
when you're quiet.

Joseph is climbing around amongst the old man's deep storage, clearly searching for something.

JOSEPH

Look, what's this!
*(studies a metal pipe)*
Oh, nothing.

MARIE
*(follows)*
What are you looking for?

JOSEPH

Rifles.

MARIE

What?

JOSEPH

Time bombs, dynamite. You know.

MARIE

Come on, get upstairs. I've got to get back
home and your aunt Ruthy will be wondering
where you are.

They come up into the kitchen and head for the back door, Marie turning off the lights as she goes.

JOSEPH

Those cops at Grandpa's funeral said he was a
revolutionary terrorist.

                    MARIE
No, they didn't. They called him an agitator.
Whatever that is. Carry that box of plates out to
the car for me.

                    JOSEPH
              *(lifts box off chair)*
Union agitator, revolutionary terrorist—same
thing. He's got to have rifles down there
somewhere.

                    MARIE
              *(closes door and locks it)*
I'm his daughter, Joseph. If Grandpa was a
revolutionary terrorist I'd have known about it.

14. EXTERIOR, PADDY DWYERS'S HOME—NIGHT

                    JOSEPH
              *(approaches car)*
Yeah, but you see, revolutionary terrorists
have to be really good at pretending to be
one thing while in reality they're something
else completely.

Marie follows and places another box of knickknacks on the back seat. She shuts the car door, pauses and lights a cigarette. She studies Joseph on the front seat, already lost in the pages of the book he's reading. Marie then leans back on the car and gazes off at Paddy Dwyer standing in the dim recesses of the backyard, looking elsewhere.

                    MARIE
              *(smokes, sighs)*
Who were you, really, Dad?

Paddy glances at her, grins, and looks away.

                    JOSEPH
              *(looks over)*
Who are you talking to?

Marie tosses away her cigarette and gets in behind the wheel.

>               MARIE
> Move this crap aside. How do you expect
> me to drive!

>               JOSEPH
> Those are Billy's library books.

>               MARIE
> Well, move 'em.

He gathers up the books and she backs out of the driveway.

15. EXTERIOR, RESTAURANT—NIGHT

Jim and Amy kiss goodnight beside her car. Then—

>               AMY
>           *(leans back)*
> You sure I can't give you a lift?

>               JIM
> No, it's not far at all. I'll just walk.

He holds the door for her and she gets in.

>               AMY
> How long is your license suspended?

>               JIM
> Another year. But it's good. I get a lot of
> exercise.

He secures the door. She rolls down the window.

>               AMY
> See you Saturday?

>               JIM
> Saturday, yes.

                    AMY
And there'll be dancing at this church thing?

They kiss once more. Then—

                    JIM
Guaranteed. And white wine. They're raising
money for something or other.

                    AMY
Can't wait. See you. Bye.

Jim smiles and waves as she pulls out and drives off. Once she's out of sight, he hustles around the building to his own car. He gets in behind the wheel and looks around carefully before pulling away.

16. INTERIOR, JIM FULTON'S HOME—NIGHT

It's a hot night and all the screened windows and doors are open. Richard is passed out on the couch with the baby asleep beside him. The TV plays with the sound turned off. Billy is reading and just finishes Daniel Berrigan's *No Bars to Manhood*.

                    JOSEPH
Psst! Billy.

                    BILLY
Hey, champ. Shh!! The baby's sleeping.

Joseph slips in the front door with a small stack of books.

                    JOSEPH
I got those library books.

                    BILLY
Great.

                    JOSEPH
                *(of Berrigan)*
Should I return this one?

BILLY
No, I'll hold on to that for a while.

JOSEPH
*(displays book)*
*Fathers and Sons*, Terr-jen-nev.

BILLY
*(corrects him)*
Terr-gain-yev.

JOSEPH
What?

BILLY
It's a Russian name. That's how you say it.

JOSEPH
*(puzzled, moves on)*
*The Rebel*, Cay-muss.

BILLY
Cay-moo.

JOSEPH
Are you messing with me?

BILLY
No, really. It's French. That's how they say it. Cay-moo.

JOSEPH
Crazy language. Why put in a letter when you ain't even gonna use it? I'm not even gonna try this one.

BILLY
Hobsbawm.

JOSEPH
Oh, that's not so weird. Hobsbawm. There's a

kid in school named Tannenbaum.
*(reads cover)*
*The Age of Revolution.* Are these school books?

### BILLY
Yeah. My friend gave me a list of books her college assigns first year students.

Jim pulls up in the driveway. Joseph looks out.

### JOSEPH
Hey! Dad's driving the car!

### BILLY
Pretend you haven't noticed.

Joseph jumps back on the couch and flips diligently through one of the books. Jim enters, sees the sleeping baby and continues quietly. He sets his car keys aside and comes over to the boys.

### JIM
What are you doing up this late?

### JOSEPH
*(feigns surprise)*
Oh, hey Dad.

### JIM
*(not fooled)*
This a new thing with you, reading books upside down?

Joseph realizes, corrects it and sighs.

### JOSEPH
It's too hot to sleep.

### JIM
Yeah, it's like an oven out there.
*(of Richard)*

He should get some proper shut eye. He's gotta work in the morning.

BILLY
No one wants to risk waking the baby now that she's finally asleep.

JIM
*(undoes his tie)*
Yeah, I'm all for that. I'm hitting the sack. See you in the morning.

He continues on to his room.

JOSEPH
*(follows)*
Dad, can I mow the lawn?

JIM
Joseph, it's eleven o'clock at night!

JOSEPH
No, tomorrow.

JIM
And not lose a foot?

JOSEPH
I did the front yard last time.

JIM
*(sits on bed, removes shoes)*
You *almost* did the front yard last time. Look, if you start a job finish it. And push the machine, don't drag it behind you. That's bad policy. You could slip on the wet grass, your foot go under the blades and that's the end of your hockey career.

JOSEPH
I hate hockey.

JIM
Yeah, well, you get my drift.

JOSEPH
Yeah.

Jim lies back on the bed, still dressed, with his hands behind his head.

JIM
Everything okay next door?

JOSEPH
I guess.

JIM
Be sure to eat what your aunt Ruthy feeds you. Don't be picky.

JOSEPH
Okay.

JIM
And make sure your sister is not even in the yard when you mow the lawn.

JOSEPH
Okay. Goodnight.

JIM
Goodnight.

17. INTERIOR, NYC DELI—DAY

Julia enters and waves hello to Yosef and Rashid.

YOSEF
*(gestures to back)*
He's back there in his office!

She weaves her way through costumers and finds Billy at a table covered in newspapers and a few books. He's making notes and doesn't notice as she comes down over him and kisses his cheek. Surprised, he leans back and smiles. She displays paperwork.

JULIA

I found it.

BILLY

City College?

JULIA

You can still apply for the fall semester.
*(puts paperwork before him)*
There.

Billy studies the five or six pages of the application as Julia gets a cold drink at the counter.

BILLY

Will I need to declare a major?

JULIA

Probably. But you can change your major, too, later. Besides, any credits you earn can go with you when you transfer to another school.

BILLY

*(convinced)*
Thank you.

JULIA

You're welcome.
*(they kiss, then)*
I had a lovely time the other night.

Billy sets aside the paperwork and takes her hand.

BILLY

Me too. You get home alright? Your parents weren't worried?

                    JULIA
I called. They were fine.

                    BILLY
I like your friends.

                    JULIA
Do you? Yeah, they're cool. We just know
one another from classes, really. But Amanda
and I are pretty close. They all think you're
*fascinating*!

                    BILLY
Qui, moi?

                    JULIA
Oui, toi! A construction worker who reads
Camus! Are you kidding me? Amanda's
terribly intrigued.

                    BILLY
         *(ironic)*
I'm just the coffee boy.

                    JULIA
Lucky me!
         *(organizes application)*
Here, let's get started on this.

## 18. EXTERIOR, JIM FULTON'S HOME—DAY

Billy and Jim pull up in the driveway. Mike and his sons do the same next door. They wave to each other across the fence and head into their homes. Standing out of the car, Billy stops and draws out his wallet.

                    BILLY
Dad, here's my rent.

                    JIM
When did you find time to cash your check?

BILLY
I got nothing but time down in the street while you guys are setting steel. I opened an account at the bank there.

Jim takes the cash but hesitates. He hands it back.

JIM
Listen, just keep putting it in the bank for the college.

BILLY
You sure?

JIM
Yeah. I drew a bit out of my annuity. I'll be able to pay back your uncle Len by the end of the month.

BILLY
I applied to a college.

JIM
*(worried)*
Oh, yeah? What college?

BILLY
City College of New York.

JIM
*(more worried)*
And how much is that?

BILLY
Not a lot. And, because it's a state school, I can apply for a New York State guaranteed student loan.

JIM
A loan! I don't like the sound of that. I'm still paying off my mortgage.

### BILLY
I can apply for it on my own. I don't have to
start paying it back till a year after I graduate
and the interest is locked at three percent.

Joseph comes around the side of the house, pushing the lawn mower, its motor turned off, the job finished.

### JIM
*(impressed)*
Nice work, Joseph.

### JOSEPH
*(long suffering)*
It took *all* day.

### JIM
Oh, the injustice of it all! Get inside and let's
see what's for supper.
    *(looks off)*
Natalie!

Natalie is at the fence in Mike's yard.

### NATALIE
Can I come home now?

Jim goes over and lifts her up over the fence and carries her to the house.

### JIM
Of course, you can! How are you, darlin?

### NATALIE
Joseph wouldn't let me in the yard.

### JIM
*(entering house)*
Yeah, he's a tyrant, I know. But do as he
says whenever he has a lawn mower in
his hands.

19. INTERIOR, JIM FULTON'S HOME—DAY

The kitchen is crowded with Catherine's little sisters, Bobby from next door and Maggie Dolan, along with Karen helping with the screaming infant.

                JIM
        *(was hoping for quiet)*
Jesus Christ.

            CATHERINE
Hey, Dad. Lizzy and Maria are with us till eight. My parents are seeing Diane give a recital at the school.

                JIM
Hello girls. Go wash your hands. Maggie, make sure they don't hurt themselves. Joseph, put a shirt on, for cryin' out loud. Bobby, don't Aunt Ruthy feed you anymore or what?

              BOBBY
        *(at stove)*
She don't let me cook.

              BILLY
      *(gets a beer from fridge)*
Ha! As I suspected! It's you who've been invading the sanctity of our tasteless and unpretentious grub with this foreign cuisine!

              BOBBY
     *(defends himself)*
Catherine does the Italian.

                JIM
       *(opens pot)*
What is it?

              BOBBY
Hungarian goulash.

JIM

Hungarian what?

BOBBY

Like a meat stew over noodles.

JIM

Fair enough. Smells good.
*(responds to a knock on the door)*
Who is that?

JOSEPH

*(off, calls)*
It's the cops!

Everyone freezes. Jim goes to the front door, shoos Joseph away and finds his parole officer, Giordano.

JIM

Hey, come on in, Officer.

GIORDANO

*(enters)*
Sorry, I know it's supper time. I was just passing by and thought I'd get this off my to-do list. Hey, everybody.

ALL

Hi.

They all wave and go back to business as usual.

JIM

You hungry?

GIORDANO

No, I gotta meet the missus and her tribe at seven. How's everything here?

JIM

Okay.

GIORDANO
*(with pad and pen)*
Working?

JIM
Everyday.

GIORDANO
Drinking?

JIM
Nope.

GIORDANO
Family situation positive?

JIM
*(gestures to the mob)*
Yeah, well, I suppose I'll get some peace
and quiet when I'm old.

GIORDANO
*(puts away notepad)*
Don't count on it, pal. These little critters
get old enough to drive and you won't get a
moment's rest. Trust me. Okay. Take care,
Jim. See you next time.

JIM
Have a nice weekend, Officer.

As Giordano goes down the steps, Richard arrives home with his Mexican co-worker, Hector.

RICHARD
Dad, this is my friend, Hector, from work.
His house burnt down. He's gotta wait for
his cousin to drive in from Patchogue.

CATHERINE
Oh my God! Hector!

                    HECTOR
Not my house. I just rent a room there. But
yeah—done. Toast.

                     JIM
Sit down. We're about to eat. Billy go get a
bench from outside for the kids.
          *(sitting, to Hector)*
Anyone hurt?

                   HECTOR
No. The old lady who owns it is away.

                     JIM
Electrical?

                   HECTOR
Probably.
          *(of food)*
Wow, this looks great.

## 20. INTERIOR, SUBWAY TRAIN—DAY

Billy and Julia ride the subway uptown to Harlem. The car is full of black people and some cast glances at the young interracial couple holding hands. Julia pretends not to notice, enjoying being seen with her handsome white boyfriend. Billy, though, is self-conscious, careful and alert. Two particularly aggressive young men are enjoying giving Billy serious attitude while appreciating Julia's beauty. One of them, wearing a Muslim skull cap, leans closer and asks, so all can hear—

                   DERRICK
Excuse me, sister, is this white man
bothering you?

                    JULIA
          *(unsmiling, strict)*
No, he's not. Thank you. Leave us alone.

Derrick backs off with a great demonstration of righteous respect, still giving Billy the evil eye. Billy shrugs and gives him the peace sign.

> BILLY
> Allahu Akbar, man.

After a moment of stunned silence, Derrick and his friend laugh out loud and, as the train doors open and they exit—

> DERRICK
> *(points)*
> Well played, brother!

When the doors close and the train rumbles on its way, Billy sees Julia is giggling and shaking her head.

> BILLY
> *(embarrassed)*
> What? That's how Rashid says it.

> JULIA
> "Man?"

Others around them laugh now, too. Billy smiles and looks across at another rider—an older man.

> RIDER
> That was the whitest way to say Allahu Akbar I've ever heard!

Much laughter. An elderly lady pokes him with her elbow.

> LADY
> That was like the Quaker Oats Nation of Islam calling, thank you very much!

The train car rocks with laughter.

21. EXTERIOR, WILSON HOME—NIGHT

Julia excitedly leads the way across the noisy street to her parent's brownstone home in Harlem.

## 22. INTERIOR, WILSON HOME—NIGHT

As they enter the main hall, Agnes approaches.

>                    JULIA
>               *(makes introductions)*
>       Mom, William.
>
>                   AGNES
>       Hello, William. And welcome.
>
>                   BILLY
>       Good evening, Missus Wilson.
>
>                   AGNES
>               *(waves to Eliot)*
>       Oh, you can call me Agnes. Thank you.
>
>                   BILLY
>       Alright. You can call me Bill.
>
>                   AGNES
>       Okay, Bill. This is my husband, Eliot.
>
>                   ELIOT
>               *(approaches)*
>       Hello, Bill. You can call me Mister Wilson
>       just for the sake of variety.
>
>                   BILLY
>       Okay, Mister Wilson.
>
>                   JULIA
>       Just call him Councilor, Billy. That's what
>       I do.
>
>                   AGNES
>       Julia, you know everyone. Introduce Bill
>       around.

As Agnes returns to the kitchen, Julia leads Billy into the large main room where seven or eight people of diverse ethnicities are standing around with drinks and chatting.

An hour later, Billy steps out of the bathroom and studies some pieces of art on the walls of the hallway leading to the kitchen. In the kitchen, Julia is helping her mom prepare a side dish. Billy overhears—

> AGNES
> He's handsome.
>
> JULIA
> He's funny too. On the subway, these two
> boys from the neighborhood tried to intimidate
> him and in like thirty seconds he had them
> cracking up.
>
> AGNES
> You should not have taken the subway.
>
> JULIA
> But even if I get a taxi at the university, they
> won't come up here.
>
> AGNES
> They will if you're with a young white man.
>
> JULIA
> But isn't that what we're supposed to be, you
> know, fighting?
>
> AGNES
> You can choose your fights. Not every day of
> the week needs to be a conflict.

Billy coughs, announcing his approach, and steps into the kitchen smiling.

> BILLY
> Can I help you with that?

                    AGNES
                *(grateful)*
        Yes, please, Bill. Just take this and place it on
        the sideboard in the dining room.

Billy takes the platter and leans close to Julia as he steps away.

                    BILLY
                *(whispers)*
        What's a sideboard?

                    JULIA
        The table against the wall by the window.

                    BILLY
        Got it.

Later: More people have arrived. There's much chatter. Billy is studying the extensive library. Eliot joins him.

                    ELIOT
        See something that interests you?

                    BILLY
        Well, yeah. I mean, a lot. But this...
                *(displays book)*
        Doctor King.
                *(indicates a framed photo on the wall)*
        Julia mentioned you worked with him.

                    ELIOT
        Yes, I did.

                    BILLY
        I'm sorry for his passing.

                    ELIOT
        Yes.
                *(then, of book)*
        *Why We Can't Wait*. Important book. Do you
        know it?

BILLY
I have it on order at my public library.

ELIOT
*(finds another)*
This, the *Collected Speeches and Essays*, is probably a better introduction to King's thinking and methodology, though.
*(hands it over)*
Keep it. Are you interested in civil rights work?

BILLY
Oh, I don't know. But I recently read some Daniel Berrigan and it's made me rethink a lot of things I thought I had solid opinions about.

ELIOT
*(impressed)*
Well, that's always good. I have nothing but respect for Father Berrigan, but he's a bit more radical than I'm prepared to go. However...
*(looks around, spots someone)*
...you should meet Desmond.

Eliot waves over Desmond, a thirty-five-year-old black man, neatly dressed in suit and tie.

DESMOND
*(approaches, to Billy)*
How do you do?

BILLY
Hi. Fine, thanks.

ELIOT
Desmond Saint-Just, Bill Fulton.

Later: Dinner is in full swing. Animated conversation about the arts, culture, current events. Billy, copying Julia, learns how to use a fork with his left hand and wield the knife with his right.

Later still: Agnes shows some people out and joins Julia on the sofa. They look off at Billy in the dining room listening to Eliot and Desmond.

> ELIOT
> But the US is scaling back the war in Vietnam and reducing the military draft.

> DESMOND
> This is political maneuvering with an eye to the next election.

> ELIOT
> Probably. But they are concessions.

> DESMOND
> Concessions made very obviously in the face of persistent militant activism, though they won't admit that.

Eliot sits back, agreeing but still not convinced.

> ELIOT
> I just worry the Panthers will sacrifice the moral high ground of fighting it out in the courts, something that gains them enormous support from more moderate allies.
> *(sits forward)*
> Look, lawyers for the Black Panthers did, in fact, get Huey Newton released from prison.

> DESMOND
> On a technicality.

> ELIOT
> All of the law is technicality, Desmond! Listen, a year ago, it was popular to say no black revolutionary could ever get a fair trial in the United States. Now, here's an example of justice won. The law is all we have to fight with.

Now Desmond sits back, smiling, as Eliot pours more wine.

> DESMOND
> Bill, Eliot and I have been having this argument for ten years.

> ELIOT
> It's an argument worth having again and again, though.

Pleasantly exhausted, Desmond grows more philosophical.

> DESMOND
> *(drinks, looks aside)*
> Lawyers, like us, like to believe that man is the sum of his laws; sociologists, that man is the sum of societal phenomena; philosophers, that man is defined by his thinking; believers, by their faith. But in order to be a man, simply, it is sometimes necessary to escape these definitions. In order to be a student, it is necessary to disrupt the college; in order to be a citizen it is necessary to march in the street, make a lot of noise and upset your fellow citizen's complacency; in order to abide by the law, it is necessary to confront that law— perhaps to break it.

> BILLY
> *Antigone.*

> DESMOND
> *(uncertain)*
> Am I quoting someone without knowing it?

> ELIOT
> The play. Sophocles.

> DESMOND
> *(realizes)*
> Oh! Sorry. Of course.

**BILLY**
*(explains)*
I read Julia's class copy.

**DESMOND**
But, yes: *Antigone*. Can lawbreaking in certain cases be a function of conscience? It's not a new problem.

**ELIOT**
But here, in Sophocles, importantly, conscience is very specifically defined as personal conscience in reaction to the mandates of the state operating in the interests of society.

**BILLY**
Where does the individual end and the community begin? Is it okay to have the consensus challenged by the individual?
*(to Julia)*
Right? Isn't that the theme or whatever?

**JULIA**
I didn't even read it yet! You tell me.

**ELIOT**
*(amused)*
That is the question, always, in a nutshell, Bill. And yes, Desmond and I are still arguing like a couple of ancient Greeks.

Meanwhile—

**AGNES**
Time to say goodnight to your young man, missy.

**JULIA**
Look at him: he soaks up everything he hears. He's forgot all about me.

AGNES
I doubt that very much. Go ask him to help
you with the coats upstairs.
*(stands)*
I'll break up this debate.

Julia hops up and catches Billy's eye, pointing to the hall.

BILLY
*(standing, to men)*
Excuse me.

He steps out into the hall where Julia takes his hand and leads him upstairs. Once there, the young people make out. Afterwards—

JULIA
I'll see you Tuesday, then?

BILLY
Yeah. But how about after work on Monday?
We could see a movie.

JULIA
I have class that night.

BILLY
Oh, right. Can you come to my niece's
christening?

JULIA
Of course! I'd love to. Will I meet Aunt
Ruthy?

BILLY
Of course. Aunt Marie too. You'll meet the
whole gang.

They kiss again. Then, very intrigued—

JULIA
Joseph?

BILLY
Okay, but you've been warned!

Later: Billy and Desmond are being shown out.

ELIOT
When's the next train, Bill?

BILLY
*(checks wristwatch)*
There's a twelve-oh-nine. I should make that easily.

ELIOT
You got money for a taxi?

BILLY
I'll just jump on the subway.

ELIOT
No, take a taxi.
*(then)*
Desmond...

DESMOND
*(agrees)*
We'll share a taxi to 67th and Broadway, then you go on to Penn Station.
*(calls)*
Agnes, thank you. And Julia, lovely to see you again.

JULIA
Goodnight!

She and Billy share a wink and a grin. And then the two young men are outside.

23. EXTERIOR, WILSON HOME—NIGHT

Billy and Desmond walk to Broadway to find a taxi.

DESMOND
When do you start school?

BILLY
If all goes as planned, September—fall semester.
    *(adds, explaining)*
I turn eighteen in October.

DESMOND
Ah! Nothing like cutting it close, my friend!

BILLY
    *(baffled)*
Yeah, I don't know what I was thinking. A year ago I actually I wanted to join the Army—at least for the better part of a day.

DESMOND
What changed your mind?

BILLY
My dad threw a fit.

DESMOND
Good for him.
    *(waving down a taxi)*
We'll have to stay in touch. I lecture at City College once or twice a semester.

The available taxi drives right by them. Billy calls after it—

BILLY
Hey!

DESMOND
Here, you get out here and wave.

BILLY
    *(with distaste)*
No.

DESMOND
Seriously.

BILLY
Let's just take the subway.

DESMOND
*(relents)*
Yeah, why not.

They start walking down Broadway.

DESMOND
How long have you and Julia been together?

BILLY
Six weeks this Tuesday.

DESMOND
No way! You two are like you've known each other for years!

BILLY
Yeah? Cool. We get on well.

DESMOND
Has she met your family yet?

BILLY
Not yet. Next weekend. She'll be coming out to my niece's christening.

DESMOND
*(sensibly)*
And how do you think they'll take it?

BILLY
Take what?

Desmond stops and looks at his new friend, frowning. Billy stops as well and turns back, realizing.

                          BILLY
             Oh, you mean because she's black?

                          DESMOND
                       *(rolls his eyes)*
             Yes, because she's black.

Billy smiles, throws out his arms and proclaims—

                          BILLY
             They love me! If I care for someone, they'll
             care for them too!

Desmond could be persuaded, but he's skeptical. He comes forward and lightly punches Billy in the chest.

                          DESMOND
             Well, I don't know these people, of course.
             But if that turns out to be the case, I want a
             full report because that, my friend, is a beautiful
             home.

                          BILLY
             Exactly.
                       *(continues on)*
             Now, here we are at the subway, where all men
             are treated with equal disregard!

                          DESMOND
                       *(laughing)*
             After you!

                          BILLY
             I have extra tokens, I think.

They skip down the steps.

24. INTERIOR, JIM FULTON'S HOME—DAY

The day of the christening. Richard is helping Billy knot his tie.

RICHARD
And what's her name?

BILLY
Julia. Julia Wilson.

RICHARD
She goes to college?

BILLY
Yeah. Columbia.

RICHARD
*(done with tie)*
There you go.

Richard sets about doing his own tie as Billy slips into his jacket.

BILLY
I'm going to walk up to the station and meet her. Then we'll walk over to the church.

RICHARD
What's she like? What's her family do? Brothers? Sisters?

BILLY
She's an only child. Dad's a law professor. And her mom has an art gallery and publishes books.

RICHARD
*(impressed)*
Fancy people.

BILLY
No. Kind of. Educated. But they're cool. Nice. Interesting thing, though: her mom's white and her dad's black.

Richard is unsure how to respond. Billy watches and waits.

RICHARD
Oh. So... So, she's... what?

BILLY
She's black.

RICHARD
*(sees Billy's concern)*
Cool.

BILLY
Am I doing something stupid here?

RICHARD
What, bringing your girlfriend home?

BILLY
My black girlfriend.

Richard finishes with his tie and pauses. Then—

RICHARD
No. It's not stupid. But... the older people might be a little rocked.

BILLY
*(loses confidence)*
Shit. I shouldn't have invited her. I shouldn't be bringing her into this.

RICHARD
*(checks time)*
She's probably already on the train.
*(then, defiant)*
And bringing her into what! Fuck that. I want to meet her. I'm sure everyone wants to meet her.

BILLY
*(grateful but worried)*
Yeah?

                    RICHARD
          Yeah. Look, man, if you care for her, we care
          for her too.

They high-five.

                    BILLY
          Yeah. Fuck it. Just got the jitters there for a
          minute. She's great. Smart, beautiful, funny.
                    *(leaving)*
          I gotta go!

                    RICHARD
          Don't be late. You're the godfather!

                    BILLY
          See you at the church!

25. EXTERIOR, DOLAN HOME—DAY

Billy walks past Marie's house. She leans out her front door and calls to him.

                    MARIE
          Hey, handsome! Where are you off to? The
          christening isn't for an hour and a half yet.

                    BILLY
          I'm meeting my girlfriend at the train station.

                    MARIE
                *(comes out to the fence)*
          Oh, my goodness! You don't tell your aunt
          anything anymore! What's her name?

                    BILLY
                *(detained, smiling)*
          Julia.

                    MARIE
          Not from around here, I assume.

                        BILLY
                     *(patiently)*
            She lives in the city.


                        MARIE
            A city girl! Look at you, wise guy. Here,
            straighten your collar.


                        BILLY
                    *(as she does this)*
            Aunt Marie, I better get going. Her train's due
            soon.


                        MARIE
                  *(knocks lint off his jacket)*
            A lot of girls around here are gonna be crying
            into their pillows when this gets out, buddy boy!


                        BILLY
            See you at the church!

She watches him go, smiling, and heads back inside.

26. EXTERIOR, TRAIN STATION—DAY

Billy reaches the elevated station platform just as the train pulls in. The hydraulic doors open and a dozen or so passengers exit. Billy looks up and down the platform and sees Julia coming towards him. They embrace and kiss. The train rolls away.

                        BILLY
            You look lovely.


                        JULIA
                       *(of dress)*
            It's appropriate for a christening?


                        BILLY
            I guess so.

Julia looks out over the town.

                    JULIA
          So, this is where you come from.

                    BILLY
                  *(points)*
          That's where I went to kindergarten. And
          over there, that's the high school I attended.

                    JULIA
               *(of a church spire)*
          Is that the church we're going to?

                    BILLY
                *(leads her away)*
          No, that's the Lutherans. We don't talk to
          them because they deny the pope has magic
          powers or something. We're headed out
          that way...

27. INTERIOR, CHURCH—DAY

The christening ceremony. Billy and Karen are godparents. Jim is with Amy. He watches everyone and appears to imagine they are disdainfully whispering to one another about Billy's black girlfriend and giving him, Jim, expressions of disapproval. Marie and Tom, Mike and Ruthy, Trish and Paul Fiore—they are, in fact, all glancing at Julia from time to time. But it could be anything; harmless curiosity, admiration for her beauty and poise. But Amy can see Jim is deeply, quietly angry and she herself is worried.

28. EXTERIOR, JIM FULTON'S HOME—DAY

A party in the backyard. Music is playing, food is cooking, beers are being drunk. Natalie is looking innocently at Julia's dark skin, touching her cheek lightly with her own white hand. Ruthy looks on, delighted.

                    RUTHY
                  *(laughs)*
          Look! She's never seen anyone with dark
          skin like yours.

JULIA
I know.
*(to child)*
Look.

Julia places their hands side by side on the table. Natalie smiles at the contrast too, fascinated.

TRISH
So, what did you make of the christening, Julia?

JULIA
It was a little spooky, I have to say.

MARIE
Oh my God! Yes. I know. When I made my first holy communion, I ran out the church and halfway home before my mother got hold of me out in the middle of Flatbush Avenue!

RUTHY
You don't need all that hocus-pocus. I can christen you right here. Ain't that right, Sister Ann-Margaret?

ANN-MARGARET
I haven't read the rule book recently, Missus Fulton. But I think so.

Ruthy dips her thumb in her glass of water and makes the sign of the cross on Julia's forehead.

RUTHY
There, now it's done.

JULIA
Now I'm a Christian?

ANN-MARGARET
Well, at least a Catholic.

RUTHY
With free admission to all church dances.

Julia gets up and, taking Natalie by the hand, wanders over to study Mike's ship looming above them all.

JULIA
That's the ship?

MIKE
*(proudly)*
Yep! That's her.

They all join her.

JULIA
That's remarkable! How are you going to get it out of here?

Mike grins and scratches his head.

RUTHY
I hope it stays there for the rest of our lives! Otherwise, I won't ever know where he is!

TOM
*(calls over)*
He's just gonna wait for the flood to come and wash us all away, I think!

BILLY
*(hosting, to Julia)*
You need anything?

JULIA
I'm good. I'll have a hotdog when they're ready, though.

MARIE
*(hands him glass)*
Billy, can you get me another white wine.

Billy goes to the cooler near the house and meets Amy just coming out the back door.

                    BILLY
                *(concerned)*
            Amy, you seen my dad?

                    AMY
                *(unsettled)*
            He's inside. He's not feeling well.

                    BILLY
            Oh.

Billy makes a move to step inside but Amy stops him.

                    AMY
            You should leave him alone for now, I think.

She moves off and Billy looks to Richard at the grill.

                    RICHARD
            I think he's just watching the game.

Billy brings Marie her wine and looks off at Julia surrounded by his extended family, perfectly welcomed and liked.

29. INTERIOR, JIM FULTON'S HOME—DAY

Inside, in the little room at the end of the hall, Jim is before the TV. But he's not watching the game. He's staring at the carpet, muttering angrily to himself. Julia comes down the hall to the phone, just outside the TV room.

                    JULIA
                *(politely)*
            Mister Fulton, is it okay if I call my parents?

Jim looks up from under at her, his patience tested, and nods. He turns away. Julia dials and waits, stepping as far away as the cord will allow. Finally—

                    JULIA

Hi, Mom. Yeah, we're here at Billy's house.
Uh-huh. We're going to take the train back in
and stay the night at Amanda's parents in
Brooklyn. That okay? Yeah, I'll be back
tomorrow night. Yes, for the holiday. Billy
doesn't have work tomorrow. Okay. Love
you. Bye.

She hangs up the phone and then, making an effort to be sociable, she leans in around the doorframe and glances at the TV.

                    JULIA

Who's winning?

Jim doesn't answer. He reaches out his arm and closes the door in her face. Julia falls back, startled—hurt and afraid. She catches her breath and walks back outside.

30. EXTERIOR, JIM FULTON'S HOME—DAY

Billy is already organizing their departure when Julia comes out to him.

                    JULIA

We should leave.

                    BILLY

Yeah, Richard's going to drive us to the
station. I just need to...
        *(sees she's upset)*
You okay?

                    JULIA

Yeah, I'm fine. Let's just go.

                    BILLY

Let me just help Catherine get these things
inside.

Billy follows Catherine and Amy into the house carrying plates and bowls. Julia gathers her things and is embraced by Ruthy and Marie, hurriedly saying goodbye to all.

31. INTERIOR, JIM FULTON'S HOME—DAY

As Catherine and Amy wrap leftovers, Billy sets the dishes in the sink and walks down the hall to the TV room, gently pushing open the door.

> BILLY
> Hey. You okay?

> JIM
> *(loudly)*
> Get outta my sight.

> BILLY
> *(nearly faints)*
> What?

> JIM
> You heard me.

And Jim slams the door shut again. Having heard this, the women in the kitchen pause. Billy comes up the hall, stunned.

> CATHERINE
> Billy?

Speechless, Billy makes his way to the front door in a daze, trying to catch sight of Julia walking down the driveway to the street. Just as he reaches the front door, Jim strides up the hall and out to the living room. He stops six feet away. Billy pauses with the screen door open and one foot out on the stoop. He looks back.

> JIM
> If you think you can ever bring that nigger bitch back into my house again you might as well never come back yourself!

Catherine drops the dishes she's holding to the floor. Amy raises a hand to her mouth, horrified. Billy just looks at his father like he doesn't recognize him. Jim comes to the front entrance and closes the door, shutting the boy outside.

# Episode Seven

## 01. INTERIOR, JIM FULTON'S HOME—DAY

Catherine drops the plates. Jim slams the door in Billy's face and then turns to see Amy in the kitchen staring at him, horrified. Catherine runs outside. Amy grabs her bag off the back of a chair and heads for the front door.

>                    AMY
>                *(passing him)*
>           I'm leaving.

>                    JIM
>           Go ahead. See what I care.

She stops at the door, looks at him in disbelief, then bursts into tears and runs from the house.

## 02. EXTERIOR, TRAIN STATION—DAY

Richard pulls up to the curb below the station. He gets out along with Billy and Julia to say goodbye. Billy is preoccupied and distant as Richard and Julia hug.

>                    RICHARD
>           It was really nice meeting you, Julia.

>                    JULIA
>                *(unsteady)*
>           Likewise. Thank you for inviting me.
>           Catherine's fantastic and your little girl
>           is adorable.

>                    RICHARD
>           We'll see you next time.

>                    JULIA
>           I hope so.

>                    RICHARD
>           You better hurry, though. I think that's the
>           train coming now.

>                    *(to Billy as Julia moves off)*
> Everything okay?

>                            BILLY
>                       *(embraces him)*
> I'll see you later.

And Billy hurries to the escalator with Julia. They run up onto the platform just as the train pulls in. Richard knows something is wrong. He waits, but then gets back in the car and drives off.

03. INTERIOR, JIM FULTON'S HOME—DAY

Jim comes into the kitchen and considers the broken plates across the floor. He kicks some of them against the wall. Marie appears in the door from the backyard.

>                           MARIE
> What happened?

>                            JIM
> Leave me alone.

And he walks down the hall to his TV room.

>                           MARIE
>                         *(follows)*
> You scared the living daylights out of Catherine.
> What's wrong with you?

>                            JIM
>                    *(drops into his chair)*
> Get the fuck out of my house, you pain in the
> ass bitch!

But when he looks up again, he sees Tom at the end of the hall behind Marie.

>                            TOM
>                   *(controlled, but furious)*
> Go home, Marie. I'll be over in a minute.

Speechless, Marie wanders back outside to the yard.

>                    JIM
> Listen, Tom...

>                    TOM
> Fuck you, asshole. Marie takes care of
> Natalie as if she were our own and she
> don't want nothing for it but to know
> that child is safe and...

>                    JIM
> Who asked her to do that, huh! I didn't!

>                    TOM
> You were in no fit state to decide anything!
> You oughta be grateful...

>                    JIM
> Get out of my house, goddamn it!

04. EXTERIOR, JIM FULTON'S HOME—DAY

Catherine, under her mother's arm, cradling her own child, has calmed down enough to relate what she witnessed.

>                   MARIE
>              *(stunned)*
> He called her that to her face?

>                  CATHERINE
> No, to Billy. She was already out of the
> house.

>                    MIKE
>              *(relieved)*
> Well, thank God for that, at least.

>                   RUTHY
> Thank God for what! He insulted the boy's
> girlfriend!

TOM
*(comes back out)*
Marie, let's go.

Tom doesn't even wait for her. He just turns and walks out of the yard. Marie hurries after him.

MARIE
Natalie!
*(takes child's hand)*
Come on with me.

RUTHY
Go talk to him, Dad.

MIKE
No. We should get out of here too.

RUTHY
How can we just go home!

MIKE
Look, it's his house. He can do as he likes. He can welcome who he pleases. If he doesn't want a black person in his house that's his right.

RUTHY
She's not a black person! She's Billy's girlfriend!

Mike has no response to this. Ruthy heads inside.

RUTHY
Well, I'm gonna give him a piece of my mind, myself, then.

MIKE
Ruthy, stop!

She does. She looks back.

MIKE
We live next door. We don't want to be
hassling with him our whole lives. Let him
be. You've got your own home to look after.

Then Richard returns.

RICHARD
What happened? Aunt Marie's all upset.

CATHERINE
I can't live here anymore.

Paul Fiore stands up, tosses away the spent ice in his drink and starts to leave.

PAUL
Your father told Billy not to come home
again unless he loses the negro girlfriend.

Richard sinks slowly to the picnic table bench and sighs. Paul pats his shoulder.

PAUL
(to Trish)
We got room for them at our house?

TRISH
It'll be crowded. But Karen's found an
apartment closer to work so that room'll
be free.

PAUL
Fine. Me? I'll go pitch a tent in the backyard.

He wanders away.

TRISH
(stands)
Richard, go gather up what she'll need for
the baby and we'll go get the room ready.

Trish and Catherine leave with the child. Ruthy and Mike hesitate, but then follow.

05. INTERIOR, JIM FULTON'S HOME—DAY

Richard comes in the back door to the kitchen and looks around at the mess. He lays the car keys on the counter, crosses to the hall and sees Jim in his chair in the TV room. Jim just glances up the hall at him and then looks away. Richard goes upstairs and gathers the baby's stuff. He stops when he finds Joseph hiding beside a chest of drawers.

>    RICHARD
> You alright?

>    JOSEPH
> Where should I be?

>    RICHARD
> Help me with this stuff.

06. INTERIOR, JIM FULTON'S HOME—DAY

Jim hears them at work upstairs and comes up the hallway to the living room. Richard and Joseph come down the stairs with boxes of stuff to take away.

>    JIM
> Where you taking all that now?

>    RICHARD
> We're moving out.

>    JIM
> Richard, don't be an idiot. You can't let this sixteen-year-old girl run your life.

>    RICHARD
> Your car keys are there on the counter.

Richard leaves, Joseph trailing in confusion. Jim hangs back, then rushes to the door.

> JIM
> *(calls after them)*
> And don't think you can just come on back
> here any time you need more help, either!

07. EXTERIOR, STREET—DAY

Richard and Joseph march blindly up the street, shell-shocked.

08. EXTERIOR, JIM FULTON'S HOME—DAY

Jim looks at the whole deserted barbecue setup in the backyard. He sweeps everything off the table and into a metal garbage can.

09. EXTERIOR, FIORE HOME—DAY

Joseph is happy and excited to be helping Paul set up a large camping tent in the middle of the backyard. Richard steps out from the kitchen and sits on the stoop.

> RICHARD
> I feel bad about all this.

> PAUL
> Don't. I should have moved out here in
> May. But Trish talked me into to buying
> the air conditioner for the master bedroom.
> Now my sinuses are all kablooey.

> RICHARD
> No, I mean, about Billy and Julia.

> PAUL
> Joseph, go get the little TV off the top of
> the fridge inside. That's an extension cord
> over there by the stoop. I think they're
> playing the Yankee game on Channel Eleven.

The kid runs off on his mission. Richard comes closer.

RICHARD
He was afraid something like this might happen.

PAUL
And he still brought her out here?

RICHARD
He almost didn't. He was gonna send her back on the train at the last minute. But I told him not to.

PAUL
*(sits in his tent)*
Yeah, that would have been a real slob thing to do, even though well-intended.

RICHARD
*(exasperated)*
She's a nice girl.

PAUL
She is. But she's black.

RICHARD
But what difference does that make?

PAUL
It makes a difference.
*(drinks, adds)*
It don't have to make sense. It don't have to be right. Or decent. But it makes a difference. As we just saw.

Joseph returns with the portable television and they start setting it up in the tent.

10. INTERIOR, JIM FULTON'S HOME—DAY

Jim finishes clearing up the scattered and busted plates all across the kitchen floor. Returning the dustpan to its place beneath the sink, he sees the whiskey. He pauses, considers having a drink, then closes the cabinet. Standing back, he hears a knock at the front door.

                    JIM

Shit. Now what?

He goes to the door, expecting more family. But instead he finds his parole officer, Giordano.

                  GIORDANO

Hey, Jim.

                    JIM

Officer Giordano. Come on in.

Giordano comes in and casts a glance around.

                  GIORDANO

All alone today?

                    JIM

I just threw everyone out. We had a barbecue. My granddaughter was christened this afternoon. Have a seat.

Giordano is alert to Jim's smoldering mood. He hesitates, then steps in and sits on the couch. Jim sits opposite.

                  GIORDANO

So, how are things?

                    JIM

For the first time in my life I don't have anyone telling me what to do.

                  GIORDANO

Is that so?

                    JIM

That's the way it is.

GIORDANO
*(pauses, opens notebook)*
Okay. Working?

JIM
Everyday.

GIORDANO
Drinking?

JIM
No.

GIORDANO
Domestic situation positive?

JIM
It's my house.

GIORDANO
Of course.

JIM
I don't have to apologize to anyone about anything—not in my own house.

GIORDANO
*(stands, investigates)*
Not usually, no.
*(looks down hallway)*
Where'd you say everyone went?

JIM
I don't know where they went and I don't give a good goddamn either.

GIORDANO
You're not driving that car, are you?

JIM
No.

GIORDANO
How do you get to work?

JIM
My son drives me to the train station.

Giordano puts away his notepad. He watches Jim who is wringing his hands and staring at the carpet.

GIORDANO
It gets easier with time.

JIM
*(looks up)*
What does?

GIORDANO
Sobriety.

JIM
*(irritated)*
Why's everyone think I got a drinking problem?

GIORDANO
Because you recently spent three months in detox after being caught driving drunk and dislocating the jaw of a uniformed officer of the law. Now excuse me for living, but a person is allowed to make a few assumptions.

JIM
I have no problem with the drink.

He stands, opens the cabinet beneath the sink and shows Giordano the bottle of whiskey.

JIM
See that? That's there all the time and I never touch it.

GIORDANO
*(lifts bottle)*
Wow, that's the good stuff.

JIM
Take it if you want it. I don't need it.

GIORDANO
*(returns it)*
No. Thanks.
*(stands back)*
Listen, Jim, can I give you a small piece of advice?
*(rushes to explain)*
I mean, I don't want to tell you what to do or anything! I know you obviously got an issue with that.
*(as Jim does not protest)*
You got a lady friend?

JIM
*(scoffs, looks away)*
Not anymore, I think.

GIORDANO
Ah! I see. You upset somebody again?

Jim turns back to tell him off but Giordano raises his hands, backing off, pleading innocence.

GIORDANO
Jim! Jim, listen to me: it is my considered opinion as an officer of the law, a recovering alcoholic, a father of five and a sports fan: you need to get laid.

Jim goes and sits on the couch in the living room. Giordano is opening doors, looking for bodies.

JIM
Are we done here?

                    GIORDANO
I guess so. Don't get up. I'll let myself out.
            *(at front door)*
See you next time.

                    JIM
            *(resentful)*
Yeah, and when might that be?

                    GIORDANO
Hard to say.

He lets himself out. Jim sits back and sighs. The house is still, quiet—empty.

11. INTERIOR, JIM FULTON'S HOME—DAWN

Jim goes through his routine: makes coffee, laces up his boots, sips his coffee and then pours it down the sink. He grabs his car keys and leaves.

12. EXTERIOR, TRAIN STATION—DAWN

Tom and Mike are on the platform already, the train approaching in the distance.

                    TOM
You talk to him?

                    MIKE
There's no talking to Jim. Never has been. It's gotta be his way or nothing at all. Useless.

                    TOM
I'm just afraid he's gonna say he wants to take the kids back in the house with him and Marie is gonna blow a gasket. She won't let that little girl go back with him carrying on like this.

                    MIKE
It might be a better thing, though.

TOM
How?

MIKE
He don't like to be in debt to anyone. And he feels like we're all doing him a favor helping out with the little ones.

TOM
We *are* doing him a favor, the fuck! What the hell is wrong with that? I'm sure he'd do the same if something happened to me or Marie.

MIKE
Let's just give it some time and let things cool down.

The train pulls in and slows.

TOM
That was a reckless thing for Billy to do, though.

MIKE
*(agrees)*
What was he thinking!

TOM
Ah, he's just a smart aleck trying be different, that kid.

MIKE
It's all this peace love and understanding malarkey they get from these long-haired rock musicians and peaceniks on TV.

TOM
*(boarding train)*
I'd throw the punk out the house too, no question. But I won't stand for Jim talking to Marie like that.

13. EXTERIOR, TRAIN STATION—DAWN

Down on the street, Jim remains in his car till the train pulls away. Then he gets out, buys a coffee and goes up to the platform to await the next train.

14. INTERIOR, JOB SITE, SHANTY—DAY

Jim buttons up his work shirt and finds his hardhat and gloves. Clarence passes by on his way out to the yard.

> CLARENCE
> *(concerned)*
> Where's Billy?

> JIM
> *(shrugs)*
> Don't know. He was coming to work on his own today.

15. EXTERIOR, JOB SITE, YARD—DAY

Jim steps outside and watches the entrance from the street, looking out for Billy as the rest of the men head for the elevator. He glances at his wristwatch, gives one more look around, then follows everyone else and goes to work.

16. EXTERIOR, JOB SITE, 51ST FLOOR—DAY

Business as usual. They set steel. Clarence and Jackie-Neal are connecting and Bear is signaling. Jim calls out instructions and directs the work as needed.

Fade to black.

17. EXTERIOR, JIM FULTON'S HOME—NIGHT

Nine months have passed and now it's late February. The sun has set and it's snowing. Jim returns from work, pulls up into his driveway and gets out, glancing around to make sure Giordano isn't surveilling him. He goes inside.

18. INTERIOR, JIM FULTON'S HOME—NIGHT

Jim throws the car keys on the table and opens the fridge. Seeing nothing he's interested in, he closes it and opens the cabinet beneath the sink and looks at the bottle of whiskey. Choosing to forego that as well, he stands back and runs water from the tap into the kettle.

19. INTERIOR, DOLAN HOME—NIGHT

Natalie is standing on a kitchen chair looking across the yards to her own house.

                    NATALIE
            *(points)*
    My dad's home.

Marie and Tom glance up from their meal.

                    TOM
    He takes a later train now.

                    MARIE
            *(annoyed)*
    And he's driving to and from the station. His
    parole officer is likely to come by any day
    and catch him at this.

                    TOM
    Marie, there's nothing we can do about it.
    Drop it.

20. INTERIOR, MIKE FULTON'S HOME—NIGHT

Joseph, Brian and two of his smaller brothers are eating dutifully while Mike smokes his pipe and plays solitaire. Ruthy is leaning over the table looking out the window at Jim's kitchen.

                    RUTHY
            *(of Jim)*
    You talk to him at all?

MIKE
No. He takes a later train these days. Doesn't want to run into anybody, I guess.

Ruthy whips her dish towel over her shoulder and turns away.

RUTHY
Sometimes you men are more childish than this lot here.

BRIAN
Hey! We're not childish!

JOSEPH
Yeah.

BRIAN
Glen's childish.

JOSEPH
He is.

GLEN
So what? I'm a child. Back off!

A loud crash is heard down the hall.

RUTHY
Good God Almighty!

MIKE
Now, what the hell is going on out there!

And he strides through the house to the garage, where Bobby and Edward are fighting brutally. Mike tries to intercede but both boys are stronger and it doesn't stop until Ruthy gets between them, smacking both in the face until they back off. The younger boys have followed and look on from just inside the house.

EDWARD
He's a faggot!

RUTHY
*(to Bobby)*
What's he going on about?

BOBBY
I'm gay.

Confused, she looks to Mike.

RUTHY
Dad, what's he mean?

Mike, speechless, just shakes his head and starts to leave. But he turns back to Ruthy, furious.

MIKE
This is all your doing. I've always told you you're too easy on him!

RUTHY
*(stomps her foot)*
What's it mean!
*(to Bobby)*
Gay what?

EDWARD
He's a sissy!

BOBBY
Mom, I'm homosexual.

This she understands. But she's still astounded.

RUTHY
And so it's *this* that you're fighting about!

EDWARD
Fucking pervert.

RUTHY
Don't you!

                    EDWARD
               *(whipped by her towel)*
          Oww!! Jesus, Ma!

                    BOBBY
          You're a fucking dick, Edward.

                    RUTHY
               *(weakly)*
          I won't have that kind of talk in my house!
          I won't have it!

But she's falling to pieces. She sits down on a toolbox and covers her face in her hands. Mike comes and places his hand on her shoulder. But she shoves him away.

                    RUTHY
          Leave me be! You're no help at all!

She stands and runs out.

                    EDWARD
          You see what you've done, pervert!

                    MIKE
          Shut up, you!
               *(to Bobby)*
          Get your things together and move out. I
          don't want to see you around here no more.

Mike goes out after Ruthy.

21. INTERIOR, JIM FULTON'S HOME—NIGHT

Jim comes down into the basement and over to the area Billy made his new room. He finds some paperback books. In one of these he finds a receipt from a bookstore with a phone number and "Julia" written across the back. He looks up when he hears the outside cellar door open. Standing, he crosses the basement and discovers Joseph leading Bobby down the steps from the backyard. They stop when Jim switches on the light.

                    JIM
             *(of Bobby's state)*
        Jesus Christ what happened to you?

                    BOBBY
        Edward.

                    JOSEPH
        They got in a big fight because Bobby's a
        *homo* sexual.

                    JIM
        Oh, Jesus...

                    BOBBY
        My dad threw me out.

                    JIM
        Come on, we gotta get those cuts taken
        care of.

He heads upstairs and the boys follow.

A little later, in the kitchen: Jim has Bobby in a chair and is tending to his wounds.

                    JIM
        Joseph, get me that bottle of whiskey beneath
        the sink.

Joseph gets it, reluctantly. He brings it to the table. Jim opens it and hands it to Bobby.

                    JIM
        Look, just take a swig of this and swish it
        around the front of your mouth. It's gonna
        sting like hell. But it will sanitize things.
        You can spit it out in here.

Bobby takes a swig, does as he's told and lurches towards a big cooking pot beside his elbow on the table, spitting furiously.

                    BOBBY
          Arrgghhh! Gross!

                     JIM
          Not a whiskey man, I see.

                    BOBBY
          That's not whiskey, Uncle Jim.

                     JIM
          That is the *best* Irish whiskey you can buy in
          the tri-state area, pal. Hold still.

Relieved, Joseph returns the bottle to the cabinet beneath the sink, looking back, worried, as Jim prepares to stitch Bobby's lip. He turns away into the hallway as—

                    BOBBY
          Arrgghhh!

                     JIM
          Easy. That's it. One more.

                    BOBBY
          Fuck!

                     JIM
          That's the worst of it. Just enough to keep
          it from leaving a scar. Joseph, gimme that
          bandage.

Joseph grabs an adhesive bandage off the counter and Jim applies it carefully.

                   JOSEPH
          Where did you learn to do that, Dad?

                     JIM
          We had to do this on the boats with your
          grandfather out for days at a time fishing.
          There was always someone with their

hand sliced open or a finger hanging off.
> *(hands kid bloodied towel)*

Here, throw this in the bathroom hamper.

Jim goes to the sink and runs water into a glass. Bobby pulls himself together and sits up straight, accepting the glass of water.

JIM
So, how did this all start?

BOBBY
I told them.

JIM
You told who what?

BOBBY
*(drinks, spits, then)*
I told my brothers and our friends that I was gay.

JIM
Now, why the hell did you do that!

BOBBY
Because it's how I am.

JIM
Yeah, well, everybody's one way or another, I suppose. But you don't have to go around telling everyone about it. Jesus. You should keep that kind of thing a secret.

BOBBY
I don't like pretending.
*(then, of stitches)*
Is this real cat gut?

JIM
Yeah. I've had that for years.
*(repackages his mini surgery kit)*

> I keep this in my wallet. I nearly sliced off
> my little finger a few years ago on the job.
> Look, there, see?
> > *(displays a small scar)*
> That could've been much worse. It's a good
> thing to have handy.

Jim fills the kettle with water.

> JIM
> What are you going to do now?

> BOBBY
> I have a friend who can get me work at a
> restaurant in Garden City.

> JIM
> Cooking?

> BOBBY
> Not yet. But kitchen work.

> JIM
> You got money to get to Garden City?

> BOBBY
> Yeah.

> JIM
> You can have the room upstairs on the right
> for the night. I'll be up and gone early. So
> when you go just lock the door behind you.

> BOBBY
> Okay. Thanks.

Bobby stands and heads for the stairs. Jim hesitates, but then calls after him—

> JIM
> You heard from Billy?

Bobby stops on the stairs, pauses, then—

### BOBBY
No.
*(waits, then moves on)*
Goodnight.

### JIM
Yeah. Goodnight. Good luck.
*(fixes coffee, to Joseph)*
How about you?

### JOSEPH
How do you mean?

### JIM
You heard from Billy?

### JOSEPH
No.

Jim comes over and sits.

### JIM
How old are you?

### JOSEPH
Ten.

### JIM
Really? Jesus. Already? God.
*(drinks, then)*
You think you can manage things around here during the day while I'm at work?

### JOSEPH
*(carefully)*
After school?

### JIM
Yeah.

JOSEPH

Like what?

JIM

I'd leave you money so you can go up to the highway and get groceries. You'd keep this place cleaned up. You'd bring the garbage cans back in out of the street, be here when the oil company delivers, do the laundry. All that kind of thing.

JOSEPH

Could I come back and sleep in my own room?

JIM

Why not.

JOSEPH

I gotta ask Aunt Ruthy.

JIM

You don't have to ask nobody nothing.

JOSEPH

No?

JIM

I'm your father. This is my house. You're my son. How we run things is up to us, no one else.

JOSEPH

Okay.

Jim grabs his keys.

JIM

Here, I made a copy of the back door key for you.
*(hands it over)*

After school tomorrow, let yourself in and
bring your stuff back over from next door.
Get a keychain for that. You got a wallet?

>                    JOSEPH
> No.

>                     JIM
> Okay, we'll get you a wallet.

22. INTERIOR, MIKE FULTON'S HOME—DAY

Afternoon. Ruthy is lying on the couch, sad, staring at the ceiling, a dish towel clutched in her hand. Joseph stands aside, holding his schoolbag.

>                    RUTHY
>               *(weary)*
> You ready to go, then, are you?

>                    JOSEPH
> Yeah.

She sits up and neatens his hair. She wipes his runny nose with her dish towel.

>                    RUTHY
> Tuck your shirt in.
>               *(he does, then)*
> Now, you'll call to me from the window if
> you get into any sort of trouble.

>                    JOSEPH
> Yeah.

>                    RUTHY
> Is there anything over there to make for
> supper?

>                    JOSEPH
> There's a piece of meat he told me to broil.

                    RUTHY
                 *(skeptical)*
            You know how to do that?

                    JOSEPH
                   *(lies)*
            Yeah. Kinda.

She's not convinced.

23. INTERIOR, JIM FULTON'S HOME—DAY

Joseph and Ruthy come in the back door out of the snow. He drops his schoolbag and lifts a hunk of steak out of the sink where it is thawing.

                    RUTHY
                 *(inspects it)*
            That's a good cut of beef.
                 *(then, at oven)*
            Now, look, the broiler is this down here. You
            put the meat in a shallow pan.

                    JOSEPH
            Like this one?

                    RUTHY
            No, that's too deep. Your mother has just
            the thing there under the sink.

She opens the cabinet and finds the broiling pan. She admires it, polishing its surface with her sleeve.

                    RUTHY
            I got her this for her tenth anniversary.
            Because she was always borrowing mine!

24. EXTERIOR, FIORE HOME—DAY

Catherine comes out the back door in her high school uniform carrying a plate of food and crosses over to Paul's tent. It's still snowing. Just as she's entering the tent, she pauses to watch Jim drive by the house on his way home from the station. Then—

                    CATHERINE
          Dad, you sure you're okay out here?

                    PAUL
          Fine.
                    *(of television)*
          The reception is excellent.
                    *(of food)*
          Thanks, darling. Was that Mister Fulton
          just drove by?

                    CATHERINE
          Yeah. If he gets caught driving, he'll be in
          more trouble than ever.

                    PAUL
          How was school today?

                    CATHERINE
          Nothing special.

25. INTERIOR, JIM FULTON'S HOME—DAY

Jim comes in the backdoor, kicking snow off his boots. He discovers Joseph at the stove watching potatoes boil.

                    JOSEPH
          How do you know when potatoes are done?

                    JIM
          Poke 'em with a fork. If they're hard as rock,
          they're not done.

He takes off his coat and only then notices Ruthy sitting alone in the living room, staring off at nothing.

                    JIM
          Ruthy?

RUTHY
*(looks up, stands)*
Oh. Jim. Sorry. I was miles away.

JIM
We knocked off work early 'cause of the weather. Mike will be back soon I'm sure.

RUTHY
*(of Joseph)*
I wanted to make sure he didn't burn the house down on his first try.

JIM
I'm sure there'll be some bumps in the road. But he'll be okay. Thanks.
*(then)*
You alright?

She's exhausted. She sits again.

RUTHY
Everything's broken. None of the boys are talking. Mike just sulks. No one even comes home for supper. The little ones wander around the house like someone just died.
*(of Audrey's picture)*
I miss her. She would've known what to do. How to talk about it. What to say.
*(to Jim)*
He's my son, Jim. Like all the rest of them.
*(disconsolate)*
Everything is broken.

And she stares off again at the snow falling outside. Jim steps back into the kitchen and moves Joseph aside from the stove. He pulls the boy out into the back porch and starts forcing him into his winter coat, whispering.

JIM
Walk your aunt Ruthy back next door. It's

icy out there. Help her along. Don't slip.

       JOSEPH
But the steak...

       JIM
I got it. Go.

26. EXTERIOR, JOB SITE, YARD—DAY

Next day, Jim comes off the elevator and pokes his head into the office trailer down in the yard.

       JIM
Kevin, I've got to get uptown to see my
brother, Mike, on the Munson job up on
East 53rd. I'll be late getting back from
lunch. The guys have work they can do in
the meantime.

       KEVIN
Right.

27. EXTERIOR, NYC STREETS—DAY

Jim walks to the subway.

28. INTERIOR, NYC SUBWAY—DAY

Jim rides uptown.

29. EXTERIOR, MUNSON JOB SITE, YARD—DAY

Jim comes into the yard. A man passing stops and turns...

       CURT
Jim!

       JIM
Hey, Curt. You know where my brother,
Mike, is at?

                    CURT
          Boltin' up probably up about twenty-five or
          twenty-six.

                    JIM
          Thanks.

Hank, the elevator operator sees him approach.

                    HANK
          Howdy, Jim. What brings you to these parts?

Jim steps up and enters.

                    JIM
          Gotta see my brother, Mike, up on twenty-
          five.

                    HANK
          Okay. I'll just wait for these guys coming
          up behind you here.

A few more men file in on their way back from lunch. The gate is closed and the cage kicks into gear. It rises up over the city, the cold wind whipping through the cage.

30. EXTERIOR, MUNSON JOB SITE, 25TH FLOOR—DAY

Jim comes off the elevator and looks for Mike. Coming across the floor, he looks up and sees Mike's eldest, John, bolting up.

                    JOHN
               *(pauses in his work)*
          Uncle Jim! What are you doing here?

                    JIM
          Where's your father?

                    JOHN
               *(points across floor)*
          Out that way last I saw him.

Jim climbs a ladder and makes his way across the job on the intermediate beams. He spots Mike in the distance. Mike tightens a bolt with the pneumatic drill and pulls it back to rest. He looks over, sees Jim approaching and scowls.

> MIKE
> Now, what are you doing here!

> JIM
> Listen, I know I'm not the best person to be giving advice about raising kids, but I think you've got to go easy on Bobby.

> MIKE
> Oh, damn the whole thing! I don't want to talk about it!

> JIM
> Ruthy's a wreck, Mike.

> MIKE
> Ruthy's a wreck? I've been warning her about this for years! He's a disgrace! He's an insult to the whole family!

Jim looks away. Mike stands and carries his bolt-gun to the next point. Finally, Jim follows.

> JIM
> He's a good kid. He's always been a good kid.

> MIKE
> He's a pansy! He's always been a pansy!

> JIM
> And, so, what's the difference between then and now? Nothing's changed!

> MIKE
> Everything's changed! Now he's going around telling everybody! Like he was

>           proud of it for crying out loud! He's a...
>                    *(looks around)*
>           Where's my wrench?
>
>                         JIM
>           Right there to your left.
>
>                         MIKE
>           He's a fucking disgrace! And...

As Mike turns, reaching for his wrench, he missteps and his foot falls short of the beam. Jim goes white as Mike falls to the floor sixteen feet below, landing on some planks cantilevered out over a shaft going all the way down to the street level. Panicked, Jim starts to climb down to him but Mike's weight tilts the planks and he falls down into the shaft. He falls ten floors before being jerked to a stop in a tangle of ropes. But these hold him only a moment before he drops again another twelve floors. He then gets caught again in a net that tears and drops him one more story to a plywood welding platform from which he just manages to tumble out onto the poured concrete of the second floor. He gets up, stunned, and staggers blindly towards the perimeter. He trips over the low cable strung across the outside edge of the building and falls out into the alley beyond. He lands on top of an overfull dumpster and rolls down off the debris, landing softly on the pavement behind the job site. A homeless man, Jed, sitting on a box in a doorway ten feet away, watches as Mike gets shakily to his feet and, cut, bruised and bleeding, wanders off in a daze.

>                         JED
>           Hey, my friend, you got any spare change?

## 31. EXTERIOR, MUNSON JOB SITE, YARD—DAY

Jim, John and a dozen other ironworkers come tumbling off the elevator and run out into the street.

## 32. EXTERIOR, NYC STREETS—DAY

They search for Mike and find the homeless man who points out the way Mike went. They search the next street and fan out.

33. EXTERIOR, NYC PARK—DAY

Jim finds Mike sitting on a bench, half-conscious. Two office workers are smoking at the far end of the bench, watching the battered tradesman curiously. Jim approaches and grabs his brother's shoulder.

                    JIM
Mike?

Mike snaps out of it and looks around a moment before sinking back into semi-consciousness. Jim stands back and waves down the other ironworkers.

34. INTERIOR, NYC HOSPITAL—DAY

Jim and John are in the waiting area. John is terrified.

                    JOHN
You gonna talk to her?

                    JIM
              *(nods)*
Yeah, I'll do it.

                    JOHN
Thanks. I can't handle it.

                    JIM
Got any more change?

They pool their quarters and dimes. Jim goes to the payphone.

35. INTERIOR, MIKE FULTON'S HOME—DAY

*(Intercut with previous scene)* Ruthy comes down the hall from the kitchen and answers the phone.

                    RUTHY
              *(busy)*
Hello.

JIM

Ruthy, it's Jim.

RUTHY
*(panics)*
Holy mother of God what happened!

JIM
*(braces himself, then)*
Mike's had an accident on the job.

She falls back against the wall and drops the phone. She claps her hands together and brings them to her forehead, speed reciting the Hail Mary. Brian looks down the hall from the living room.

BRIAN

Ma?

JIM
*(off, on phone)*
Ruthy?

The boy comes down the hall and lifts the receiver.

BRIAN
*(into phone)*
Hello?

JIM

Who's this?

BRIAN

Brian.

JIM
Brian, it's Uncle Jim. Your mother okay?

BRIAN
*(studies Ruthy)*
I don't know. She's praying or something, I think.

Done praying, Ruthy stands and grabs the phone back.

> RUTHY
> Give me that phone. Jim?

> JIM
> Listen, Ruthy, he's okay. But he's in the hospital.

> RUTHY
> Where's he at?

> JIM
> Any of the boys out there with a car handy? John and I can't get him home on the train.

> RUTHY
> I'll call Marie.

> JIM
> *(now he panics)*
> Marie! No, don't call Marie.

> RUTHY
> Never you mind whatever! I'll call whoever I want. You stay with Mike till she gets there!
> *(calls)*
> Brian, get me something to write with!
> *(into phone)*
> Now, where's he at?

36. EXTERIOR, MARIE'S CAR—DAY

Marie speeds to New York City on the Long Island Expressway, weaving recklessly in and out of lanes, terrifying other motorists, lighting herself a cigarette and dialing through the radio stations.

37. INTERIOR, NYC HOSPITAL—DAY

Marie comes striding in off the elevator and approaches the desk. She sees Jim, but ignores him.

                        MARIE
You, I'm not even talking to.
            *(to Nurse)*
I'm here to see Mike Fulton who's due to
be released. I'm driving him home.

                        NURSE
Let me just check.

                        MARIE
            *(glances at Jim)*
And you have nothing to say for yourself yet?

                        JIM
I thought you weren't talking to me?

                        MARIE
            *(turns away)*
I'm not.

                        JIM
Good.

                        NURSE
            *(hangs up phone)*
They're walking him out now.

Two orderlies walk Mike out. He's got a neck brace, a crutch, a cast on one arm and bandages down one side of his face. Jim and John take over and assist him to the elevator.

### 38. EXTERIOR, MIKE FULTON'S HOME—DAY

Marie pulls up before the house and they get Mike out of the car. All his boys, their cousins and the neighbors crowd around and parade into the house behind him.

### 39. INTERIOR, MIKE FULTON'S HOME—DAY

Mike is in his place at the head of the table, still dazed and confused, a cold beer in one hand and his unlit pipe in the other. Jim is beside him. The kitchen is overflowing with family, friends and neighbors, everyone looking on silently, hopeful, afraid, curious. Finally—

                    RUTHY
              *(waits, watches, then)*
         You hungry, Dad?

He looks across at her, then away. He nods vaguely.

                    RUTHY
                *(encouraged)*
         Yeah. We'll get some stew into you and
         set things right.
                *(to the boys)*
         What are you all standing around for! Sit
         down and eat. Brian, get some bowls down
         from there. Glen, get up and let Aunt Marie
         sit down.

                    MARIE
         I have to go, Ruthy. Don't bother. Tom will
         be home soon.
                *(embraces her)*
         I'll check in tomorrow.

                    RUTHY
         Thanks, Marie.

Most everyone drifts out the front and back doors, mumbling their best wishes. When the crowd thins out, Bobby is revealed. He's still almost as banged up as his dad. Ruthy freezes as she crosses the room with a bowl, glad to see Bobby but afraid of another fight.

                    BOBBY
              *(looks from Mike to Ruthy)*
         Is he gonna be okay?

At this, Mike looks over and sees him. Uncomfortable, Edward and John look down at their boots and frown.

MIKE
*(to Bobby)*
Where's Edward?

BOBBY
*(points)*
Right there.

Mike looks and finds Edward right there beside him.

MIKE
*(to Edward)*
You two shake hands and be done with it.

Edward scowls and turns away. Jim punches him in the arm.

JIM
You heard your father.

With a great show of reluctance, Edward stands and shakes hands with Bobby. Then, looking back at his father—

EDWARD
There: done. Okay?

But Mike has moved on.

MIKE
*(to Jim)*
Remember cutting lumber up the hill that winter when we chopped off the bough we were sitting on?

Jim is baffled at this non sequitur but relieved too.

JIM
Yeah. I do.

JOHN
*(greatly amused)*
Get outta here! Are you kidding me!

JIM

We were up high too. Higher than this house, probably.

BOBBY
*(laughs, sitting)*
How old were you?

JIM
*(of Joseph and Brian)*
Oh, no older than these two—maybe younger. Not the sharpest two knives in the drawer, I'm afraid.

MIKE
The only thing is saved us was the snow. It was five feet deep and new fallen. So it was like landing in a pillow.

JIM
But the axe came down after us and nearly split my skull open then and there.

MIKE
We didn't find that axe again till the spring thaw.

JIM
The old man was furious.

MIKE
*(eats)*
Yeah. That was his good axe.

And now everything's back to normal. Ruthy buzzes around the room, feeding people. Smaller sons clamber up between the older ones and jostle for space.

40. INTERIOR, JIM FULTON'S HOME—NIGHT

Having washed up, Jim comes out to the kitchen and finds Joseph

totaling up receipts and counting money. He starts making himself
a coffee as he watches the kid at work.

>                    JIM
> We still in business?

>                  JOSEPH
> We have seven dollars and thirty-five cents
> left over from this week's budget.

>                    JIM
> That means we're ahead.

>                  JOSEPH
>              *(uncertain)*
> And that's good?

>                    JIM
> Yeah. That's good.
>              *(then)*
> Do you have homework or something you
> have to do?

>                  JOSEPH
> It's Friday.

>                    JIM
> Oh, right. Look, here, I got you a wallet.

>                  JOSEPH
> Cool!

>                    JIM
> You know how to use one of these things?

>                  JOSEPH
> I guess.

>                    JIM
> No guessing. Look, put the seven dollars in
> here like this, see?

JOSEPH
What about the coins?

JIM
Coins don't go in a wallet. They go in your pocket. You righty or lefty?

JOSEPH
Righty.

JIM
Okay, so your wallet goes in your left back pocket.

JOSEPH
Always?

JIM
Always. You know why?

JOSEPH
No.

JIM
Because you're righty and you'll use your right hand, like this, to count the money while you hold the wallet in your left. Like this. Here, try it.

Joseph practices drawing out his wallet from his left back pocket like a gunslinger pulling a six-shooter out of his holster.

JIM
Good. So, you see, the wallet falls open like that and you can get the money out in as few moves as possible. At the grocery checkout there's nothing worse than someone who doesn't know how to use their wallet and stands there looking down into it not knowing what they'll find. It backs everything up. Slows things down.

JOSEPH
What goes in here?

JIM
That's for, like, your identification. You got
identification?

JOSEPH
Yeah. My school ID.

Joseph goes to one of the two kitchen counter drawers and gets
his ID.

JIM
*(surprised)*
You keep your ID in the kitchen drawer?

JOSEPH
Yeah. That's where everyone's is.

Jim comes over and looks. Sure enough, he finds—

JIM
*(reads cards)*
Richard. William...
*(then)*
This is Natalie's birth certificate.
*(hands it to Joseph)*
That goes in the bottom right hand drawer
of the bureau in my bedroom. Face down.
*(then)*
What is all this junk in here? Hey! Look,
here's my five-eights hex wrench. I've been
looking for this.
*(pockets it, then)*
Okay, so your ID goes in here. Let me see it.
*(studies it)*
When's that from?

JOSEPH
Couple of years ago.

Jim flips it over and reads—

> JIM
> "I am a Catholic. In case of an accident, please call a priest and notify Audrey Fulton."
> *(fits it into wallet)*
> Well, you gotta get the nuns to update that for you.

> JOSEPH
> Who should I put?

> JIM
> Me, I suppose. Right?

> JOSEPH
> I guess.

> JIM
> Bring that garbage pail over here.

Jim reviews what remains in the drawer, then pulls it out and dumps all its contents into the trash. He shoves it back into place.

> JIM
> Okay, so this is now the bank. Put your wallet, keys, spare change and that little notebook in here.

> JOSEPH
> And I'll keep receipts in there too.

> JIM
> Right. Good idea.
> *(closes drawer)*
> Okay, go watch TV. I got some stuff to take care of.

A little later, Jim closes the TV room door as Joseph watches an old movie. He studies the bookstore receipt with Julia's number. He dials the phone and stretches the cord across the hall so he can stand in his bedroom.

41. INTERIOR, WILSON HOME—NIGHT

*(Intercut with previous scene)* Agnes is reading when the phone rings. She sets it aside and comes up the hall to answer.

                    AGNES

Hello?

                    JIM
               *(braces himself)*
May I speak to Julia, please?

                    AGNES
Who may I ask is calling?

                    JIM
Jim Fulton. Billy Fulton's father.

Agnes realizes this is tricky.

                    AGNES
               *(carefully)*
Hold on, Mister Fulton.

She sets the receiver down and goes up the hall to where Julia is playfully, amateurishly, performing a violin duet with her best friend, Amanda.

                    JULIA
               *(looks up)*
For me?

                    AGNES
               *(wary)*
It's Bill Fulton's father.

Julia is surprised too. She composes her thoughts before standing. Then, setting aside her instrument, she gets up but pauses again in the doorway. Finally, she goes to the phone.

JULIA
*(into phone)*
This is Julia.

JIM
Hello. This Jim Fulton, Billy's father.

JULIA
Yes. How may help you?

JIM
I wanted to talk to him, to Billy.

JULIA
I'm sorry, I haven't seen him in many months, Mister Fulton. We're no longer together.

JIM
Oh. I see.

JULIA
Is everything okay?

JIM
Do you know where I might be able to find him?

JULIA
No. I'm afraid not. Did you try the college? He was enrolled.

JIM
No, I didn't. But thank you. I'll do that.

JULIA
Okay. Goodnight then.

JIM
*(stammers)*
Miss. Julia.

JULIA

I'm still here.

JIM

Listen, I wanted to—apologize for my behavior that day we met. I might have said things—things I now regret.

She is impressed by his effort, but not forgiving.

JULIA

You never said a word to me, Mister Fulton. But, yes, I understood I was not welcome. Whatever it was you said to Billy, though, upset him terribly.

JIM

Yes. Yes. Well, I'm sorry for all of it.

JULIA

You should try to find Billy and apologize to him.

JIM

Yeah. I'll try. Goodnight.

JULIA

Goodnight.

He hangs up and sighs with frustration. He opens the door to the TV room and discovers Joseph asleep in the chair. He nudges him awake.

JIM

Go on up to bed. It's late.

Joseph gets up and wanders away, sleepily, leaving the TV playing. Jim goes back to the kitchen and tosses the receipt with Julia's number into the trash. He leans on the counter and has a brief, little, silent argument with himself. Then he reaches down and opens the cabinet beneath the sink. The whiskey bottle is waiting. But he leaves it there and turns on the gas beneath the kettle. He prepares himself an instant coffee while the water boils. Finally, he turns off the gas, takes out the whiskey bottle and pours himself a drink. But he just stands there and looks at it. He reaches for it but then stops. He crosses to the table and sits.

> JIM
> *(hangs his head)*
> What have I done?

Exhausted, he looks up and sees Audrey seated across from him at the table, looking off towards the hall. She doesn't seem to notice him.

> JIM
> Go ahead, say it.

Audrey gets up and walks down the hall towards the TV room.

> JIM
> Yeah, of course—ignore me!

He gets up and lifts the drink off the counter, defiantly. But then he has a better idea and, placing it back down, goes to follow Audrey so he can tell her off. He stops at the top of the hall and sees her seated in his chair in the glow of the television.

> JIM
> You think I'm stupid. That's the short and long of it.

She pays no attention and looks off at the television. Jim gives up and wanders into the living room where he stops before the front window and looks out at the falling snow.

> JIM
> I can never do anything to your liking.
> Nothing's ever good enough.

And this reminds him of something else he wants to say. So, he goes back to the hallway, not seeing Joseph crouched on the staircase. The kid comes forward and peeks around the edge of the wall. At the top of the hallway, Jim raises his finger to make his point, but stops. Audrey is gone. He comes down the hall and into the small room. Finding no one there, he glances at the television and sees a teaser for the eleven o'clock news playing. An announcer is talking over footage of a group of young people in handcuffs being led into a police van. Jim is startled to see Billy, briefly but clearly, is one of the offenders.

> ANNOUNCER
> Eighteen youths arrested in Newark on drugs
> and espionage charges in what appears to be
> a Black Panthers subsidized bomb factory.
> Details at eleven.

More commercials follow. Astonished, Jim throws the lights on and looks at his wristwatch. He looks back up the hall and sees Joseph standing there.

> JOSEPH
> Who are you talking to?

Jim's not sure. And he is deeply shaken.

# Episode Eight

01. INTERIOR, JIM FULTON'S HOME—NIGHT

Jim fixes a cup of instant coffee in a hurry, keeping an eye on the clock above the stove. It's 10:57. Joseph is looking around for whoever Jim has been talking to.

> JIM
> Toss that booze down the sink, Joseph.

Joseph does so, happily.

> JOSEPH
> What's going on? Who were you talking to?

> JIM
> Never mind. Come on, we gotta watch the eleven o'clock news.

> JOSEPH
> I hate the news.

> JIM
> Well, that's too bad.
> *(heads down the hall)*
> Keep your eyes peeled and your ears open. We're looking for something.

> JOSEPH
> On the news?

> JIM
> Yeah.

Jim knocks everything off a table and plants it before the TV set.

> JIM
> Get a chair. You got anything to write with?

> JOSEPH
> Why would I have something to write with? I was sleeping.

                        JIM
            Go find something to write with.
                    *(aside)*
            Goddamn, kid.
                    *(to Joseph as he returns)*
            You always have books and paper and what
            not, making a mess of things.
                    *(as Joseph sits at table)*
            Now, look, there's gonna be a story about
            some punks arrested in Newark, New Jersey.
            And we need to know everything we can
            about it.

                        JOSEPH
            Why?

                        JIM
            Never mind why right now. Just get ready
            to take notes. Shhh! Here they go.

The news starts. Jim sits in his chair. Joseph sits poised with his pen above a sheet of paper.

                        ANNOUNCER
            Good evening and welcome to *News at Eleven*.
            Earlier today, in Newark, New Jersey, FBI
            agents raided what they suspect is another
            weapons depot for a domestic terror organization
            affiliated with the Black Panther Party.

There is footage of a school.

                        JIM
            Where is that? Is that...

                        JOSEPH
            Looks like a grocery store.

                        REPORTER
                    *(on screen)*
            This building behind me, once a grocery store...

                    JOSEPH
        See!


                     JIM
        Shut up. Listen...

                   REPORTER
        ...was recently taken over and allegedly used
        as a grammar school for underprivileged
        black children in this violently divided city
        where racial tensions have barely eased since
        the riots here three years ago. But federal
        investigators insist the school is in fact a
        cover for a weapons storehouse supplying
        splinter groups related to the Black Panther
        Party.

They rerun the footage of the young people being led to the van and Billy is clearly glimpsed.

                     JIM
        Look! Look! In there... In that crowd...

                    JOSEPH
             *(jumps up)*
        Billy! That's Billy! Look, Dad, look! They
        got Billy!


                     JIM
        I know I know! Where are they taking him?
        Where are they going?

Joseph now has his nose an inch from the television screen, looking for clues.

                   REPORTER
        Eighteen people associated with the school
        have been apprehended on drugs and
        espionage charges until further notice and
        held in Newark's Criminal Courts Detention
        Center.

                              JIM
That's it!

                            JOSEPH
                          *(writing)*
Criminal Courts Detention Center.

                              JIM
We got a map of Jersey here somewhere, I
know it.

                            JOSEPH
Yeah! Yeah! I'll get it!

He goes running. Jim strides back up the hall to the kitchen and puts his empty cup in the sink just as Joseph runs in with a shoebox full of maps.

                              JIM
We got one when we went to go see your aunt
Eleanor in Neptune on the Jersey Shore.

                            JOSEPH
I know. I saw it in here. Here.

Joseph finds it. They toss away the shoebox and spread the map out across the kitchen table.

                              JIM
                          *(pointing)*
Look, no, over here.

They find Newark and start tracing the way there.

02. EXTERIOR, JIM FULTON'S HOME—NIGHT

Jim walks up the street through the snow to the Fiore's.

03. EXTERIOR, FIORE HOME—NIGHT

Jim stops outside the door, hearing a fierce quarrel. He peeks in the window and sees Richard on the couch, hanging his head in despair as the baby bawls and Catherine sobs and yells. Richard stands and gestures hopelessly—

RICHARD
What do you want me to do!

Pausing a moment to reconsider, Jim knocks. The door is thrown open immediately by Trish who is on her way out.

TRISH
Hey, Jim. I gotta get out of here.

JIM
What's the problem?

TRISH
*(lights a smoke)*
They're children. And now the children have
a child of their own. And no money. Or
privacy. And then, of course, there's the
changing of the diapers. I think this has to
do with all that. I'm outta here.

Now Catherine sees Jim outside and slams the door. Jim falls back but the door is opened again and Richard looks out at his father.

CATHERINE
Don't let that man in this house!

Richard tries to keep cool and closes the door behind him, stepping out onto the front steps.

RICHARD
*(shakes his head clear)*
Hey, Dad.

JIM
Listen, we've got to go to Newark. Billy's in
some sort of big trouble with the cops.

                    RICHARD
He's what?

                    JIM
I saw it on the news. He's tangled up with
the Black Panthers or something and they've
tossed him in the lockup. Come on, get your
coat. I need you to drive.

                    RICHARD
I can't, Dad.

Jim is already walking back to his house. But now he stops, turns and comes closer.

                    JIM
She'll be alright. Call one of her sisters to
come over and help with the baby.

                    RICHARD
No. I can't.

                    JIM
          *(amazed at this defiance)*
Look, I'm still not allowed to drive. I'm not
even supposed to leave the state. This is
important. Your brother's mixed up with a
crowd of terrorists!

                    RICHARD
          *(with difficulty)*
Sorry. I have to take care of things here.

He goes back inside. Jim is dumbfounded.

04. INTERIOR, JIM FULTON'S HOME—NIGHT

Jim comes in the front door, furious, and finds Joseph fitting himself out for adventure. He has his boots on, his coat, the map of New Jersey in his pocket. He reaches into the kitchen drawer and gets his wallet, keys, spare change and notebook. He turns to Jim.

                    JIM
          What do you think you're doing?

                    JOSEPH
          We're going to Newark to spring Billy, right?

Jim sighs and looks away. Then, weighing his options—

                    JIM
          Okay.

                    JOSEPH
          Will we need a flashlight?

                    JIM
          There's one in the glove compartment. Tie
          your bootlace. You got a hat?

05. EXTERIOR, JIM FULTON'S HOME—NIGHT

Joseph follows Jim out of the house.

                    JIM
               *(looks back)*
          That door locked?

Joseph goes back, checks, locks it, closes it again and follows to the car.

                    JIM
          Now, you just keep a look out as I drive.

                    JOSEPH
          What am I looking for?

                    JIM
               *(sitting into car)*
          For anything that looks like a policeman.

                    JOSEPH
          Maybe we should check the brake lights.

                    JIM
        What? Why?


                    JOSEPH
        You'd be surprised how many outlaws get
        apprehended by being pulled over for routine
        violations.

He's got a point.

                    JIM
        Okay. Go check. They working? That's on,
        that's off. That's on, that's off.

They're working. Joseph comes back and gives Jim the thumbs up. But before he can climb in—

                    JIM
        Let's check the directionals too.

                    JOSEPH
        Oh yeah!

He gets out and runs around the front of the car. Jim signals one way and then the other. Joseph gives him a double thumbs up.

                    JIM
        Okay. Get in here.

Joseph climbs in and Jim backs out of the driveway.

                    JIM
        We're not outlaws, though.

                    JOSEPH
                (disappointed)
        No?

                    JIM
        We're just regular people in a screwed up
        situation.

                    JOSEPH
          We're rebels! Desperadoes!

                    JIM
          Well, I don't know about that. But some-
          times society is outta whack and you gotta
          do the right thing all on your own. Sit down.
          Uh-oh. That your aunt Marie getting into
          her car?

                    JOSEPH
          No, that's her neighbor next door, Missus
          Sheppard.

                    JIM
          Okay. Keep your head down till we pass her
          house, though.

They pass without incident and are on their way.

06. EXTERIOR, HIGHWAY & JIM'S CAR—NIGHT

Jim drives and Joseph navigates with his map and flashlight.

07. EXTERIOR, NEWARK JUSTICE BUILDING—NIGHT

Jim pulls up before a complex of dark municipal buildings. Joseph is roused from sleep as the car stops.

                    JOSEPH
          We there yet?

                    JIM
          I think so. Everything looks closed up. What
          time is it?

                    JOSEPH
               *(checks wristwatch)*
          One thirty-five and...
               *(counts)*
          Twenty seconds.

JIM
What's that over there?

JOSEPH
There's a light on.

JIM
You stay here and I'll go check.

Jim walks to the lighted entrance of the Criminal Justice Building. Peering inside, he sees a white night watchman, Collins, seated in the lobby tuning a transistor radio. Jim knocks on the glass door. Collins looks over, alarmed. Jim displays himself in the overhead light. The man stands and comes forward. Just inside the heavy safety glass doors he pauses once more to size up Jim. Then he leans towards an intercom off to the side.

COLLINS
Can I help you?

JIM
*(locates intercom on wall)*
Yeah. Is this the Criminal Justice Detention Center Building?

COLLINS
Who's asking?

JIM
I think my son is supposed to be here.

COLLINS
Only me working here tonight.

JIM
No, I mean he's a prisoner.

Collins leans back and sizes Jim up again, skeptical.

COLLINS
What's he done?

JIM
*(impatient)*
Is this where he'd be?

COLLINS
*(with attitude)*
Well, it depends what he done. That's why
I'm asking.

JIM
He was mixed up with that bunch got
apprehended in the school that was really
a grocery store where they're hiding guns
and making bombs and all.

COLLINS
Oh, that bunch. Saw it on the TV. Yeah,
they was here earlier. Just as I was coming
on duty. Lots of to-ing and fro-ing and
lawyers arguing in the hallways. You know,
I ain't got no authority around here. I'm just
the night watchman. But I seen some things
that'd make a hit TV show in a minute flat.

JIM
He in there?

COLLINS
Could be, I suppose. But I doubt it. If they
was to be fingerprinted and charged and all
whatever, it would've been done across the
way there in the precinct.

Jim looks where indicated and sees nothing but the dark demolished city neighborhood. Turning back—

JIM
Where's that exactly?

COLLINS
Make a left at that burning garbage can, drive

halfway down the block, past the bombed-out church, and you'll see it there on the right—Precinct Six.

                    JIM
Thanks.

                  COLLINS
            *(eager for more talk)*
I ain't got no authority around here, as I say. Just the night watchman. But I'd say this is a hell of a place for a man to let his son wander into.

                    JIM
               *(affronted)*
Well, that's what I'm here for: to get him out.

                  COLLINS
           *(nods, not convinced)*
Yes. Yes. There is that, of course. Well, good luck to you then.

Jim nods and starts back to the car.

                    JIM
Thanks.
              *(under his breath)*
Goddamn nut case.

Walking back, he sees the area is really like a war zone. Joseph is asleep again in the passenger seat but wakes up as the car door opens and Jim gets in.

                  JOSEPH
What happened?

                    JIM
            *(increasingly anxious)*
We gotta get to the precinct over there. Your door locked?

                    JOSEPH
    Yeah.

08. EXTERIOR, NEWARK PRECINCT SIX—NIGHT

Jim slows to a stop outside the heavily barricaded building.

09. INTERIOR, NEWARK PRECINCT SIX—NIGHT

Jim enters and approaches the front desk, dragging along Joseph who is asleep on his feet. A black policeman, Robinson, looks up from his paperwork.

                    ROBINSON
    Can I help you?

                    JIM
    I think my son might be here.

                    ROBINSON
    Name?

                    JIM
    Mine?

                    ROBINSON
    Your son's.

                    JIM
    Billy.
        (corrects himself)
    William. Fulton.

Robinson flips through pages on a clipboard. Then—

                    ROBINSON
    Yes. Fulton, William: seventeen. Probably
    a lie. Caucasian: indisputable. No listed
    domicile: deeply suspicious.
        (looks up)
    He's not here.

                    JIM
        No? But they said...

                  ROBINSON
        They've all been released. There were
        irregularities with the warrant. And the
        search of the premises turned up no evidence
        of...
                *(reads warrant)*
        "...drugs and espionage related activities."
                *(sets aside clipboard)*
        Just a school for little kids after all. You'll read
        all about it in the papers tomorrow.

Now Jim doesn't know what to do. He checks the time: almost two-thirty in the morning.

                    JIM
        Where is this school?

                  ROBINSON
        Hold on.

Robinson grabs a pen and a scrap of paper and begins writing.

10. EXTERIOR, NEWARK SCHOOL—NIGHT

Jim drives up the street slowly, checking addresses against the scrap of paper. Joseph is sound asleep in the back seat. Finding the address, Jim pulls up and parks at the curb in front. It is a grocery store with a handmade banner stretched over the entrance identifying it as the Newark Community School. It's starting to snow again, getting very cold. As Jim steps out of the car, he removes his big winter coat and leans back in to drape it over Joseph. He shuts the door quietly, makes sure they're all locked, then heads into the school. People are coming and going and the front entrance is wide open.

11. INTERIOR, NEWARK SCHOOL—NIGHT

Volunteers are putting the place back in order as it's been torn up by the police and FBI during their search. A sixty-year-old black woman, Rachel, notices him.

                    RACHEL
          Hello. Are you looking for someone?

                    JIM
          Yeah. I think my son is supposed to be
          working here.

                    RACHEL
                    *(as he's white)*
          Billy?

                    JIM
          Yeah. You know him?

                    RACHEL
          You better hurry.
                    *(shows him to the back)*
          They're getting ready to drive them away
          to safety.
                    *(calls)*
          Billy!

She leads Jim to what was probably the stockroom but which is now a makeshift dormitory. Entering, Jim stops. Billy looks up from where he is stuffing a duffle bag with clothes and books. He's thin, pale, with long hair and unshaven. A few bunks away, a young black man named Kurt is also preparing to flee.

                    BILLY
                    *(surprised)*
          Dad.

                    RACHEL
          He just walked in the door.

Jim is speechless. Billy is concerned for time. He glances at Kurt, who nods, takes his stuff and heads out, giving them privacy. Rachel steps back outside with him.

BILLY
What are you doing here?

JIM
I saw it on TV. They showed you being taken away.

BILLY
It was nonsense. They raid places like this once a month, trying to discredit any kind of black resistance.

JIM
*(looks around)*
Is this the... Black Resistance?

Billy pulls the drawstring of his duffle bag and sets it on the floor.

BILLY
You could say that, yeah. Educating poor black kids in a safe environment—that's called terrorism on TV.
*(then)*
Look, I couldn't tell you where I was because of the draft board situation.

JIM
They're sending notices to the house almost every day now.

BILLY
Yeah, I figured. I didn't want to put you in a position where you'd have to lie if you were asked where I was. How's it with Richard?

JIM
I heard they've deferred his call-up again.

BILLY
*(skeptical)*
You *heard*?

JIM
*(sits on a bunk)*
No one's talking to me anymore. Catherine and him moved out. Won't let me see the baby. Marie and Tom are holding Natalie hostage. The Fiore's, my friend Amy. The whole nine yards. I don't see anyone.

BILLY
Well, I'm not going to ask what you might have done to deserve such a thing.

But they both know. Jim looks at the floor.

JIM
I called her, your girlfriend.

BILLY
Her name is Julia.

JIM
Yeah. Julia. I found her number down with your stuff in the basement. I apologized.

BILLY
For what?

JIM
For being rude.

BILLY
Not for being racist?

JIM
*(offended)*
Hey, I am not racist.

BILLY
Right: and you've never had a drinking problem.
*(let's this sink in)*

Or ever lost your temper.
      *(waits again, adds)*
And you never just shut up and stared at your shoes when the neighbors were waving flags and cheering on our brave nation's attempt to wipe out a country of poor people in Vietnam.

### JIM

Those people are communists.

### BILLY

So were a lot of people who started unions in this country—probably even your own. Besides, what do you know about communism?

### JIM

Hey, I can't be expected to know the ins and outs of all this!

### BILLY

Why not?

### JIM

I know what I read in the newspaper.

### BILLY

Read a different newspaper and you're bound to learn something. Choose a different radio program and you're sure to hear something you didn't know before. Try listening to anyone who is not just like you.

### JIM

*(stands, angry)*
And what, in your high and mighty estimation of things, do you think I'm like!

### BILLY

*(even tempered)*
You're a frightened, semi-educated, working class white man. Choose to have an honest

conversation with anyone who is not *that*, and
you are bound to learn a lot more about the real
world you actually live in. That's all I'm saying.

                    JIM
              *(punch-drunk)*
Look, Bill, I'm a man of my time and place.
All this violence and confusion happens
around me and I can't keep up. What am I
supposed to do about that? I didn't make the
world. I just live in it.

                    BILLY
No, that won't do anymore. You did make
the world. We all made the world. We keep
on making it. And the world is broken. And
if it's going to be fixed, it's us who have to
fix it—here and now.

Jim relents. He's at a loss for words. Billy watches him compassionately but offers no consolation. Finally—

                    JIM
Where are you going now?

                    BILLY
Can't tell you. Now that they've identified
and fingerprinted us, it's just a matter of
time before the draft board shows up. There's
a network we're all part of anyway. They'll
help us get somewhere safe and find us work.

                    JIM
A network?

                    BILLY
Yeah.

                    JIM
              *(worried)*
Like... a conspiracy?

### BILLY
If you like. Don't worry. It's not unlike a union. People with similar aims. Collective bargaining sort of thing. Forceful negotiation. We don't make bombs. We don't have guns.

### JIM
*(relaxes)*
It might all pass, you know. The draft is winding down.

### BILLY
They're still killing Vietnamese women and children and getting away with it.

Jim is dizzy from the force of Billy's conviction. He decides to get practical—

### JIM
You got any money?

### BILLY
A few bucks.

Jim fishes out his own wallet and hands the boy all he's got. Billy hesitates but Jim glares at him and so he takes it.

### JIM
Are these sensible people, this network?

### BILLY
They've got enough sense not to put up with things as they are.

### JIM
And apart from draft evasion, you gonna break the law?

### BILLY
Not if I don't have to. But, you know, it's likely.

Jim nods and gets on with it, accepting the situation.

> JIM
> Okay. Do what you gotta do. And don't get caught. Let us know how you are from time to time.

> BILLY
> I'll do my best.

> KURT
> *(leans in door)*
> Billy. We gotta go.

Billy and Jim shake hands and Billy walks out. He runs to catch up with his friends and disappears in the crowd. Jim wanders out to the entrance and notices the school room is pretty much put back together. Rachel is in the entrance watching the boys flee. She glances back at Jim.

> JIM
> *(of school room)*
> That was quick work.

> RACHEL
> Yes. You get used to setting things to rights when they so often get wrecked. He's a wonderful young person, that boy of yours.

Jim looks off at Billy climbing into a van with his compatriots. They drive off.

> JIM
> It's his mother's doing, I'm sure.

> RACHEL
> He's got brothers and sisters, no?

> JIM
> *(proudly)*
> Oh yeah. There's his little sister, Natalie,

>           who's five. And then there's his older
>           brother, Richard, recently married, and their
>           first girl. Then there's the number three
>           boy, Joseph, who's asleep in my...
>                    *(looks around, panics)*
>           Jesus Christ Almighty, where's my car!

## 12. EXTERIOR, NEWARK IMPOUNDMENT LOT—DAY

The sun is just coming up as Jim's car is towed in. Its front end is let down and the vehicle released from the tow truck. In the back seat, Joseph huddles, peeking out from under Jim's coat. Outside, two lot employees, Lonnie (50, black) and Edgar (30, black, lame) take possession. Lonnie takes the paperwork from the tow truck driver and puts it on his clipboard. He confirms the license plate number as Edgar inspects the car.

>                    EDGAR
>           Late model Chevy, good condition, small
>           dent on left back panel, blue... Is this blue?
>
>                    LONNIE
>           That's some sort of spaceship vomit green
>           to me, Edgar, but I ain't had my coffee yet.
>
>                    EDGAR
>                    *(stops)*
>           Uh-oh!
>
>                    LONNIE
>                    *(prepared for hassles)*
>           Damage in transport?
>
>                    EDGAR
>           No, we got a passenger here.

Joseph pushes open the passenger side door with effort and stands up on the running board, proud and defiant.

>                    JOSEPH
>           Am I under arrest?

13. INTERIOR, NEWARK CITY BUS—DAY

Jim rides the bus with Rachel. He's the only white person on it and is keenly aware of this. The bus stops and the Driver leans over and looks back down the aisle—

> DRIVER
> Madame, this is your stop. The impoundment lot is three blocks down this street here.

Jim and Rachel step off the bus.

> RACHEL
> Thank you, sir.

> JIM
> Thanks, pal.

> DRIVER
> *(pulls door closed)*
> Have a good day.

14. EXTERIOR, NEWARK STREETS—DAY

The bus pulls away. Jim and Rachel find themselves in the middle of nowhere: wrecked buildings, garbage tumbling down the street in the wind, abandoned sofas on sidewalks, cars on fire. They walk on towards the lot.

15. INTERIOR, NEWARK IMPOUNDMENT LOT—DAY

In the tiny one-room office, Joseph is at the battered old desk eating a bacon and egg sandwich from a diner as Lonnie studies the kid's ID.

> LONNIE
> *(reads)*
> "Joseph Fulton, third grade, Our Lady of Perpetual Help, Lindenhurst, Long Island."
> *(of picture)*
> This you?

JOSEPH

I'm in the fifth grade now. I was just little then.

LONNIE
*(flips card over)*
"I am a Catholic. In case of an accident, please call a priest and notify Audrey Fulton. TU8-7661."
*(reaches for phone)*
That your mom?

JOSEPH
*(hesitates, then)*
Yeah. But—she's not home right now.

EDGAR
*(replaces phone)*
Who was driving?

JOSEPH

My dad.

LONNIE

What are you guys doing so far from home on this freezing cold Saturday morning?

JOSEPH

We're trying to break my brother, Billy, out of jail.

Lonnie and Edgar trade glances, amused.

EDGAR

And what did he do?

JOSEPH

He's a revolutionary trying to save poor inner city black kids from the evils of fascist capitalism.

LONNIE

All by himself?

JOSEPH
No, he's part of a nationwide conspiracy of like-minded freedom fighters. Can I, please, have milk in my tea?

Edgar comes forward, knocks around in a bag and finds a few plastic single-serving creamers.

EDGAR
There you go.

JOSEPH
Thank you. But he's a drug dealer too.

EDGAR
Is he?

JOSEPH
Yeah.

LONNIE
You mean, Billy?

JOSEPH
Yeah. We all were last summer, my little sister and me too, when my brother Richard needed money for a wedding ring.

Lonnie sips his coffee and scratches his head.

LONNIE
And what about your dad?

JOSEPH
He was in a mental institution for beating up a policeman. But that was just a cover-up to disguise really high-level corruption in local government...

They're interrupted by a knock at the door. Looking over, they see see Jim and Rachel outside. Edgar stands and opens the door.

JOSEPH
Hey Dad!

JIM
*(enters, relieved)*
Wow, that was a close one. Thank you, gentlemen.

EDGAR
Oh, he's been entertaining us no end.

LONNIE
Hey Missus Lambert.

RACHEL
Hello, Lonnie. We ain't seen you at church recently.

LONNIE
I'm gone over to the Presbyterians, Rachel.

RACHEL
*(mock insulted)*
Oh, is that so.

LONNIE
They're quieter. Too much singing and hollering over at the Baptist for me.

Rachel sits and opens her bag.

RACHEL
The school is lending our friend here, Mister Fulton, the money to get his car out of the lot.

LONNIE
Okay. Let me get the book.

RACHEL
*(hands card to Jim)*
Mister Fulton, this is the address to send a

                    check to when you can. It's not the school...
                         *(for Lonnie to hear)*
                    It's that very loud Baptist church around the
                    corner from it.

                              JIM
                    Thanks. I'll take care of that right away.
                         *(to Joseph)*
                    You gonna finish that?

                              JOSEPH
    No.

Jim takes the last third of Joseph's breakfast and wolfs it down as—

                              EDGAR
                         *(throws on coat)*
                    If you'll follow me, I'll show you where
                    the car is.

They exit. Jim leans back in.

                              JIM
                    Missus Lambert, we'll take you back to the
                    school or straight home?

                              RACHEL
                    To the school, thank you. The children will
                    be arriving in a couple of hours.
                         *(then to Joseph)*
                    Boy, you sure did give your dad a scare!

16. EXTERIOR, NEWARK IMPOUNDMENT LOT—DAY

Edgar and Jim walk along. Edgar has a pronounced limp and so Jim checks his own anxious gait to wait up for the younger man.

                              EDGAR
                    That's a hell of a family you've got there
                    it sounds like, Mister Fulton.

                    JIM
          They're alright, I guess.
                *(then, of Joseph)*
          But you can't believe a word that one says,
          though.

                    EDGAR
                *(laughs)*
          Oh, I'm sure there's some small truth in even
          the tallest tale!

                    JIM
                *(of Edgar's lameness)*
          What happened you?

As they make their way off into the field of lost automobiles, Edgar explains...

                    EDGAR
          I got wounded over in Nam. My foot there,
          see? Shot to hell. I'm not much good for a lot
          of things these days. And I gotta get out of
          the house. So—this work suits me.

Dissolve to—

17. INTERIOR, FIORE HOME—DAY

The baby, Audrey, is screaming. The little girls, Maria and Lizzy, are having a fight and Catherine is sobbing at the kitchen table over her homework with her head in her hands.

                    RICHARD
                *(as patient as possible)*
          You can't just yell at her and then give her
          whatever she wants just because she starts
          crying!

                    CATHERINE
          That's easy for you to say! You're never
          here!

RICHARD
What can I do about that! I gotta work! And
I'm here...
*(then, to child)*
Don't touch that!

The one-year-old is reaching out to touch a tall stack of dirty dishes perched precariously at the edge of the sink. She stops wailing and looks at her father.

RICHARD
Come over here.

The child shakes her head—no.

RICHARD
Audrey, come over here to me.

But the child just shoves the dishes and they crash to the floor.

RICHARD
That's it!

He lunges forward, picks up the child and carries her out of the kitchen, screaming wildly. Catherine screams too. The sisters look on in terror. Richard carries the child upstairs and places her in their bedroom.

RICHARD
Now, you stay here until you say sorry.

But, of course, the child just screams louder. Richard steps out of the room, closes the door, and looks down to see Catherine at the foot of the stairs.

CATHERINE
No!

RICHARD
She stays in there until she stops crying and understands she did something wrong!

                    CATHERINE
    I can't stand it!

She throws herself face down on the couch and Richard sits at the top of the stairs, guarding the door, behind which the child howls violently.

                    RICHARD
    Me neither.

18. EXTERIOR, JIM FULTON'S HOME—DAY

Jim pulls into the driveway and stops. Home at last. Joseph tumbles out the passenger side and moves to the back door, taking out his key. Jim shuts the ignition and sighs. Then, in his rearview mirror, he sees Giordano sitting in his car across the street, looking right at him.

                    JIM
    Son of a bitch!

He gets out of the car as Giordano gets out of his. They both come forward and meet at the fence. Giordano takes out his notepad and pen.

                    GIORDANO
                *(looking aside)*
    Morning, Jim.

                    JIM
                *(looking aside)*
    Constantine.

                    GIORDANO
    Working?

                    JIM
    Yeah.

                    GIORDANO
    Drinking?

JIM

No.

GIORDANO

Domestic situation positive?

JIM
*(hesitates)*
Well, that's a more complicated question.

Giordano now looks back at Jim who is exhausted and unshaven, then at the car and, finally, up the street.

GIORDANO

I suppose you just drove up to the store to get milk and diapers for the granddaughter, huh?

JIM

Yeah.

GIORDANO

Helping out the struggling younger couple.

JIM

Something like that.

GIORDANO
*(nods)*
Yeah, that's what I thought.
*(pockets notepad)*
Okay, Jim, see you next time.

JIM

Next time.

Giordano gets in his car and drives away. Jim leans on the fence and hangs his head.

JIM
*(relieved)*
Goddamn.

## 19. INTERIOR, FIORE HOME—DAY

Catherine is still face down on the couch with the pillows over her head, shaking with sobs. Upstairs, behind the closed door, the kid still wails. Lizzy and Maria sit huddled together in the hallway, terrified. Richard maintains his vigil, eyes closed, hands over his ears. And suddenly—silence. The crying stops. Catherine sits up, wide-eyed, sniffling. Richard lowers his hands from his ears. They wait. Finally, he stands and reaches out to the door handle. He turns it slowly. Opening the door and stepping inside the room, Richard discovers the child sitting on the floor, preoccupied with a puzzle book. She lifts her tear-stained face to him, grins, and goes back to work on the puzzle book. Richard comes down on one knee and kisses her head. A moment later, he comes down the stairs with the child in his arms. He places her in Catherine's lap and leaves the house.

## 21. EXTERIOR, FIORE HOME—DAY

Richard practically falls out through the front door and staggers down the street.

## 22. INTERIOR, JIM FULTON'S HOME—DAY

Jim finishes shaving at the bathroom mirror. Natalie is seated on top of the laundry hamper. He towels off his jaw and puts on a fresh shirt.

> NATALIE
> *(nonstop chatter)*
> And Bobby got accepted to a cooking school in the city.

> JIM
> Oh yeah?

> NATALIE
> *(climbs down)*
> He made us tacos.

Jim leads her out to the kitchen.

JIM

Tacos? Were they good?

NATALIE

Like sandwiches but with this funny bread
that's crispy like potato chips.

Jim sits at the kitchen table and lifts the lid off his financial shoebox, removing the checkbook. Joseph carries over a new cup of coffee.

JIM

Thanks.
*(of Rachel's card)*
Can you read that?

JOSEPH

*(reads)*
Cooperative Baptist Fellowship.

JIM

Okay.

NATALIE

Joseph's in trouble again at school.

JIM

*(writing the check)*
Oh, yeah? So what else is new?

JOSEPH

No, they just put me in the advanced class
for English.

JIM

*(studies towing receipt)*
But that's good, isn't it?

JOSEPH

Maybe. I might have to read Shakespeare,
though.

JIM
He's an all-star. I've heard about him.

They look up as someone enters the front door.

RICHARD
*(off)*
Dad?

NATALIE
*(jumps up)*
Richard!

She and Joseph run out to greet him. Jim finishes writing out the check, sips his coffee, then stands and goes to the living room. He finds Richard seated on the couch, head in his hands, demoralized. Nathalie and Joseph are on either side of him, worried. They look to Jim.

JIM
Joseph, get some money from the bank. Take
your sister up to the highway and get a slice
of pizza and a Coke for the two of you.

Joseph runs to the drawer and takes a few dollars from the bank, fitting them carefully into his wallet. Then he hesitates, uncertain. Jim is about to sit opposite Richard when he glances back at Joseph.

JIM
What?

JOSEPH
Is that one slice and a Coke for each of us or
one slice and a Coke to split?

JIM
Jesus. Whatever. Get lost for a while, will ya!

JOSEPH
Okay.

The kids run off with two more dollars. Jim waits, then:

> RICHARD
> *(exhausted)*
> I can't take it anymore.

Jim considers this, sips his coffee and sits.

> JIM
> Well, that's not an option.

> RICHARD
> It's too hard.

> JIM
> You and her need a home of your own.

> RICHARD
> But how? I mean…

> JIM
> We'll figure something out. Have you been able to save anything?

> RICHARD
> No. Nothing to speak of. There's always something needs to be got.

> JIM
> What's the situation at work?

> RICHARD
> They laid some people off.

> JIM
> They kept you, though.

> RICHARD
> Yeah.

Jim looks aside and shrugs.

                    JIM
          Well, that's something.

                    RICHARD
          The economy and whatnot. Everyone's worried.

                    JIM
          Yeah. They say we're in for a few lean years.
                    *(sips coffee, then)*
          When does Catherine graduate?

                    RICHARD
          June.

Jim hesitates before suggesting this, but—

                    JIM
          Might be the two of you have to work.

                    RICHARD
          Yeah.

Jim stands with his coffee and looks out into the street.

                    JIM
          Listen, I was thinking to finish renovating the
          basement. Put in a bathroom and kitchen
          down there.

                    RICHARD
          Oh, yeah?

                    JIM
          Could she live in a basement apartment, you
          think?

Richard gradually allows himself to be hopeful. He thinks it over a moment, then—

                    RICHARD
          Probably. I mean—yeah.

                        JIM
                  *(sits back down)*
            I'm not sure we can manage a separate
            entrance, though.

                      RICHARD
            That'd be okay.

                        JIM
            There's some permits we'll need to apply
            for. Maybe Catherine can look into that
            during the week...

And so on. They set to work making a plan. Outside, we hear the banging of metal.

23. EXTERIOR, MIKE FULTON'S HOME—DAY

Mike and his older sons are at work on the ship that looms like an enormous trapped whale amongst the little houses of the neighborhood. Out in the street, Marie is leaning back against her car, smoking a cigarette, contemplating their work while Ruthy plays baseball with her younger sons and Marie's two girls. Maggie pitches. Ruthy swings and gets a hit. A neighbor's garage door window gets busted and Ruthy drops the bat, horrified. But the kids are jumping around like maniacs, cheering.

                      BRIAN
            Oh man, Ma! Look what you did!

                      MARIE
                *(drops her cigarette)*
            Run Ruthy! Run! That's a fair ball! Run!

24. EXTERIOR, FIELD—DAY

Meanwhile, Joseph and Natalie tramp quietly away from the highway and wander back towards home through the field, passing abandoned furniture, rusted shopping carts and discarded building materials. As they make their way across this plain of cracked asphalt and weeds, Joseph soliloquizes—

JOSEPH
And from all these things, you see, something can be made. From these highways and gas stations. From these fast food restaurants and parking lots. From these lines of houses of whole families and people with problems, from this darkness and squalor and comedy and the brave things that troubled people do—something, I think, can be made. And remain. From this, I think.

Natalie pauses and looks around, skeptical.

NATALIE
From *this*?

JOSEPH
*(convinced)*
Yes. Even this.

The End ~